BITHELL SERIES OF DISSERTATIONS
VOLUME ELEVEN

Expressionist Poetry and its Critics

CHRISTOPHER WALLER

Headmaster, Eltham College

INSTITUTE OF GERMANIC STUDIES
UNIVERSITY OF LONDON   1986

British Library Cataloguing in Publication Data

Waller, Christopher
Expressionist Poetry and its Critics. —— (Bithell series of
dissertations, ISSN 0266–7932; v.11)
1. German poetry —— 20th century —— History and criticism
2. Expressionism
I. Title   II. University of London, *Institute of Germanic
Studies*   III. Series
831'.912'0931   PT553

ISBN 0 85457 132 9
ISSN 0266-7932

© The Institute of Germanic Studies

Printed by W. S. Maney & Son Ltd, Leeds, England

TO MY WIFE, ROSEMARY

CONTENTS

ACKNOWLEDGEMENTS

This book is an adaptation of a doctoral thesis submitted to the University of London in 1978. I should like to thank first and foremost my parents-in-law, Mr and Mrs Arnold Clark of Great Missenden, Bucks, without whose financial assistance I should never have entertained the idea of writing the original thesis. My thanks to many friends in England and Germany who have furnished me with invaluable material. The library staff at University College London, at the Institute of Germanic Studies, and at the Wiener Library responded most patiently and helpfully to my many questions and requests. I should also like to thank Liz Thomas, Lynda Mitchell, and Ann Weaver who uncomplainingly devoted long hours to typing and checking the text. It is difficult to believe that I could have had a more solicitous or interested supervisor than Peter Stern who gave most generously of his time to encourage and cajole and to wade through undisciplined first drafts. I am also grateful to Martin Swales whose advice and comments have been most stimulating and illuminating. To my wife, Rosemary, and three children, Jane, Claire, and Peter, who have had to put up with many absences and no little financial hardship at times, I owe more than I can say.

REFERENCES

References in the notes at the end of each chapter are given with bibliographical details at the first occurrence in the book and thereafter merely with author's name or short title. But complete bibliographical details to such references are listed in the Bibliography (pp. 171–86). Abbreviations for periodical titles are in accordance with those used in *The Year's Work in Modern Language Studies*.

I EXPRESSIONISM — INTRODUCTION

> It is a word like a sack in which one would like
> to catch the winds of Aeolus.[1]

The indefinability of the word 'Expressionism' has become a topos of literary criticism. This has not deterred critics and writers from venturing a definition, even though such definitions invariably issue into a kind of despairing lament about the diffuseness and ultimate futility of the term. Nevertheless I should like to begin with two assertions. The first is that between 1910 and 1925 the literary scene in Germany was dominated by the phenomenon Expressionism. The second is that the dispute about definition and terminology is bound to become an endless round of qualifications and balancing-acts, unless the label 'Expressionism' is accepted with all its debilities and accretions — accepted as what it was, a label appropriated by and apportioned to the most unlikely people, and accepted for what it has become, of dubious value as a style category and indispensable as a historical and descriptive term. Its confusing versatility can perhaps be illustrated by quoting Kurt Hiller's 'Some of the rabble who ruled the Nazi party were considered to be Expressionists'[2]alongside Goebbels's 'Our decade is thoroughly Expressionist in its internal structure. This has nothing to do with the new cult-word. We who live in the modern world are all Expressionists'.[3]

As a historical term 'Expressionism' has three main uses: first, it is part of the contemporary currency of self-understanding among writers and intellectuals, who may or may not employ it, who may or may not heed the programme broadcast in its name, but for whom it indicates the sense of cohesion which they seek; secondly, it may be used to describe what H. R. Jauss calls 'an horizon of expectation'[4] — no writer writes in a vacuum, he writes with a view to a public which reads him and expects certain things from him, what he writes is repudiatory or affirmative in relationship to literary modes available to him, and thus he finds himself dealing with particular themes, perhaps in a particular way; thirdly, it may be employed to indicate the way in which disparate talents engage in a debate with given expectations which change and evolve — only hack writers will fulfil expectations completely, in the same way as (according to T. S. Eliot) a truly individual talent interlocks with tradition *and* changes it. If the healthy mistrust of literary terms and the dissatisfaction with their vagueness become an obsessive and inevitably frustrated search for ideals of definition, what happens is that a great deal of dust is raised which ends by obliterating whatever merits individual writers and particular works may have. Moreover, one is in danger of losing any sense of the historicity of the individual writer's undertaking. Perhaps, to some extent, this is what has happened

I

to Expressionist literature. Some critics have responded with sharp hostility to it. Even those who have attended to individual writers have often begun by belabouring the term 'Expressionism' for its elusiveness and ultimate uselessness and then, paradoxically, used it as a stick to beat the writers they propose to discuss. In an attempt to escape from the eternal wrestle with literary -isms, I have founded my account of Expressionist poetry and its critics in a small number of *particular* criticisms and *individual* poets.

Rarely, if ever before, can a group of poets have declared in such strident detail what their intentions and hopes were. The poets of German Expressionism preceded, accompanied and followed their anthologies with a multitude of newspapers, magazines, pamphlets, essays and manifestos which have probably attracted more attention than the poetry itself. They were above all a self-conscious generation of poets and felt an urgent need to articulate their theories and aspirations unambiguously and fiercely. Indeed, sometimes, it is difficult to determine where the poetry ends and the programme begins, so nearly does the former enact the latter, so similar is the tone of voice which informs both. For some years the collective reputation of the Expressionist poets (like that of the Georgians and pre-Raphaelites) has been at a very low ebb, perhaps deservedly so. Perhaps, on the other hand, that reputation has suffered from a widespread acceptance of over-simplified stereotypes and vast generalizations or from critical spleen. The question of changing literary tastes as part of the historical process is relevant here, a process that was exacerbated in the post-1945 'Kahlschlag' with its pervasive sense of a culpable Weimar. The almost universal obloquy which has been poured upon the heads of the whole group has made the task of salvaging individual reputations (should any deserve to be salvaged) a very strenuous undertaking. The law of poetic averages alone suggests that not all the twenty-three poets in Kurt Pinthus's famous anthology, *Menschheitsdämmerung*, are iconoclastic barbarians or, to use Erich Heller's phrase, 'intellectual asthmatics'.[5] This book does not presume to be a salvage-operation (though, in the case of two of the poets selected, it *is* an attempt to haul from critical oblivion), but to study the work of five poets against the background of a series of cogent criticisms. This should provide an opportunity to consider and illuminate Expressionist poetry as exemplified by a small group of poets and to discover how appropriate and justified the general criticism is when applied to particular, individual cases.

It is worth asking why literary Expressionism has often met with hostile criticism. Expressionism was primarily a public and well-publicized affair, it advertised its activities and intentions (poetic, moral, practical), it sought to intervene in and influence many sphere of life, it raised all kinds of expectations (political as well as literary) in those who were swept along by it: in short, it offered a large target, or indeed two large targets, the theoretical programmes, manifestos, articles etc . . . *and* the poetic practice. What has borne the full weight of the literary critic's attention has not been, as might have been expected, the gap between theory and practice, for on occasions that gap is not wide. Instead he has concentrated on four aspects: what the movement was, what is was not, what it claimed to be and what its consequences were. What was the Expressionist movement in practice, to one side of all -isms? Who and what were the Expressionist poets, who did they claim to be, to one side of all definitions? They were a kind of international arts-alliance which was sustained by the ambition of combining with more or less anarchist revolutionary politics and transforming the world. Throughout Germany, indeed throughout Europe, there were from about 1910 onwards pockets of feverish artistic activity to which scores of writers, painters, sculptors and musicians rallied. Composed of a bewildering assortment of talents and personalities, Expressionism was a dynamic movement which dealt consciously and unconsciously in naive dialectical opposites — championing irrationality and passionate feeling as against rationality and temperate thinking, spontaneity and heedlessness as against deliberation and sobriety, intensity and dogmatism as against gentleness and debate, the excessive and the sensational as against the orthodox and the soft-hued, the fragmentary and the shapeless as against the self-contained and the coherent. Its literature was a literature of global assertion, easily susceptible of political meaning, partly because it so frequently spoke in political categories, and partly because it sought not simply to intervene in the political sphere but to merge the two worlds — literary and political — in a welter of intensely personal feeling. For example, in 1919, the Expressionist writer and theoretician, Kasimir Edschmid, proclaims that the artist has a duty to *all* the aspects of the age in which he lives:

The artist has never stood so much at the centre of the universe as he does today. Never, in such overwhelmingly tragic circumstances, has his responsibility for his age been so binding upon him. Seen from his point of view, with art as his central problem, any depiction of present objectives becomes a depiction of the age. Political questions, religious questions, any matter of urgency merge, indissolubly, with questions of art.[6]

There was an almost perverse determination about the way in which the Expressionist writers, by their public endeavours to realize their grand ambitions in art and in the world of practical affairs, set themselves up as critical targets and, predictably, invited the kind of captious unpopularity and criticism which attends political parties. They aspired to politics without entering its discourse, or more accurately for Weimar, they and so many like them *were* the political discourse. Peter Gay argues this brilliantly in *Weimar Culture* (1969; reprinted Harmondsworth, 1974) in connection with such figures as Rathenau, Meinecke and Hintze.

They were extraordinarily volatile and disorientated outsiders, they offered an overheated challenge to the given and were passionately committed to . . . anything which aroused their sympathy or enthusiasm. This generation's feeling of homelessness and isolation is balanced by a craving for a community, *any* community, and there was no shortage of available communities at that time — Becher and Walden turned to Communism, Brod to Zionism, Johst, Bronnen and Benn to National Socialism, Werfel to Catholicism. Expressionist writers were intensely dissatisfied with the status quo — before the First World War they loathed the tedium and meretricious superficiality of Wilhelminian Germany, after the war they played out ambiguous roles on the fringes of the Revolution and then they came to resent or ignore the Weimar Republic. They cast their dissatisfaction into quasi-religious statements and visions. Placing unconditional trust in 'the authority of their poetic powers of clairvoyance',[7] they adopted a messianic stance. They were

3

herald and magician, leader and legislator, thaumaturge and redeemer, God's 'silver sons' and 'soldiers in the army of the only salvation'.[8] They purveyed panaceas, political bromides and slogans. Having placed their art and their enthusiasm in the service of politics and social amelioration, they came to regard it as a *superior* form of political activity:

Modern poetry [is] a political poetry — poetry of a more exalted kind — for it is concerned not with the rise and fall of political parties and individuals, but with the politics of mankind and human charity, which alone can impose (both in art and in the political administration of nations) the necessary order after the chaos through which we are now living.[9]

The astonishing (*and* exclusive) claims which Pinthus, writing in 1915, makes for 'modern poetry' hardly need underlining. Yet, at the same time, Expressionist writers like Pinthus were bored by mundane practicalities, they could not be bothered with the minutiae of everyday political life, not did they show the slightest interest in the political and public as realms involving institutions, open debates, contracts, compromises, various democratic curbs and balances, and the interchange of ideas. The result was that whole areas of political discourse were obliterated, and *their* political discourse, in spite of all the claims it made for itself, was anything but political. Every utterance was couched in a heavily sustained and overwritten language, celebratory, rhetorical, foreclosing all cautious deliberation and demanding immediate assent; this-worldly ('diesseitig') and otherworldly ('jenseitig') vocabulary, the practical and the metaphysical were scrambled together so that statement became exclamation, idea became dogma, suggested pragmatic solution became urgently proffered chance of salvation, exhortation became irresistible imperative.

Moreover, in many of the major cities at least, Expressionist writers had a fervent and impressionable audience in Germany, traditionally a country which pays great heed to its poets, thinkers and philosophers: recalling in 1934 the vertiginous early days of Expressionism, Klaus Mann distends it into a national phenomenon and, even allowing for the fact that he offers no supporting evidence for his assertions, presents an interesting picture:

A great part of the nation was, of course, amazed, perhaps even repelled by the Expressionist movement. But everybody sensed its very potent presence . . . On the way home we had screamed poems by Klabund and Werfel into the night, and the next morning . . . hung a cubist painting in the classroom . . . volumes of verse, dramas, anthologies, almanacs, magazines poured onto the market and found a bewilderingly wide readership . . . young people sustained this literature, and for a short while it seemed as if the whole nation might be caught up in such enthusiasm.[10]

Amazingly for such a self-conscious generation, the Expressionist writers never asked themselves what effect their continual recourse to histrionics and a kind of monumental idiom might be having either on language, which even in the poetic mode is public property and a medium for thought and for thinking, or on public sensibilities and the reservoir of feeling. Literature, like the other arts, is not a self-contained, isolated thing; reflecting the times it helps to shape them, it offers

4

diversion and amusement *and* it presents a model for behaviour and values, it portrays *and* recasts the sensibility of an age. The Expressionist writers of all people subscribed to this affective view of literature — Gottfried Benn, for example, brooks no doubt when he asserts: 'It was from works of art that problems issued into the age, thrust their way into the age. Far from expressing the age, works of art created the age. Art, not war, shapes history'. [11]

By invoking two recent books I can perhaps indicate the way in which my reading of Expressionist writers has led me to interpret the role they played and the area they sought to occupy in German life and literature. Roy Pascal in his *From Naturalism to Expressionism* (London, 1973) argues from the conditions of society obtaining in Germany at the time (1880–1918) and illuminates thereby the kind of literature produced. Amongst other things he shows how intense the self-loathing of the German bourgeoisie was (and the Expressionist writers, almost to a man, were recruited from this class), how the bourgeoisie's hatred of philistinism, pre-war complacency and materialism was self-directed, and how the bourgeoisie's reaction against these was in the name *not* of a revolutionary proletariat, but of such bourgeois values and talismen as culture, literature, intellectual élitism and 'Geist'. The result was that the bourgeoisie worked up a complex head of steam, but had nowhere to go, and came to treat society and social problems as kinds of literary metaphor. J. P. Stern in his *Hitler: The Führer and the People* (London, 1975) sees the Hitler-phenomenon not in terms of economic or social conditions, but of personal values (especially that of authenticity) injected into politics, and demonstrates how politics became a personal quasi-literary metaphor. The Expressionist writers occupied a kind of middle-ground between these two positions: they loathed their own bourgeois background and shared with others of their class a profound discontent with the bourgeois style of life and with a status quo which was sustained by bourgeois values; they made various futile attempts to step out of their isolation and to link arms with the proletariat, and they not only sought to understand the public, political, social realm exclusively in terms of private, personal, quasi-literary values, but they intimated that this was the only way to understand it. Passionate intensity was a crucial category in the Expressionist writers' scale of values: Werfel's line 'The more intensely we live here in this life, the more intense shall be our existence in the next' [12] was applied indiscriminately to *all* spheres of life.

If, in this introductory chapter, I have drawn attention to the connection between literary Expressionism and politics, I have followed the example of many Expressionist writers (for whom the connection was axiomatic) and of many critics (for whom the connection ousts almost any other consideration). However, this connection does not always apply, or rather it does not always apply to any significant extent. For example, two of the five poets selected for detailed analysis cannot primarily be regarded under this aspect of a literary/political dialectic. My principal concern will always be with individual poems and will touch upon political questions only when the particular poet under discussion overtly makes the connection or when the poetry is plainly susceptible of political significance. I do not focus attention upon any of the predominantly activist Expressionist poets: moreover, this book is not intended to be an elaborate, all-inclusive 'Rezeptionsgeschichte'. It is deliberately selective — in its choice of poets, of poems and of relevant biographical details. Given the particular nature of the Expressionist movement, I think it inevitable that reference must constantly be made to the historical context and to the social ambience.

All five poets are well represented in *Menschheitsdämmerung*,[13] the most authoritative of the Expressionist anthologies. Though the poets in question may have resisted the label 'Expressionist poet' and may not have even heard the word 'Expressionism', Pinthus's ascription was clearly right: all five belong most appropriately within the literary-historical framework of Expressionism. Three of the poets, it is true, moved into different contexts, but a significant part of their work is typical of important facets of the Expressionist movement, and in the case of one of the five (August Stramm) the poetry is generally acknowledged as the most successful practical demonstration of the theories of one of the leading Expressionist 'schools'. The reasons why these five have been singled out should emerge during subsequent discussion of their work. Ultimately, though, the choice is founded in the belief that because they are very different talents, an examination of their work will suggest the range and multifariousness of Expressionist writing and provide illuminating criteria, against which the validity of the criticism assembled in the following chapter can be measured.

Anyone concerned to characterize the work of August Stramm has to see clearly through a thicket of apparent contradictions and paradoxes and to seek answers to three questions: is Stramm a wilful iconoclast or an intense, self-disciplined craftsman struggling to render his 'imperfect penance'[14] and wrenching some of his best poetry (like the English writer Ivor Gurney) from the horrors of front-line warfare? Is his poetry merely an uncontrolled volcanic eruption or does it represent a passionate endeavour to regenerate what he sees as an ailing language? Having 'brought the language into flux', as Radrizzani maintains,[15] having 'tortured' it, as Muschg argues,[16] what does he do with it?

Georg Heym is usually bracketed with Trakl as the best of the early Expressionist writers. If Stramm offers the not uncommon picture of an Expressionist writer whose poetry, drama and far from conservative syntactical experiments shock and alienate his circumspect family, then Georg Heym is his counterpart, but no less a representative figure — never and nowhere at home, resolutely self-destructive, self-consciously lawless and mutinous, and yet, most interestingly if critics are right, very conservative as far as poetic form is concerned. For reasons of self-preservation, the argument goes, he consciously or unconsciously subscribes to Stefan George's cult of strict form as the only means of subjugating otherwise intolerable visions and of banishing otherwise all-conquering evil. He is of special interest as a representative of early Expressionism's deep fascination for 'big city' life. Critics remain sharply divided about the precise nature of his attitude to the world in which he lives. He has been cast as a prophet, a seismograph, a perspicacious social critic, a visionary poet, a twentieth-century Büchner, a gloating voyeur of catastrophe or so enmeshed in his own obsessions that he cannot see beyond himself.

Franz Werfel is the great charismatic figure amongst Expressionist writers. His contemporaries regard him as their natural leader. Kafka, for example, writes in a letter dated December 1922: 'You are without doubt a leader of your generation, and that's no flattery . . .'. Werfel's poem 'An den Leser' (1911) is supposed to have triggered off literary Expressionism on the night of 16 December 1911. Heym is dead by January 1912, Stramm by September 1915, and if only because he survives until 1945, Werfel appears a much grander, more expansive, cosmopolitan figure. There is a very constrained and embattled quality about some of the earlier Expressionist writers, whereas Werfel is all volatility and versatility, fluency and uninhibitedness. His introversion is a well publicized affair, his private agonies and prejudices are flaunted brazenly. His speeches and writing throughout the 1920s and 1930s plead earnest concern with political and social issues. He constantly invokes the word 'reality', he raises all sorts of extra-literary expectations in his avid audience, and his words acquire and are frequently invested with a political patina. He comes in for harsh criticism from Karl Kraus, to whom he seems a publicity-seeking charlatan (peddling emotionality and religiosity) and a slipshod craftsman. For Kraus, Werfel is living proof of the conviction that moral turpitude and linguistic negligence are inextricably bound together and that Werfel's apparent insistence on spontaneity and immediacy as poetic values in themselves inevitably leads to syntactical carelessness and emotional sloppiness. A thorough discussion of Werfel's work should certainly include an examination of his relationship with language and his attitude to poetic form in general terms and from the point of view of those critics who, like Kafka, believe that his poetry has a dangerously hypnotic and confusing effect: 'All yesterday morning my head was as if filled with mist from Werfel's poems. For a moment I feared the enthusiasm would carry me along straight into nonsense'.[17]

It is not really until 1969 that Kurt Heynicke accepts rather reluctantly the label 'Expressionist poet'.[18] Yet his 1936 volume *Das Leben sagt Ja* is still replete with characteristic Expressionist motifs which are typical of, for example, Werfel's poetry and of his own early collections. His kin *are* the Expressionist writers, and his uneasy relationship first with *Der Sturm* and then with Expressionism as a whole can be interpreted as a symptom of the Expressionist generation's intellectual and spiritual rootlessness. Being rootless, it is a generation which becomes peculiarly vulnerable to the siren call of any party, any cause, any community which seems to offer the promise of a sustaining strength and integration. In the 'twenties there are a host of such communities and causes demanding and acquiring passionate alle-giance. Sokel is not alone in declaring[19] that Heynicke was a member of the National Socialist party and that there is a significant connection between National Socialism and Expressionism[20]: 'the confluence of late Expressionism with Nazism was neither a chance happening nor a reversal of the Expressionist current, but a natural dénouement of basic Expressionist tendencies'.[21] The charge is usually couched in general terms: a historian, for example, concludes that 'in Expressionism we see in preparation the themes, the state of mind, the intoxication . . . of a youth that found itself ready to plunge into the great adventure of the Third Reich'.[22] Heynicke always strenuously denied that he was ever a member of the National Socialist party. What *is* certain is that in the 1930s he wrote two plays apodeictically in honour of the National Socialist régime. Detailed consideration of his poetry will perhaps

7

provide an answer to two questions: first, by virtue of which essentially Expressionist qualities might we feel able to predict his subsequent support of the National Socialists? And secondly, does a close examination of his work enable us to flesh out the invariably unsubstantiated charges that Expressionism somehow 'paved the way for' or 'issued naturally into' or 'provided a basis for' National Socialism? Because there is something intensely confessional and self-absorbed about Heynicke's poetry, it will not be easy always to make a clear distinction between preparing the way for Fascism in the biographical sense and the wider sense in which certain features of the poetry appear to prefigure the Nazi ideology.

If Werfel was included in this selection because he could not be left out, Wilhelm Klemm offers the lure of the unknown, the attraction of having been largely ignored by literary critics and historians, though Jan Brockmann's 1961 dissertation ('Untersuchungen zur Lyrik Wilhelm Klemms', University of Kiel) is a much needed pioneer and corrective after decades of perhaps undeserved neglect. With nineteen poems Klemm is better represented in *Menschheitsdämmerung* than any other poet apart from Werfel and Ehrenstein, and Robert Newton does not doubt that he is 'one of the good poets of *Menschheitsdämmerung* who has enjoyed more that his share of oblivion'.[23] Any reader of Klemm's poetry might, therefore, seek to determine the justice of Pinthus's generous representation and of the subsequent critical neglect. Brockmann in his dissertation suggests a way of approaching Klemm's work by reference to Lukács's attack on Expressionism for its abstraction and bloodlessness (see the following chapter). Moreover, parallels with the life and work of Gottfried Benn suggest themselves continually, and it might be helpful and illuminating to bear such parallels in mind in any consideration of Klemm's poetry. As with Heynicke there is a challenge to be met: 'The almost fully matured and deeply moving Wilhelm Klemm is waiting to be discovered anew . . . '[24]

These five poets represent a manageable cross-section of Pinthus's choice in *Menschheitsdämmerung*. Assessment of their work should involve the attempt to do critical justice to individual texts which they produced — rather in the spirit of F. R. Leavis's advice: 'In dealing with individual poets the rule of the critic is, or should (I think) be, to work as much as possible in terms of particular analysis — analysis of poems or passages, and say nothing that cannot be related immediately to judgements about producible texts'.[25] But poems, as Eliot eloquently argued, have implications — 'moral, social, religious'[26] *and* political — and effects:

Poetry may effect revolutions in sensibility such as are periodically needed; may help to break up the conventional modes of perception and valuation which are perpetually forming, and make people see the world afresh, or some new part of it. It may make us from time to time a little more aware of the deeper, unnamed feelings which form the substratum of our being, to which we rarely penetrate.[27]

The tentativeness which informs Eliot's verbs ('*may* effect . . . *may* help . . . *may* make') can be dispensed with in the land of poets and thinkers and at a time when 'the word still had power'.[28]

NOTES

1   R. Musil, *Der Mann ohne Eigenschaften* (Hamburg, 1952), p. 458.
2   K. Hiller, 'Begegnungen mit "Expressionismus"', *Der Monat*, XIII/148 (January 1961), 55.
3   J. Goebbels, *Michael. Ein deutsches Schicksal in Tagebuchblättern* (1929), fourth edition (Munich, 1934), p. 77.
4   H. R. Jauss, *Literaturgeschichte als Provokation* (Frankfurt a.M., 1970), p. 175.
5   Erich Heller, *The Disinherited Mind* (1952; reprinted, Harmondsworth, 1961), p. 207.
6   Quoted in: P. Raabe, *Die Zeitschriften und Sammlungen des literarischen Expressionismus* (Stuttgart, 1964), p. 186.
7   Carl Sternheim writes of 'die Autorität meiner dichterischen Seherkraft' in: 'Die deutsche Revolution' (1918–19); *Gesamtwerk*, 9 vols (Berlin, 1963–70), VI (1966), 86.
8   Klabund, *Die Weißen Blätter*, 5 (July–September 1918), 106–08.
9   K. Pinthus, 'Zur jüngsten Dichtung', *Die Weißen Blätter*, 2, Heft 12 (July–September 1915), 1509.
10   K. Mann, 'Der literarische Expressionismus' (1934), in: *Prüfungen* (Munich, 1968), pp. 193–95.
11   G. Benn, 'Marginalien' (no date); *Gesammelte Werke*, 4 vols (Wiesbaden, 1958–61), I (1959), 391.
12   See his poem 'Die Leidenschaftlichen' ('The Passionate Ones'); *Das lyrische Werk*, edited by A. D. Klarmann (Frankfurt a.M., 1967), pp. 230–31.
13   K. Pinthus (ed.), *Menschheitsdämmerung* (1920; reprinted Hamburg, 1959. All references are taken from this edition).
14   The phrase ('eine unvollkommene Sühne') is Georg Trakl's. It is quoted in: 'Frühlicht über den Gräbern', *Der Brenner*, 18 (1954), 251.
15   R. Radrizzani, *August Stramm: Das Werk* (Wiesbaden, 1963), p. 438.
16   W. Muschg, *Von Trakl zu Brecht* (Munich, 1963), pp. 64–65.
17   Entry for 23 December 1911; *Tagebücher 1910–1923* (New York, 1948/49), p. 202.
18   Kurt Heynicke, *Das lyrische Werk*, 3 vols (Worms, 1969–74), III (1969), 7.
19   W. H. Sokel, *The Writer in Extremis* (Stanford, California, 1959), p. 209.
20   Thomas Mann, Adorno, Willett, Samuel, Hinton Thomas, and Furness — among many others — all point to a more or less close relationship between the two.
21   Sokel, p. 229.
22   E. Vermeil, *The German Scene* (London, 1956), p. 142.
23   R. P. Newton, *Form in the 'Menschheitsdämmerung'* (The Hague and Paris, 1971), p. 211.
24   F. Usinger, 'Die expressionistische Lyrik', *Imprimatur*, 3 (1961/62), 125.
25   F. R. Leavis, *Revaluation*, seventh edition (London, 1969), pp. 2–3.
26   T. S. Eliot, 'The Age of Dryden', in: *The Use of Poetry and the Use of Criticism*, twelfth edition (London, 1959), p. 64.
27   T. S. Eliot, 'Conclusion', in: *The Use of Poetry . . .* , p. 155.
28   Stefan Zweig, *Die Welt von gestern* (Stockholm, 1941), pp. 250–51.

II THE CRITICISMS

> Literary criticism ought to be a history of man's
> ideas and imaginings in the setting of the
> conditions which have shaped them. [1]

This book takes as its starting-point, and will use as a framework, a series of criticisms of Expressionism by contemporary writers, who have something pertinent and incisive to say about the movement. There are two principal bands of criticism, the formal and the thematic. Rilke and George, who focus their attention on formal considerations, regard Expressionism as a cult of formlessness, whereas Lukács and Thomas Mann argue that Expressionism claims a vital involvement in the political and social spheres, but has no insight into the practical responsibilities which are the inevitable concomitants of such involvement. It is rare for a critic to object to Expressionism on both counts, although it is certainly possible to see the objection of formal irresponsibility as analogous to that of political irresponsibility: indeed, by 1930, Thomas Mann, who makes his original criticism of Expressionism in 1918, is deeply aware of the analogy. The five writers, whose reservations are recorded here, are not some kind of unimpeachable critical idols. Issue will be taken with their criticism; they are, after all, very much part of the same literary and social ambience from which Expressionism emerged, and the charges which they level at Expressionism can frequently be turned round and directed at their own work. What is particularly interesting is that, from an early date, these writers demur to be swept along by the fervour of the latest literary fashion; they resist it, they raise important objections to it, and, no matter how loosely they may voice their objections, they offer potentially fruitful ways to approach Expressionist writing.

(a) *R. M. Rilke*

> . . . this salutary antagonism . . . there must be not only a partnership, but a union; an interpenetration of passion and of will, of spontaneous impulse and of voluntary purpose. [2]

Rilke's life represents one long repudiation of the political branch of Expressionism known as activism. Where he interprets any commitment to his own age or to philanthropic goals merely as a source of inauthenticity and as a potentially fatal impoverishment of his uncompromising view of his poetic mission, the activist Expressionist writers derive their literary sustenance and existential justification from a feeling of commitment and responsibility. In his memoirs, Erich Mühsam, an activist Expressionist, recounts how he was once chided by Wedekind for dissipating his time and energies, for dividing his efforts, for seeking to play two roles in life — that of a 'Caféhausliterat' and that of a fighter for proletarian rights:

'You are standing on the back of two horses straining in different directions; they will rip your legs apart'.
'If I let one go,' I replied, 'I shall lose my balance and break my neck'.[3]

Against this determination to 'ride two horses' Rilke sets the example of Rodin and the image of 'the mighty course of the river which refuses to divide into two branches'.[4] This image appears in a letter written in 1903, but it could easily have been written in 1913 or 1923 (though not with reference to Rodin) as a counter-example to the likes of Mühsam, Pinthus, Pfemfert, Rubiner and Hiller. Expressionism's will-to-diffuseness, which Rilke regards as fissiparous and wastefully arrogant, is offset by his monumental will-to-be-all-of-a-piece, will-to-create-whatever-one-is. His rejection both of political activism and of the whole movement of Expressionism is contained in one particular letter, written on 12 September 1919. The actress Anni Mewes had sent him a 'carefully and beautifully sealed little parcel'. In it was a pamphlet entitled *Die Silbergäule* written by Heinrich Vogeler, a painter, whom Rilke had visited in Worpswede in 1900. In his reply to Anni, Rilke sharply dismisses the pamphlet and its message of Expressionist love for all mankind. His use of the image of the train leaping off the rails soon indicates that his main objection to Expressionism is going to be concerned with poetic form. Expressionism, according to him, is uncontrolled and undisciplined, it takes an appearance of intensity to be the actual quality of intensity, it is a premature outer manifestation of inner dynamism, and Rilke dismisses Vogeler's grandiose philanthropic project as a paradigm of just this sort of wilful scattering of inner resources. It is not fortuitous or self-contradictory that four years earlier, in his warm praise of the early Expressionist poet Georg Trakl,[5] Rilke should use such words as 'Zäune' (fences), 'eingezäunt' (fenced in) and 'Einfriedungen' (enclosures) to signal the kind of control which characterizes Trakl's best work. Rilke's criticism of the Expressionist poet is founded in precisely the same objections as those which he levels against Vogeler and other activists:

The Expressionist, this explosive spirit pouring its boiling lava over all things and insisting that the arbitrary form into which the crusts harden is the new, the future, the veritable outline of being, — is a desperate soul . . . (12 September 1919)

Expressionism, Rilke argues, is like an erupting volcano and is an example of that 'imageless act' ('Tun ohne Bild') in the Ninth Elegy, activity without necessary intellectual curb and concomitant mental picture. The Expressionist poet, like the volcano, may indeed by overwhelmed by a kind of inner necessity to gush forth, but the whole point is, Rilke implies, that he should *not* be like a volcano. By patience and craftsmanship he should shape his inspiration (which Rilke does not for a moment deny him) and should eliminate all arbitrariness and adventitiousness — these are the qualities which Rilke repudiates above all in Expressionist poetry. It is a question of finding Coleridge's 'salutary antagonism', of matching deeply felt emotion with painstakingly sought form and coherence.

The appropriateness of Rilke's criticism of Expressionist form can be gauged from the fact that Expressionist writers continually avail themselves of the same image of the volcano when they define their attitude to poetic form. Max Deri, for example, in a 1918 article entitled 'Expressionismus und Idealismus', explains how intensity of feeling is a value in itself in Expressionist poetry: 'all the dams of Classical restraint are burst asunder. Dynamic feeling seeks an outlet, "expression" in an upsurge of almost unchecked ecstasy. Anything which does not course down from the peaks with an incandescent glow has no worth'.[6] Yet Rilke's repudiation of Expressionist form should not be accepted uncritically. Given that Expressionist poets do write in the way Rilke portrays in his image of the volcano, why should that self-evidently make their poetry into a 'bad thing'? The genesis of a poem tells us nothing about the quality of the poem as artifact. What of the *Elegies*, for instance? Arriving with whirlwind force in January 1912, finished in what reads by Rilke's own account like an excess of Expressionist fervour almost exactly ten years later, do they not represent a powerful counter-argument to Rilke's criticism of Expressionist poetry? Is there not something intensely Expressionistic about their genesis, something of Expressionism's intensity about them? The answer is plainly yes and no: they did pour forth, but they had, after all, 'fermented' for ten years, ten years of single-minded concentration and strenuousness. There is no question in them of a sort of inspirational slopping-over, of what Rilke in his poem 'Doute' calls a 'premature exaltation', or of settling for the first stammering, faltering words which adventitiously enter the poet's mind and of which Valéry, a great contemporary poet and an important influence on Rilke's thought, warns:

Il faut prendre garde aux premiers mots qui prononcent une question dans notre esprit. Une question nouvelle est d'abord à l'état d'enfance en nous; elle balbutie: elle ne trouve que des termes étrangers, tout chargés de valeurs et d'associations accidentelles; elle est obligée de les emprunter.[7]

Only the trance-like act of hearkening to and recording the dictates of inspiration bears the hallmark of Expressionism, as Rilke defines it. Like all his work from the *Neue Gedichte* onwards, the *Elegies* are 'a fully matured configuration, pervaded by the glow of the poet's inspiration'.[8] To which Expressionist poems can one apply a similar description? To those of Heym and Trakl, to some poems by Werfel, to all the poems of Stramm (whose work Rilke did not know), and to very few others. Rilke's criticism of Expressionism is all of a piece with his general views on poetry *and* with his own poetic practice. This criticism can be interpreted as a corrective to those among the Expressionist poets who believed that immediacy of inspiration and heedless intensity *of themselves* produced a good poem. As a contemporary poet who felt that such a corrective was needed, Rilke renders the same kind of service to twentieth-century German poetry as Eliot does to twentieth-century English poetry — the same kind, but not to the same degree. Eliot with his conviction that 'the "greatness", the intensity, of the emotions, the components are not what counts, but the intensity of the artistic process, the pressure under which the fusion takes place' provided precisely the sort of stabilizing influence and corrective to excesses which twentieth-century German poetry lacks — in spite of the example and achievement of Rilke. And in the famous lines from the fifth section of 'Little Gidding', ' . . . every word is at home, / Taking its place to support the others . . . ', Eliot underlines the very qualities which Rilke misses in Expressionist poetry: an indissoluble harmony between felt emotion and articulated word, balance, symmetry and proportion — all antitheses to the arbitrariness and luxuriance of 'the Expressionist, this explosive spirit . . . '

(b) *Thomas Mann*

Only reality, though certainly not every reality — but a selected reality.[9]

Reality —, Europe's demonic concept.[10]

Thomas Mann, on the later of the two principal occasions in *Betrachtungen eines Unpolitischen* (1918) where he discusses Expressionism, reiterates part of Rilke's description of the Expressionist poet:

Expressionism . . . is that artistic trend which, in violent contrast to the passivity, the meekly receptive and reproductive methods of Impressionism, has the utmost scorn for any attempt to imitate reality and, resolutely repudiating any obligation to reality, places in its stead the sovereign, explosive, heedlessly creative authority of the intellect/spirit ('Geist').[11]

Even more categorically than Rilke, Mann rejects the movement: his parody of the Expressionist poets, as represented by Daniel Zur Höhe in *Doktor Faustus*, is blatant and crude. Unlike Rilke, however, Mann's criticism offers metaphysics instead of concrete insight, generalization instead of detail, rhetorical bluster instead of conveyed understanding. Nevertheless it should be borne in mind that Mann's reservations about Expressionism are voiced as early as 1918 (that is, at a time when many were still rallying to its banner) and also that his criticism yields two categories —those of 'reality' and 'responsibility' — which are central to any understanding of Expressionism and consequently need further elaboration.

Mann uses the protean term 'reality' twice in the quoted extract. He is certainly right to insist that Expressionism, if it means anything at all, is a rejection of the mimetic approach in art. Expressionist writers are intent on destroying the prestige of empirical reality; they scorn any idea of merely reproducing the visible world and indeed regard reality and art as mutually exclusive — 'the era of modern art is founded in the burgeoning insight that reality and art are not dependent on or conditioned by each other: on the contrary, they are incompatible'.[12] What does Pinthus mean here by 'reality'? What does Mann mean by 'reality'? Mann is clearly using the word in the conventional, quotidian sense which Pinthus defines on another occasion, in 'Rede für die Zukunft' (1920), an unwitting retort to Mann's charge and an endeavour to demonstrate how 'responsible' Expressionism is to 'reality'. Pinthus writes:

Reality means to man everything which is and has been outside him, around him, in front of him. Reality is nature and all manifestations of nature, the form and workings of which he perceives through the exhilarating and yet wretched apparatus of his senses — perceives and takes to be true. Reality means man's past and man's history, and, at any given time, he regards himself as the last link in that history. When man talks of reality he means all those associations and institutions which he created for himself (state, economic system, social order) in order to relieve the agony of living and which, subsequently, dominated him as if they were his god.[13]

This, or something like this, is what Thomas Mann understands by the 'reality' for which the Expressionist writer is denying all responsibility. It is, moreover, precisely this 'reality' which Expressionist writers dismiss as . . . 'unreal'. Pinthus in 'Rede für die Zukunft' provides an example of the Expressionist polemicist's habit of setting up a series of alleged dialectical opposites from which he then derives a kind of intense, emotional momentum. On one side there is Mann's 'reality' which is dismissed variously (by Pinthus and other Expressionist writers) as 'so-called', 'infinitely inferior to the reality created by the poet', 'bogus', 'chimaerical', 'a mistake', 'non-existent', as the tedious old world of the senses with its wearisome 'social conditions', fit only to be destroyed or to be 'the plaything of the poet's grotesque games'. On the other side is the Expressionist writer's view of 'reality' — 'real reality', 'inner reality', abstract, timeless, higher, ethical, new. These stereotyped oppositions are rehearsed again and again by Expressionist writers, who hedge the word 'reality' round with a series of qualifying adjectives intended to underline its otherness.

As for the second category to which Mann introduces us — 'responsibility' — Expressionist writers, too, talk of 'responsibility to reality'. Pinthus, for example, in 'Rede für die Zukunft', enjoins the artist to 'acknowledge his task and responsibility', and Rubiner expatiates on the artist's 'personal responsibility to his fellow-men'.[14] A contemporary of Thomas Mann, Max Weber, illuminates this elusive word 'responsibility'. In his 1918/19 essay 'Politik als Beruf' Weber establishes a nice difference between 'gesinnungsethisch' which represents a category of uncompromising, chiliastic idealism and 'verantwortungsethisch' which amounts to a much more pragmatic and rational kind of idealism. Weber argues that, whilst passion is an integral part of any good politician's character, it must be tempered by such qualities as a sense of proportion ('Augenmaß') and a sense of responsibility ('Verantwortungsgefühl') which, in turn, are sustained by objectivity and distance.[15] It is true that Weber is writing about politics, and that Mann is writing about literature and art, but the whole point is that for the Expressionist/activist writer any dividing-line between politics and art is erased. In a quite definite way, Weber's depiction of the 'responsible politician' recalls Rilke's poetic criteria and Coleridge's 'salutary antagonism'. Weber could well have Expressionist writers in mind when he discusses politics and politicians:

For the problem is precisely this: how can ardent passion and cool judgement be harnessed together in the same cause? The politician must use his head, not other parts of his body or soul. And yet devotion to politics, if it is to be a genuinely human activity and not some frivolous intellectual game, must be born of passion and sustained by passion. That powerful taming of the soul which distinguishes the passionate politician and differentiates him from the merely 'sterile sensationalism' of the political dilettante can be achieved only if an attitude of detachment is adopted. (p. 436)

'Tamed passion' as against 'sterile amateurish sensationalism' — this is the kind of opposition which Rilke's criticism of Expressionism sets up, and Rilke's emphasis on craftsmanship, patience and scrupulous work is paralleled by Weber's 'Politics is a steady, slow drilling of hard planks, using passion and a sense of proportion at the same time' (p. 450) and by his 'Politics is a difficult business, and anyone who takes it upon himself to interfere with the spokes of the wheel of the political development of his country must not be so sentimental that he cannot practise earthly politics'.[16]

Mann's categories of 'responsibility' and 'reality' are extremely helpful, even though he provides little elaboration of them. Weber offers valuable insights into the concept of political responsibility, and Expressionist writers define, even if they do not make altogether clear, what *they* mean by 'reality'. What remains to be examined is the extent to which Expressionist theorizing about 'reality' is distilled in the poetry — in other words, the extent to which Expressionist poets take issue with reality in the conventional sense and keep faith with their professed intention of concentrating on a 'superior' reality. As far as 'responsibility' is concerned, this is essentially a nebulous, extra-literary concept and becomes a vital factor only because the Expressionist poets were keen to make it so by arrogating all kinds of poetical, ethical and moral responsibilities to themselves and thus unhesitatingly making their literature available to the political sphere. By 1944 the Expressionist writer's impetuous arrogation of responsibility has issued, in at least one instance, into a penitential *mea culpa*. Franz Werfel unambiguously acknowledges the responsibility which he and his generation bear for the greatest catastrophe of all:

I have come to know many kinds of arrogance, in myself and in others. Yet there is no more consuming, more brazen, more disdainful, more diabolical arrogance than that of the avant-garde artists and radical intellectuals, bursting with the vain passion to be profound and obscure and difficult, and to cause pain: all this I can confirm from my own experience, since in my youth I myself was of that company for a while. Mocked in amused indignation by a few philistines, we inconsiderable men were the first to bring fuel to the hell-fire in which mankind is now roasting.[17]

Where Werfel speaks of his generation's 'bringing fuel to the hell-fire in which mankind is now roasting', Thomas Mann in his 1930 speech 'Deutsche Ansprache' writes that extra-political causes have assisted National Socialism, that it has been sustained by 'succour from intellectual/spiritual sources'. Mann elaborates on what these sources might be. In fact, he concentrates on one source, namely the economic decline of the middle class and the intensely anti-bourgeois attitude of those who in pre-war Germany had proclaimed 'a new spiritual situation for all mankind'. This proclamation, this revolt against all that the bourgeoisie stood for, found its artistic voice in 'the Expressionist soul-scream'.[18] Mann's undefined charge of 'irresponsibility to reality' has, by 1930, sharpened into an altogether more incisive and pertinent accusation, for by that date he has come to see Expressionism as a precipitate of all that was worst in Romanticism, as a powerful force for irrationalism and as an accomplice of National Socialism.

(c) *Georg Lukács*

Expressionism offered the revolutionary gesture, the uparaised arm, the clenched fist in papier-mâché.[19]

Marxist literary theory has always looked at Expressionism from one angle — as an ideological phenomenon. However much individual insights and judgements of

Expressionism may differ, the method of regarding Expressionism as a political and ideological phenomenon has persisted. Georg Lukács's 1934 essay '"Größe und Verfall" des Expressionismus' triggered a series of assenting and dissenting articles which were printed in the pages of the periodical *Das Wort* in 1937 and 1938. Lukács's essay, in spite of the expectations raised by its title, is primarily a work of demolition, and, as if to reinforce his 1934 essay, Lukács repeats many of the same points four years later in his contribution to the 'Expressionismus-Debatte', namely an essay called 'Es geht um den Realismus', and in his much later *Deutsche Literatur im Zeitalter des Imperialismus* (1950).

He founds his whole case against Expressionism in what he sees as the latter's defective response to reality. It is an anaemic, solipsistic 'abstracting away from reality'. Transferred to the political sphere, Expressionism represents the literary form of the USP ideology in all its subjective idealism, has no authentic point of contact with the proletariat, offers only abstract and Bohemian opposition to the bourgeoisie and, because it is under the sway of some 'mystic objective idealism' or 'a subjective idealism', it has no grasp at all of social, historical, economic and political forces. Lukács quotes Lenin to the effect that any search for that Expressionist ideal, 'the pure essence' (devoid of a socio-politico-economical context) is bound to be futile. He might also have quoted from that section called 'German, or "True", Socialism' towards the end of the *Manifesto of the Communist Party*, where Marx and Engels inveigh against the abstract German Socialism of the 1840s which emphasizes 'not true requirements, but the requirements of truth' and 'not the interests of the proletariat, but the interests of Human Nature, of Man in general, who belongs to no class, has no reality, who exists only in the misty realm of philosophical fantasy'. Expressionism, Lukács argues in the manifesto, is an epigonal manifestation of this kind of Utopian Socialism, a seam in what Marx and Engels describe as 'the robe of speculative cobwebs, embroidered with flowers of rhetoric, steeped in the dew of sickly sentiment, this extravagant robe in which German Socialists wrapped their sorry "eternal truths", all skin and bone'.

Expressionism, Lukács maintains, is parasitic upon the bourgeoisie, it flees the battle-field of the class-struggle, it distends and distorts all contemporary questions into eternal abstractions. Its fight against the war and the bourgeoisie is a cheap masquerade, because it is a fight against War and the Bourgeoisie. Lukács sets up a litany of arraignment in which phrases like 'abstracting poverty of content', 'extraordinary meagreness of substance' and 'abstract distortion of basic questions' are continually rehearsed. In denying causality and logic, and in aiming for totality, the Expressionist writer leaves out a living context: his resort to simultaneism in an effort to replace that context is a desperate and futile manoeuvre. The end-result of all his manoeuvres is that Expressionism assists in the growth of Fascism: Expressionism is 'without doubt one of the numerous bourgeois-ideological currents which subsequently issue into Fascism, and the part it plays in preparing the way for Fascist ideology is no greater — and no smaller — than that played by many other contemporary currents'.[20]

And Expressionist form? It is 'arbitrary' and 'subjective'; detached from empirical reality, devoid of substance, the Expressionist scream amounts to no more than 'an empty aggregate of emotional effusions', 'the hysterical distillation of inflated images and symbols which jostle haphazardly together and lack all intrinsic coherence'. Seizing upon Nietzsche's interpretation of 'style de décadence' in the seventh section of *Der Fall Wagner*, in which stylistic decadence is seen to arise when the word is made sovereign at the expense of the whole, Lukács turns his attack on Herwarth Walden, the editor of the Expressionist magazine *Der Sturm*. He belabours Expressionist writers for neglecting the 'living context' of the sentence — in the same way as he haf belaboured them for ignoring a living social and political context. Here, once again, as with the Rilke-Weber-Mann criticism of Expressionism, the movement's formal irresponsibility is set on a parallel course with its political irresponsibility. The papier-mâché poetry of Expressionism is, according to Lukács, a faithful reflection of the whole movement's catchpenny response to political issues and social problems: the poetry, heavy with apocalyptic promise, proves to be as nugatory as the political opposition to capitalism and imperialism.

The following points ought to be made in answer to Lukács; his criticism represents the habitual charge of any literary-critical conservatism against any poetic revolution; in castigating Expressionism for being 'abstract' and 'timeless', he employs many of the epithets which Expressionist writers *liked* to use of themselves (Pinthus, for example, in his 1915 essay 'Zur jüngsten Dichtung', repudiates as 'the hotchpotch of our social, cultural, political, economic relations and institutions' precisely that 'reality' for which Lukács searches in vain in Expressionism); there is nothing in Lukács's formulations that could not be turned round and used against him and his literary-metaphysical jargon; his assertion that Expressionism was 'one of the bourgeois ideological currents which subsequently issue into Fascism' should be weighed against the fact that the Communists disrupted Weimar no less than the National Socialists with whom they were allied in 1932. Lukács's criticism of Expressionism is, moreover, clothed in the same kind of abstract language which he finds so objectionable in Expressionist writing: this is partly because he, like Expressionist writers, relies on the terminology of idealism to do his work for him and partly because he gleans almost all his material from diffuse Expressionist theoreticians. Consider the following glaireous slab which contains the nub of his criticism:

This abstracting impoverishment of content is not only an indication of Expressionism's line of development and, thus, of its fate, it is from the very beginning Expressionism's fundamental, insurmountable stylistic problem, for the extraordinary meagreness of content which is the direct result stands in screaming contrast to the pretentious claims of the delivery.[21]

How can it be '*Verarmung*' 'from the very beginning' when the German prefix 'ver-' implies gradual, subsequent deterioration? Why the portentousness of 'fate' when all he means is 'development'? Why, of all words, '*screaming* contrast' without a hint of irony and humour? This is exaggerated, pretentious, and . . . Expressionist stuff. So why bother with it? First, because Marxist criticism (of which Lukács is the leading practitioner) represents a major, influential dissenting voice and secondly, as with Thomas Mann's criticism, crucial and productive critical categories come to the surface — for example, the invertebrate and abstract quality of Expressionism's political involvement.

(d) *Stefan George/Friedrich Gundolf*   Man screams — not for the sake of screaming, but in order to rouse himself and his fellow human beings into offering help.[22]

Stefan George never belonged to the artistic avant-garde, yet he was a close observer of the contemporary literary scene. His career ran parallel with that of Expressionism, and many Expressionist writers admired George and were fascinated by him. Edschmid, in his 1918 speech 'Expressionismus in der Dichtung', asserts that 'after George it could not be forgotten that a great form was indispensable to a work of art', Benn's 1934 speech, 'Rede auf Stefan George', is emphatically pro-George, and Heym once tried to join the George circle. The implicit *and* explicit reverence felt by some Expressionist writers for George the poet and exemplary teacher is not reciprocated, for he despised and dismissed all Expressionist poetry wholesale. His repudiation of Expressionism is succinctly recorded by Edgar Salin: 'Expressionism as it was called also appeared to represent [between 1918–23] . . . a genuine resurgence of art — the disciples were strongly influenced by it. George listened to them patiently, scrutinized many Expressionist poems and rejected the lot'.[23] Early in his career George declares that 'art cannot concern itself with world reform and dreams of universal happiness which, at the present time according to some people in this country, contain the seed of everything new and yet, however attractive they may indeed be, belong to a different realm from that of poetry'[24] and subsequently remains faithful to this credo for much of his life. And as a poet who is concerned with transforming experience in the medium of art and with *in*direct expression of that experience by specific artistic means, he is set on a collision course with a political, activist movement which enthusiastically makes art available to a social purpose and, moreover, seeks to cast feelings, immediately and unmediated, into poetic form. A short piece of prose which George wrote in 1896 contains ante facto his critique of Expressionism. He takes it up again in 1903 and, with more relevance to our theme, in 1933 when clearly, in republishing it, he may be casting a retrospective glance at Expressionism. It is called 'Über Kraft':

One should be on one's guard against excessively violent eruptions of power in a work of art . . . behind such eruptions there is often no trace at all of authentic, deep feeling, but only festering immaturity or the strenuous effort to persuade oneself by means of one's own screams of something which is not present. True power is demonstrated if these eruptions are controlled . . . art is not pain, nor is it sensual pleasure, it is the triumph over the former and the transfiguration of the latter . . .[25]

In this quotation many of the threads of Expressionist criticism and of general poetic theory which we have used come together: Coleridge's 'interpenetration of spontaneous impulse and of voluntary purpose', Rilke's image of the volcano, Eliot's emphasis on due proportions and harmony, Weber's appeal for 'tamed passion', and the whole Valéryan ethos of maturity and his admonition that 'il faut prendre garde aux premiers mots . . .'.

Durzak, in his excellent book[26] on George, does not doubt that 'Über Kraft' contains George's critique of Expressionism. He is probably right. What is certain is that Friedrich Gundolf in *his* fierce condemnation of Expressionism is representing Stefan George's view of Expressionist poetry. That condemnation is to be found in the first chapter of Gundolf's *George* (Berlin, 1920). In this first chapter Gundolf is concerned to achieve three objectives: to eulogize the poetry of his master, to level a broadside at Expressionism, and to play down (or to unmask as a misunderstanding) the influence which George had on certain Expressionist writers. Gundolf's assault is vituperative. He draws up an inventory of Expressionism's sins — 'fanatical humanitarianism and overblown compassion', 'the demolition of all forms in a spiritual or material pulp', 'a lack of restraint, moderation and nucleus', 'luxuriating narcissism', 'abstract, all-inclusive philanthropy', 'repudiation of all standards' etc. etc. and the Expressionist writers themselves are 'puffed-up, second-rate school-masters', 'demented priests', 'ranting charlatans' etc. etc. Their characteristic noise is the scream. Then he continues:

The scream is at one and the same time an animal reaction, a political social programme and spiritual tension. They are screaming for the unattainable, for utopia, because the act of screaming itself is already an unburdening, a release, no matter what is being screamed for. Language is shattered into its illogical, sightless components, its pre-spiritual infantine babble because this very act of shattering is an expression of something.[27]

This is the conventional picture of the Expressionist poet — straining at the leash, pent-up passion bursting forth, yearning for unrealizable dreams, screaming for the sake of it, bestial, primitive, purely destructive, wreaking all sorts of havoc on language. It is the conventional picture in 1920 and the one arrived at and propagated ten years later in a seminal National Socialist work —

The freakish excrescence called Expressionism — a whole generation screamed for expression and found it no longer had anything to express. It called for beauty and had no ideal of beauty any more. In a new creative spirit it sought to thrust its way into life and had lost all real power to create. So expression became mannerism; no new power, no new style was evolved; instead, the process of atomisation was continued. Rootless, emotionally adrift, people devoured 'primitive art' . . .[28]

It is neither fortuitous nor arbitrary that the names of Gundolf/George and Rosenberg, set up by Hitler as the official National Socialist philosopher/historian, should be linked in the same context: Gundolf and George, courted without ultimate success by the National Socialists, who with characteristic eclecticism took from everywhere whatever could be made to serve their purpose, *and* Rosenberg, representing that wing of National Socialism which saw Expressionism as an integral part of degenerate modern art, come together in endorsing the standard image of the Expressionist poet. The names of Gundolf and Goebbels (much less hostile than Rosenberg to Expressionism) had already been linked in 1920/21 when Goebbels was working on his dissertation ('The Dramatist Wilhelm von Schütz. A Contribution to the History of the Romantic Drama') under Gundolf's direction in Heidelberg.

(e) *Robert Musil*

Let us avoid big words; we have too frequently
seen such words in league with vile deeds: let us
not conjure the unconjurable![29]

Musil's antipathy toward Expreṣsionism is total and culminates, in *Der Mann ohne Eigenschaften*, in the figure of the young poet Friedel Feuermaul,[30] an amusing parody of the activist philanthropic branch of Expressionism in general and of Werfel in particular. Feuermaul is 'gifted, young, immature'. He is also a pathetic figure, 'a little lambkin running to fat before its time', a careerist for ever mouthing 'Man is good' and other bromides, a Messiah, a 'man of feeling' not concerned to explain anything by rational argument or reasoned debate, an 'exponent of the spirit of the times', a champion of revolutionary views ('only so long as it doesn't actually come to any sort of revolution'), a man motivated by a profound 'sentiment towards "the old country" and its mission to mankind' — a sentiment, Musil adds caustically, 'that would as easily have turned to bringing back the obsolete omnibus with its three-horse team as to propaganda for Viennese porcelain'. Musil's satire is acrimonious and pertinent, for he believes that Feuermaul and poets like him are dangerous. Feuermaul raises huge expectations and claims all sorts of powers, yet, in practice, does nothing except add to universal moral chaos and to what Musil calls 'the general rubble of futile feelings'. Ultimately, when it matters, when a stand has to be taken, he and the message he brings are useless: he pales beside other characters in the novel, for example the fiercely pragmatic and hard-headed Bremshuber. Through another character, Arnheim, Musil speaks of 'modern youth's craving for stability and leadership': Feuermaul arrogates to himself the reins of moral, political and poetic leadership and, in his very small way, joins the ranks of those 'intellectual dictators' who Musil, in the 1930s, retrospectively believes have played a disproportionately large and fateful role in Germany's history: 'Long before the dictators our age brought forth a veneration for intellectual dictators. Think of George, Kraus and Freud, Adler and Jung. Add Klages and Heidegger to the list. The common factor here is probably a need for domination and leadership, for the essential characteristics of the saviour'.[31]

In a series of articles, reviews and essays written between 1912 and 1920, Musil is for ever taking the side of the intellect and rational thinking against passion and emotion. For example, in his 1912 essay 'Das Geistliche, der Modernismus und die Metaphysik', he writes scathingly of 'the soul's attempt to erupt' and of 'a shapeless excess of feeling from whose gelatinous mess modernism, too, draws its sustenance'. He reserves his real venom for those 'sceptics and reformers who dispense with precise thinking and then, with the help of an alleged "emotional intuition", invent a universal spirit or a cosmic soul or a god to satisfy their temperament or to achieve the "necessary" harmony or to round off their theory of life'. He believes that modern artists have not only renounced precise thinking, but have ceased to think altogether. In a 1913 review entitled 'Pilgrimage into the Interior'[32] he expresses anxiety about the modern writer's preoccupation with metaphysics and mysticism — the review begins 'Metaphysics is on the increase; woe to anyone who offers shelter to metaphysics! Quest by writers everywhere for God . . .'. People, he argues, are peculiarly vulnerable at this time (' . . . blithe defencelessness in the face of purveyors of doctrines of salvation'), the hawkers of pseudo-mystical panaceas are not accountable to anyone, and feeling is all. In Margarete Susmann's *Vom Sinn der Liebe*, one of the two books under review, the question 'Do you love me?' has been ousted by 'Do you love?', the stability of a belief in God by 'the dispossessed, consistently religious feeling in search of a new Lord'. A great deal of raw and fervent emotion is waiting, homeless and expectant, for the right strong cause.

Musil, like Thomas Mann, regards Expressionism as a force for irrationalism and unchecked emotionality. Expressionism, according to him, feeds into, and is in turn nourished by, the reservoir of hectically expectant public feeling and is symptomatic of what, in *Der Mann ohne Eigenschaften*, is characterized as 'the new generation's attack on objectivity. intellectual responsibility and the balanced personality' (p. 405). Its humanistic-philanthropic attitudes amount to little more than a pathetic gesture, exemplified by the fiasco of the 1918 revolution ('it lacked even the seriousness with which people turned out to watch the fire-brigade'; p. 630). Musil's particular scorn is reserved for Werfel: his diaries, essays and aphorisms are littered with more or less snide remarks about Werfel whom he regards as a charlatan. Yet, for a time he is at least outwardly close to early Expressionism because of his work on the Leipzig-based periodical *Der lose Vogel*. His recorded comments on Expressionism are without exception hostile and very dependent on Thomas Mann. There is, however, at least one occasion when Musil writes at length and in his own voice about Expressionism, in a 1921 essay entitled 'Geist und Erfahrung. Anmerkungen für Leser, welche dem "Untergang des Abendlandes" entronnen sind' (*Tagebücher, Aphorismen . . .*, pp. 651–67). Having completed a diagnosis of his age and rehearsed some of the themes which had appeared in his pre-war reviews, he turns to Expressionism:

This age, to give another example of it, has combined with Expressionism to vulgarize and dilute one of art's basic insights because those who sought to introduce spirit ('Geist') into poetry were not capable of thinking. They were not capable of it because they think in empty slogans ('Luftworte') which lack content, the restraint imposed by empiricism. Naturalism offered reality without spirit, Expressionism spirit without reality: both are un-spirit ('Ungeist'). (p. 666)

Lack of true content, lack of regard for practical experience, opposition to Naturalism — these are familiar comments, though they are strikingly well stated. Defective thinking, a fondness for heady bombast, and the primacy given to 'Geist' —these charges are certainly implied in the four other principal criticisms, but not with Musil's force. What is 'Geist'? Whole chapters have been devoted to skirmishing with the word's accretions and contradictions,[33] but Musil himself is in no doubt — at least, on the evidence of a letter to Adolf Frisé in January 1931, he is in no doubt that it is composed of reason and feeling and amounts to a mutual interpenetration of both. But for the Expressionist writers it has a mystical, all-purpose, incantatory quality which resides partly in its elusiveness and indefinability as its meaning distends to include irrationality, intuition, spirit, subconscious, passion *and* intellect, rationality, mind etc . . . The fundamental credo of Expressionism is that empirical reality is inferior to 'geistig' reality, but Musil, too, shares the same credo. He may disapprove of the *kind* of metaphysics practised by the Expressionist writers, he may come to voice his reservations about contemporary reverence for 'geistig' dictators, but he himself is involved in a spiritual quest, a search for some all-embracing 'geistig' reality (note how in the above extract, he rejects both Naturalism and Expressionism as 'Ungeist') composed of mysticism and reason, punctiliousness and soul, ratio and emotion — a reality which is as difficult to envisage as all the Expressionist blather about 'essence' ('Wesen'). There is very little trace in his *Verwirrungen des Zöglings Törless* or in *Der Mann ohne Eigenschaften* of a stringent condemnation of the fastidiously 'geistig' protagonists. The Expressionist credo, at all events, culminates in Hiller's loudly proclaimed project of founding a 'Bund der Geistigen' in 1918. Various seminal Expressionist works parade the word: Heinrich Mann's *Geist und Tat* (1910), Kandinsky's *Über das Geistige in der Kunst* (1912) and Hiller's *Tätiger Geist* (1917/18) are obvious examples. Ironically, Musil, by employing 'Geist' in his critique of Expressionism, is echoing one of the most popular slogans (i.e. 'Luftworte') of the day,[34] popular not only with Expressionist writers and artists, but also part of the common currency amongst intellectuals like Henry Pachter who, looking back in 1971 to the stance he and people like him adopted in the 1920s, *still* resorts to this mysterious and untranslatable talisman:

We too were Romantics about the state; we too agreed that the Republic had no Geist; we too lacked real contact with the masses; we too saw ourselves as members of the elite; we too ridiculed the Republic as an ugly thing. We agreed: The Republic had no style.[35]

It remains to determine whether it is merely another Expressionist 'Luftwort' or can stand as a useful and fruitful critical category in any consideration of the movement.

The criticisms assembled in the preceding pages also embrace the principal charges which have been levelled at Expressionism by commentators other than those quoted. Without exception, the criticisms are either directly or indirectly adverse and cast in general terms. The fact that on occasions they can be turned round and directed at the critic's own work or that profound reservations may be expressed about their tone or their terminology does not necessarily diminish their validity or importance. The critical categories can be distilled to: formal arbitrariness and adventitiousness, political irresponsibility culminating in some kind of complicity in the rise of National Socialism, thematic insubstantiality, irrationalism, excessive emotionality, syntactical iconoclasm and heady rhetorical effluvium.

NOTES

1 E. Wilson, *Axel's Castle* (London, 1964), dedication.
2 S. T. Coleridge, *Biographia Literaria*, edited by J. Shawcross, 2 vols (Oxford, 1973), II, 49–50.
3 E. Mühsam, *Unpolitische Erinnerungen* (Berlin, 1961), p. 12.
4 Letter to Lou Andreas-Salomé, 8 August 1903; *Briefe aus den Jahren 1892–1904* (Leipzig, 1939), p. 380.
5 See the letter to Ficker of 8 February 1915; *Briefe aus den Jahren 1914–1921* (Leipzig, 1938), pp. 33–35.
6 Quoted in: E. Kolinsky, *Engagierter Expressionismus* (Stuttgart, 1970), p. 78.
7 Paul Valéry, *Variété V* (Paris, 1945), p. 131.

8 Rilke (1903–04), quoted in: P. Zech, *Rainer Maria Rilke: Der Mensch und das Werk* (Dresden, 1930), pp. 113–14.

9 F. Nietzsche, *Menschliches, Allzumenschliches II; Nietzsche Werke: Kritische Gesamtausgabe*, edited by G. Colli and M. Montinari, 30 vols (Berlin, 1967–), IV/3, 62. Unless otherwise stated, all quotations from Nietzsche's work will be taken from this edition.

10 G. Benn, 'Expressionismus'; *Gesammelte Werke*, I (1959), 246.

11 Thomas Mann, *Gesammelte Werke*, 13 vols (Frankfurt a.M., 1974), XII, 564.

12 K. Pinthus, 'Zur jüngsten Dichtung', *Die Weißen Blätter*, 2, Heft 12 (July–September 1915), 1503.

13 K. Pinthus, 'Rede für die Zukunft', *Die Erhebung*, 1 (Berlin, 1920), 411.

14 L. Rubiner (ed.), *Kameraden der Menschheit* (Potsdam, 1919), p. 173.

15 Max Weber, *Gesammelte Politische Schriften* (Munich, 1921), p. 435.

16 Quoted by G. Hufnagel, *Kritik als Beruf. Der kritische Gehalt im Werke Max Webers* (Frankfurt a.M., 1971), p. 121.

17 F. Werfel, *Zwischen oben und unten* (Stockholm, 1946), pp. 361–62. Note this passage is quoted by Joachim Fest in his brilliant *Das Gesicht des Dritten Reiches* (Munich, 1963), p. 353, to clinch his argument that culture played a part in its own destruction and in the rise of National Socialism.

18 For all these quotations from Mann's 'Deutsche Ansprache' see *Gesammelte Werke*, XI, 876–77.

19 W. Benjamin, 'Linke Melancholie', in: *Lesezeichen*, edited by G. Seidel (Leipzig, 1970), p. 255.

20 Georg Lukács, '"Größe und Verfall" des Expressionismus'; *Werke*, 17 vols (Neuwied and Berlin, 1962–75), IV (1971), 121.

21 '"Größe und Verfall"'; *Werke*, IV, 121.

22 K. Pinthus, 'Rede für die Zukunft', p. 419.

23 E. Salin, *Um Stefan George* (Munich and Düsseldorf, 1954), p. 216.

24 S. George, *Blätter für die Kunst*, Preface to first series, 1 (1892).

25 *Werke*, 2 vols (Munich and Düsseldorf, 1958), I, 531–32.

26 M. Durzak, *Zwischen Symbolismus und Expressionismus: Stefan George* (Stuttgart, Berlin, Cologne and Mainz, 1974).

27 F. Gundolf, *George* (Berlin, 1920), p. 20.

28 A. Rosenberg, *Der Mythus des zwanzigsten Jahrhunderts* (Munich, 1930), p. 284.

29 H. Carossa, *Ungleiche Welten*, in: *Sämtliche Werke*, 2 vols (Frankfurt a.M., 1962), II, 838.

30 See chapters 36, 37 and 38 of Book 2, third part.

31 R. Musil (1934–37), *Tagebücher, Aphorismen, Essays und Reden* (Hamburg, 1955), p. 398.

32 To be found in: *Die Neue Rundschau*, 24 (1913), vol. 1, 588.

33 For a discussion of the word, see Pascal, *From Naturalism . . .*, pp. 297–305.

34 Thomas Mann uses the word in his critique of Expressionism, and note how the article from which Musil's critique is extracted is headed 'Geist und Erfahrung . . .'.

35 Quoted in: R. G. L. Waite, *The Psychopathic God Adolf Hitler* (New York, 1977), p. 320.

C

III AUGUST STRAMM

> Don't ask for a formula that might open
> worlds; just a few maimed syllables dry as a
> twig.[1]

Stramm was born in Münster on 29 July 1874, a decade before most of the other leading Expressionist poets.[2] In 1893 he left school and entered the postal service. In 1902, five years after completing his military service, he married Else Krafft, a popular novelist. He continued a successful career in the Reserve and in the postal service. Between 1897 and 1903 he worked in the 'Seepostdienst' plying between Bremen, Hamburg and New York. In 1905 he began attending lectures at Berlin University. Four years later he completed a doctoral dissertation and had by this time reached the highest possible position in the postal service for a man of his age. He had also been promoted to 'Oberleutnant' in the Reserve. Since 1902 he had been writing plays, but in 1910 he seems to have become aware of new poetic gifts, though the real breakthrough of creative powers and a new style did not occur for another two or three years. With the exception of one poem and the songs in *Die Bauern* (1902/07), his earliest extant poems date from 1914. In March or April of that year he met Herwarth Walden, the editor of the magazine *Der Sturm*, and a close friendship began. Soon afterwards he sent some poems to Walden and spoke of an intended cycle. Between March and July 1914 he wrote *Du*, a collection of love poems. He was called up in August 1914 and was soon fighting in the Vosges and Alsace. By August 1915 he had written *Tropfblut*, a collection of war poems. His other works include the long poems *Die Menschheit* (1914) and *Weltwehe* (1914–15), eleven other poems, two prose pieces, nine plays and the fragments of another play. After the battle for Ostrow in May 1915 he was awarded the Iron Cross first class. In August he was on leave in Berlin: he rejected Walden's offer to have him removed from further fighting. Full of grim premonitions he returned to the front line on 17 August and, after a total of seventy engagements since the August of the previous year, he was killed in action, the last surviving member of his company, in the Rokitno marshes. There was something almost wilfully suicidal about his final stand.

When asked in a radio interview why his characters never seemed interested in politics or general ideas, Harold Pinter replied:

I'm dealing with these characters at the extreme edge of their living, where they are living pretty much alone, at their hearth, their home hearth . . . We all, I think . . . may have sexual relationships or go to political meetings or discuss ideas, but when we get back to our rooms and we are faced with a bed and we are either alone or with someone else, then

. . . I don't think we go on long about ideas or political allegiances . . . I mean, there comes a point surely, where this living in *the* world must be tied up with living in *your own* world, where you are — in your room . . .[3]

People 'at the extreme edge of their living', 'pretty much alone', 'faced with a bed', 'living in *your own* world', all thoughts of the outside world driven out by immediate personal concerns, this is certainly the world of *The Caretaker* and *The Birthday Party*: it is also the world of Stramm's poetry and plays and, in quite definite ways, of Stramm himself. During the last two years of his life, according to his daughter Inge,[4] he had no friends, he was never a member of a literary circle (although *Der Sturm* welcomed and adopted him, this seems to have been a purely professional arrangement), he was a stranger to Bohemian life and the coffee-house atmosphere, he felt stifled by the tedium of his bourgeois existence, and he was not understood by his wife whose success and uninhibited fluency as a writer of vastly popular cheap novels was a shaming reminder to him of his failure to find a publisher. The poetry which an inner power suddenly drove him to write and which came to dominate his life alienated his family: 'Poetry seethed in him like a disease which frightened us all. His earnestness would all of a sudden cut across our laughter like hoar-frost.'[5] He would shepherd his bewildered children (the only audience which, 'when compelled to listen to him, did not tap its forehead'[6]) into his study to hear his poetry. It is a poetry founded in a desperate sense of isolation, a fascination for the sexual and instinctual, a profound disillusionment with twentieth-century culture and the present state of 'German intellectual life',[7] and a bitter impatience not only with 'everything called art',[8] but also with existing vocabulary and syntax. Early particular political interests (expressed in his plays) disappear behind generalized metaphysical concerns, and yet, all the time, the reader is aware of Stramm's anguished voice. His painstakingly wrought verse is a strange, hybrid creature: it is a haven *and* the cause of further alienation; it is the sole repository and source of reality *and* agonizing testimony to his inability to 'fix the smallest mood'[9] with the verbal means available to him, it mirrors fundamental truths about man's existential suffering *and* yet clearly issues from the intensely personal distress of one struggling human being. There is no vestige of self-pity: indeed there is no palpable self. The panic-striken 'I' of the letters from the front line does not reappear in the poetry which is written, as it were, by another August Stramm: 'Dear fellow! Who are You? Man or woman! I never find what I am looking for! I am man and woman! I have been reading the poems of an August Stramm . . . they have moved me dreadfully.'[10] The mental and emotional turmoil of the letters is distilled into the spare, meticulously constructed poems of *Tropfblut*, but in all other respects — in mood, tone and syntax — the poetry is an extension of the letters: 'The lamp flickers and squints the stars float hazily' is not the first line or an early draft of a poem (though it could be either), but a sentence in a letter home (to the Waldens, 20 August 1914; Pörtner, p. 46). The sense of annihilating loneliness which pervades *Du* (with the exception of such poems as 'Trieb' and 'Erhört'), far from being alleviated by the community and companionship of fighting, is intensified. The war pushes Stramm and 'his boys' further to 'the edge of their living'. What perhaps began as a means of self-justification or as a kind of escape from routine and a sense of personal inadequacy leads to something vastly different from a Baudelairean aestheticism or what Pound calls 'maudlin confession . . . irresponse to human aggression . . . the faint susurrus of . . . subjective hosannah.'[11] The poems of *Tropfblut* represent the precipitation of Stramm's deepening awareness of man's ineluctably tragic existence and of his own part in it. At the same time, and with a dreadful irony which is not lost upon Stramm, war is felt to be the paradigm of life lived in extremis and, as such, is an ideal source of poetry, is *already* poetry — on 6 October 1914, two months after joining up he writes home from the front line: 'Where are words for what we are experiencing. Cumbersome wretched things. I do not write poetry anymore, everything around me is poem' (to the Waldens; Pörtner, p. 47); and six weeks later he writes: 'Yes, indeed! Awful days! . . . Life is quite uniquely intensified' (to the Waldens, 22 November 1914; *Erinnerungsbuch*, p. 81). His strenuous attempts to render, against the odds, an account of the experience of war meet with derision: the letter of 6 October continues 'Miserable craven insidious horror and the air looks on with a scornful snigger gurgling and thundering down from the mountains'.

Stramm's gratitude to Walden for publishing the poems of *Du* and *Tropfblut* in the pages of *Der Sturm* was immense. In the course of eighteen months with the periodical in 1914 and 1915 he was represented by seventy-five poems, seven plays and two short prose pieces. Walden for his part looked to Stramm to put poetry on the same footing as the plastic arts. He felt the greatest respect for Stramm's work and was quick to acknowledge its crucial importance to *Der Sturm*: 'One must have a guiding-light. I provide them with such a light by giving them [the members of the *Sturm* school] the name of this artist August Stramm'.[12] And Lothar Schreyer, another of the leading theoreticians, underlined Stramm's achievements on behalf of *Der Sturm*, for Stramm 'has raised word and language from the decay of uncreative daily usage and rediscovered the word as a resonant symbol' (Rittich, p. 55). To the men who ran *Der Sturm*, 'the leading organ of Expressionism' (as its own advertisement proclaimed in 1918), Stramm was the most successful practitioner of the 'Wortkunsttheorie', the magazine's autonomous theory of poetry. There seems to have taken place a remarkably timely coincidence of theory and practice. Walden and the others had spent years of furious, glum pedantry spinning their interminable theoretical webs and looking round desperately for someone with talent to practise what they were preaching. Stramm had spent even longer listening to his wife's 'singing type-writer'[13] and searching for a sympathetic publisher and audience. Little readjustment was needed on either side. The magazine, first published in 1910, began with a negative social criticism of the most general, ineffectual sort, passed through an entirely aesthetic, apolitical period and ended by 1932 with a whole-hearted championing of Communism. Stramm's contribution was to the second of these three stages, the period of the so-called '*Sturm*lehre'.

Early in his career, however, Stramm had shown an interest in social problems. His life from 1903 onwards is very reminiscent of that of many young English poets who came down from the universities in the first decade of the new century and pledged themselves to Fabian Socialism. His left-wing tendencies nearly involved him in a duel with a right-wing officer in the Reserve. He attended lectures on history, philosophy, economics and finance at Friedrich Wilhelm University in Berlin, where he became particularly interested in the doctrines of Karl Marx and the agrarian reforms of Adolph Damaschke. Inge confirms that her father was an ardent Social Democrat, and certainly his plays reveal that there was no hint of 'on the left above the parties'[14] about his concern with the plight of the socially deprived. For example, in his first play *Die Bauern* (1902/07) which is clearly influenced by Hauptmann, Stramm aligns himself with the downtrodden peasantry. The play *Der Gatte* (1909) demonstrates the lengths to which poverty drives the lower classes, whilst *Die Unfruchtbaren* (written 1910–1914, published 1916) combines a grimly naturalistic depiction of the life of four students in seedy Berlin lodgings with unsubtle propaganda for the ideas of Damaschke, guileless moralizing about the licentiousness of modern students, praise for the institution of marriage and fierce social criticism of a general kind. This criticism has nothing in common with the abstract and ultimately futile schemes for social and universal amelioration purveyed, for example, in the pages of another major Expressionist magazine, *Die Aktion*: Stramm's plays convey an understanding of the human problems they depict, they are sustained by a rigorous attention to detail and do not slither off into grandiose master-plans for the whole of mankind. Radrizzani (p. 423) places another of Stramm's plays, *Rudimentär*, alongside Strindberg's *Miss Julie* as the best written one-acter of Naturalism. It is not simply a naturalistic attack on miserable social conditions, but a commentary on man's parlous metaphysical situation, isolation and inability to communicate. Money and sensual enjoyment are the only determining factors of the characters' actions. Even the death of a child does not distract the characters for long from thoughts of money and sex. Their consciousness shrivels until it is nothing more than the marionette of material need. Twitches, convulsions, sudden accesses of nervous excitability replace the normal currency of civilized social behaviour. Stramm has an accurate ear for the linguistic solecisms of the vernacular: he recaptures the repetitiousness, the discontinuity, the inflections, the circularity of everyday speech; language in his plays loses almost all of its rhetorical informative element and becomes the medium through which a contest of wills is fought out and brief victories and vicious betrayals are registered. All dramatic motivations, all personal constants are absent: 'The play is set as it were in the Hades of capitalism and shows the skeleton of modern humanity in ghastly highlight.'[15] Here we have, in no uncertain terms, a retort to Mann's charge of 'irresponsibility to reality' and to Lukács's contention that Expressionism fails to provide a 'social, political, economic context' or 'the concrete social determinants' which shape the lives of ordinary people.

Some of Stramm's other plays (for example *Die Haidebraut, Erwachen, Sancta Susanna, Kräfte* and *Geschehen*) concentrate on man's metaphysical plight, but *not* to the exclusion of a portrayal of social conditions. Frequently Stramm is concerned to show how the petty restrictions and philistine hypocrisies of bourgeois society inevitably collide with natural instincts and the vast cosmic visions to which the characters are prey. He is expert at evoking a fetid atmosphere, heavy with sexual tension, where the embattled characters talk past each other, and violence (physical and psychological) lies barely concealed beneath the surface. Until recently it was thought that only two prose-works (*Der Letzte* and *Warten*) had survived, but, a few years ago, Peter Michelsen found an essay by Stramm entitled 'Auswanderer' ('Emigrants') in the *Vossische Zeitung* of 6 August 1903. This essay[16] initially looks like being a pedestrian recitation of statistics: mundane descriptions of people emigrating and immigrating are accompanied by unspectacular insights into their motivation. Then, abruptly, a political attitude and a social conscience begin to obtrude. For example, Stramm points out that many emigrants work on the land and are fleeing their homes because of wretched wages. He warns that problems will inevitably arise unless emigration and immigration are officially curbed. He describes the conditions on board the ships conveying the emigrants: these conditions used to be dreadful, he maintains, and continue to be bad for certain passengers, because a notorious system of class distinctions prevails. Moreover, there is something extremely adventitious about the immigration process at New York. Those who do stay have unsuspectingly become 'nature's tool for bringing about the stable, balanced distribution of the masses' (*Euphorion*, p. 210) — man's complete subjection to an extraneous power, in this case personified Nature, becomes a recurring theme in Stramm's poetry. It would be absurd to exaggerate the importance of this slight essay and make it out to be a kind of twentieth-century equivalent of Büchner's polemical tract *Der hessische Landbote*, but in his use of such phrases and concepts as 'an equal distribution of people', 'the most important tasks of social welfare', [alleviation of] 'need, poverty and race-hatred' and 'unsatisfactory apportionment of landed property', Stramm demonstrates a more than superficial concern for his fellow-men and an unsophisticated awareness of continuing twentieth-century problems. A thoroughly drab recital of statistics gives way to a series of grim (and grimly accurate) predictions and humane insights which, for their detailed research alone, contrast starkly with the raucous protestations and melodramatic advocacies of the early *Sturm* social criticism.

Moving on from a vague, generalized, hectoring and crude assault on the bourgeoisie, Walden insists that art, *Sturm* art, should become the magazine's sole concern and he is so successful and determined in this severing of art from all political, social and economic factors that he and those around him on the magazine remain studiedly and blissfully unaware of the 'threatening clouds' of the First World War (*Erinnerungsbuch*, p. 61). Walden comes to regard art as the distillation of inspired intuition and as totally independent of the rationalistic and moral doctrines enshrined in the middle-class concept of 'Bildung': Stramm, too, places art, *his* art, above all other considerations.

The '*Sturm*lehre' is based in, and derives sustenance from, a series of hostilities — hostility to the past, to the bourgeoisie, to any mimetic theory of art, to traditional and habit-created textures of thought and feeling, to moderation and rationality, to current linguistic structures and to all types of mechanical prosodic patterns. Art is not regarded as communication, but as a rhythmic composition — colour, tone, word, optical and acoustic elements are its material. Although portrayals of external reality are to be avoided and although the *Sturm* artist's first movement is always away from the object because he is endeavouring to offer not 'an account of existence' but 'judgement on existence',[17] the *Sturm* theorists maintain that they are not fleeing reality, 'real' reality:

. . . modern art is not a turning away from reality, not a flight to an ideal of beauty outside the world. On the contrary, the full vital meaning of the age is that we must strive to penetrate to the very core of reality, to the skeleton which bears that reality . . . the spirit of the modern age aspires beyond the earth to that reality which challenges man to act and to make himself master of it. [18]

This statement of the aims of modern art is no different from the customary Expressionist injunction (common to writers who had nothing to do with *Der Sturm*) to penetrate beyond the surface of things to their essence: at this important point *Der Sturm*'s privately evolved project is of a piece with general Expressionist theory. If the surface of things is to be ignored, then abstract Expressionism (Walden and the others argue), devoid of all religious, political and ethical elements, is the ideal. The goal is to objectivize subjective states (but then surely there is a sense in which all literature does this?) with the highest degree of precision and to achieve a pellucid concreteness of detail and what Sokel calls a kind of 'translogical reality'. [19] The means to this goal are linguistic experimentation and distortion, ruthless compression and avoidance of the kind of rhetorical bluster practised by Werfel and Becher whom the *Sturm* poets despised, the adoption of a fastidiously atomistic approach to language, exploitation of the acoustic and rhythmic possibilities of words, and apparently blind faith in inspiration and intuition. Form issues from a kind of inner necessity: the artist does not select a poetic form and squeeze his words into it. Form grows with content and is inseparable from it. Content is unimportant — in his obituary for Stramm, Walden writes: 'Your art is thought-less. And therefore it is art, therefore it is.' (*Erinnerungsbuch*, p. 70). Critics have accordingly tended to dismiss the content of Stramm's poetry as merely derivative of his two favourite books, Prentice Mulford's *Der Unfug des Sterbens* (translated into German in 1909) and Ralph Waldo Trine's *In Harmonie mit dem Unendlichen* (written in 1897). Furthermore, the *Sturm* poet stands outside time, his work should aim to 'shock through ecstasy' (Soergel, p. 598) and should issue from and in intense feeling. Walden, Schreyer and the other theorists continually rehearse a dialectical pattern in which primacy is given to the irrational, the intuitive, the unconscious, the rhythmic and organic, the unique, the single word, the inner vision. Implicit in Stramm's poetry is a firm, but not slavish, allegiance to the premises and presuppositions of the '*Sturm*lehre'. And whilst examination of the *Sturm* theorists does bring forth explicit pointers to an understanding of Stramm's poetry, it will be surprising if it does emerge that Walden is wholly right in maintaining that Stramm's poems have no sustaining content or theme.

Amidst all the theorizing one paradox in particular obtrudes, and incidentally touches upon Rilke's criticism of Expressionism. On the one hand, according to the '*Sturm*lehre', the artist becomes merely the medium of an insight which does not impinge upon his will or his understanding; he plays host to his art and is sacrificed for its sake: 'Art is not created, art creates. It bears the artist who bears it. Art lives the artist who dies for it' (*Erinnerungsbuch*, p. 71), he is purely passive, 'the tool which has been made ready by the urgent necessity of the vision to shape the poem . . . the will-less servant' [20] whose duty it is to 'release feelings, not to shape them' (Schreyer; Soergel, p. 598). On the other hand, phrases such as 'the form-giving man' (which the true *Sturm* artist is supposed to be) and 'the inner law' (which he is supposed to obey), suggestive of some kind of conscious ordering, are bandied about with such earnestness that they assume amuletic qualities. The whole '*Sturm*lehre' with its meticulously elaborated rules is underpinned by a fierce will-to-construction and by a dread of the adventitiousness and arbitrariness which, as Walden is keen to demonstrate, ruin Goethe's and Heine's poetry: The very sight of a poem by any of the now virtually unknown *Sturm* poets betrays a shaping hand and a controlling mind:

> Beile geilen Treten
> Sande beten
> Sande leben
> Sande heben
> Sande herrschen
> Weihen sonnen
> Weihen binden
> Weihen kränzen
> Weihen ketten
> Rote Tannen irren rote Tode.[21]

Axes lust stepping. Sands pray. Sands live. Sands raise. Sands rule. Consecrations sun. Consecrations tie. Consecrations garland. Consecrations chain. Red firs stray red deaths.

We are left with an odd picture — placing absolute faith in his senses and unmediated inspiration, surrendering to emotion and to the visions invoked in him by some power over which he apparently has no control, the *Sturm* poet makes an idol of unconsciousness and spontaneity. Then, abruptly, he proceeds to stall inspiration and sets to work shaping, condensing and imposing a pattern upon the vision with which he has been blessed. Will-lessness, suddenly and apparently without transition, yields to a strenuous will-to-shape and an access of rationality. One thinks again of Coleridge's idea of a 'salutary antagonism' (rather appropriately Stramm has a poem called 'Frostfeuer' — 'Frostfire'), but this 'salutary antagonism' amounts, in the case of Stramm and other *Sturm* poets, to a bewildering compound of the kind of eruptive inspiration which Rilke denigrates and of a fierce commitment to formal control which he misses in Expressionist poetry. By this token, the *Sturm* poet 'bears and is borne by his visions',[22] and Stramm is a poet who 'proceeds from will-less visualization, but files and hammers at his visions' (Soergel, p. 604). This implies the presence of heedful thought and rationality, the very qualities which Stramm and the others are at pains to repudiate ('Every thought is a reflecting. Every thought is a remembering . . . But your art is thought-less . . . The creative artist does not know rational logic'; (Rittich, p. 26) and which are so obviously at work in their own poetry. Schreyer categorically denies that the *Sturm* poet is ever out of control or that there is anything heedless about Expressionism as it is practised by the *Sturm* artists:

Expressionism is not the uninhibited communication of an inner world of images which takes shape in the psyche. Only if the artist controls his inner life, allying himself to the formative powers and thus ordering the world of images which appear to him so that it is not an arbitrary but an organic and harmonious work which is created — only then will the full meaning of Expressionism be realized. (Rittich, p. 12)

But how can a 'will-less servant and tool' 'control his inner life' or 'order the world of images which appear to him'? Will he not thus be jeopardizing the autonomy, the purity of the original vision? The 'salutary antagonism', the 'heat and cold' which marked Stramm's private life as husband and father, has intensified into an apparently irreconcilable conflict between uncritical passivity and fastidiously imposed will.

The thirty-one poems of *Du* were written in the Spring and Summer of 1914 before the outbreak of the war. The volume was compiled in January 1915, when Stramm was on leave in Berlin, and printed by the '*Sturm*verlag' in the same year. They express a yearning and striving for harmony with a 'Du', a seeking for love. Sometimes the quest is successful and the poem culminates in an ecstasy of sexual fulfilment, more often the poet's search is futile and ends in bitter disillusionment, but always the search continues, frantically and urgently:

> Mein Suchen sucht!
> . . .
> Und Du und Du und Du
> Viel tausend Du
> Und immer Du
> Allwege Du ('Wankelmut')

My seeking seeks . . . And You and You and You. Many thousand You. And always You. All ways You.

The 'Du' has been variously interpreted as Stramm's wife, as God, as the cosmos, as somebody/anybody of the opposite sex, as the opposite sex, as somebody/anybody outside the poet's self. Bozzetti (p. 129) argues that the longing for a 'Du' represents a 'longing for the unity of all being', 'for the confluence of everything disparate,' 'for the removal of all boundaries' and 'for the suspension of time' and he quotes the line 'Du bannt die Zeit' ('"You" banishes time') from the poem 'Wunder' to support his argument. Perhaps it is more helpful to interpret the 'Du' as Woman who exerts an irresistible sexual attraction on the poet and whom he regards as the only potential mediatrix between Man and the mysteries of the cosmos. If, according to the *Sturm* theorists, the essence of all being is movement and emotion, and if Man is to harmonize his feelings with the movement of all being, then he can do so only with the assistance of a 'Du'. In many of the poems there is a constant striving for an undefined cosmic harmony beyond the realm of sensual experience. Stramm is the opposite of prudish: he sees sex as a source of ecstasy *and* as a perfectly appropriate theme for poetry, though he denounces gratification by prostitution in the poem 'Freudenhaus':

> Lichte dirnen aus den Fenstern
> Die Seuche
> Spreitet an der Tür
> Und bietet Weiberstöhnen aus!
> Frauenseelen schämen grelle Lache!
> Mutterschösse gähnen Kindestod!

Lights wench out of the windows. Contagion/Straddles at the door. And offers moaning whores for sale! Women's souls shame shrill laughter! Mothers' wombs yawn child-death!

The poems 'Erhört' and 'Erfüllung' are about sexual fulfilment, but such poems are outnumbered by those which have sexual incompatibility, betrayal and conflict as their themes. It is perhaps significant that the last poem in the cycle, 'Erinnerung', ends on a note of heavy defeat:

> Dir
> Den
> Weg
> Den unbegangenen
> Nie
> Gefundenen Weg
> Zu
> Mir!

To You The Way The untrodden Never Found way To Me!

Occasionally the poet's partner is compliant, occasionally she yields to his importunate demands. But her usual ploy is to be coquettish and unfaithful: verbs like 'kichern' ('giggle'), 'lächeln' ('smile'), 'tändeln' ('flirt') and 'lachen' ('laugh') recur. She scorns and rebuffs him, she plays at reconciliations, and then she abandons him:

> Du
> Wendest
> Fort!

You Turn Away.

Or they argue and fight, he demands and she resists: sometimes their contests end in reconciliation as in 'Zwist', but a more typical conclusion is that of 'Begegnung' where the poet is left with an annihilating sense of failure and deprivation ('Blödes Zagen lahmet fort / Beraubt beraubt!'; ('Craven wavering limps away / Bereft bereft!') and 'Schwermut' where life peters out into cavernous silence. Stramm is concerned to catch and condense moments of acute emotional crisis and ecstasy — moments when feelings are running high, moments of passionate reconciliation after passionate strife, moments of abysmal defeat in the quest for sexual satisfaction or psychological harmony. His poems are highly concentrated visions. There are no descriptions of scenes or people, no circumlocutions: there is no question of cluttering the background or foreground with superfluous biographical or descriptive elements. The intention is not to pose language before us, but to short-circuit our expectations of it, to induce a response direct from the nerves. The dynamic brevity, issuing from an agonized apprehension of reality, is an accentuation of detail, amounting to something far beyond a sympathetic and careful photography. It is misleading to call Stramm 'a lyrical Naturalist'[23] or to declare that his poems are 'life-like structures'[24] as if he were interested in offering snapshots of reality. He is not intent on showing the external world to be an objectively present and fixed phenomenon. The development in his two volumes of verse is from the extensive to the intensive, from a conceptual apprehension of reality to a determination to allow reality to stand for itself. Thus he avoids adjectives and participles (which give width to descriptions) in favour of verbs which have a dynamic character and which are capable of expressing permanent intensity, especially if they are used intransitively. To underline his argument that descriptions of external reality decrease sharply in Stramm's poetry, Bozzetti shows that, while three out of ten adjectives in the early poems are colour adjectives, none at all is to be found in Stramm's later poetry. The poems of *Du* (all written before August 1914) contain some, not many, conventional adjectives, whereas the poems of *Tropfblut* (all written during the war) contain fewer adjectives, and almost all of these are neologisms. Verbs, which of their nature place reality under the aspect of time and enable us to see it as a constantly evolving process, are best suited to capture the essence of something for ever moving and for ever moved. Stramm's view of reality as a 'becoming' and not a static 'being' is pure Nietzsche, as is his habit of downgrading and repudiating as inauthentic everything which claims to be completed, to be stationary, to be known or merely to be.

The climactic moment which the poem 'Untreu' seeks to catch is that of a perfidious betrayal:

> Dein Lächeln weint in meiner Brust
> Die glutverbissnen Lippen eisen
> Im Atem wittert Laubwelk!
> Dein Blick versargt
> Und
> Hastet polternd Worte drauf.
> Vergessen
> Bröckeln nach die Hände!
> Frei
> Buhlt dein Kleidsaum
> Schlenkrig
> Drüber rüber!

Your smile weeps in my breast. The fire-wrought lips ice over. In your breathing leaf-wither weathers! Your look coffins And Hurls words rattling down on top. Our hands crumble Forgetfulness after it! Loosely The hem of your dress woos Dangly Thither hither!

The poet meets his faithless lover who betrays her faithlessness in her very gestures. The words of the poem form an abstract pattern which corresponds to the poet's inward state, and that pattern is a dynamic one. This is an example of what T. S. Eliot calls poetry of the first voice, that of the poet talking to himself or no one, and devoid of didactic or social function. In such a poem, Eliot maintains, where 'the first voice . . . dominates, the "psychic material" tends to create its own form.'[25] In 'Untreu' we see that the 'psychic material', the creative germ of a vision or experience, has indeed shaped the form — and thus, incidentally, fulfilled one of the main precepts of the 'Sturmlehre'. The gradual realization of infidelity and withered love is reflected in the accelerating and shortening first four lines; then comes the abrupt hiatus provided by the thud of 'und' as suspicion becomes confirmed fact. The girl rattles off excuses; the gloom of *his* passion is enshrined in the heavy, stranded word 'vergessen', whilst her couldn't-care-less attitude is captured in the saltatory last lines as she sways away seductively and coquettishly. The crumbling of the earth over the grave of their love is echoed in the crumbling lines: the impetuous haste, beginning with the brutal 'und' and ending in the equally harsh 'drauf', fades into the softer sounds of the unstressed end-syllables of 'Vergessen' and 'Hände'. Furthermore, the theme of the poem (betrayal, the whole appearance-reality dichotomy) is reflected in the form, in the way in which the sentences are built around opposites: smiling-crying, passionate lips-ice, breath-decay, her hectic words and swift movements — his apparently numb, shell-shocked state. The verse pattern is iambic during the initial period of contemplation, but breaks into the trochaic rhythm typical of Stramm's poetry once the girl starts moving. There is only one adjective — 'glutverbissnen' — which is a neologism: the predicative function falls almost entirely upon the array of wonderfully evocative verbs, the intensity of the mood is in no way inhibited or diluted by static descriptions. Instead, the metaphors build up a world from which reality is interpreted.

The poem has a startling immediacy and offers a direct apprehension of a sense of betrayal. The girl is dynamic, a node of energy and sexual attraction: without exception, parts of her body and clothing form the subject of every verb, evoking a response in the poet's mind. She works a series of physical changes in him, whilst he seems reduced by the certain knowledge of her infidelity to a static object. Her mastery is apparent from the first line, where her specious smile causes grief in his heart. The paradox of a 'weeping smile' demonstrates the extreme ambiguity of the relationship between the man and the girl: the smile is a surface reaction, it is not 'accepted' by the man's innermost self, it is transformed into its opposite. Her lips, fresh from her illicit passion, turn his feelings to ice or, perhaps, are now turned to ice *for him* — the link with 'Eisen' ('iron') and all that that word connotes of unbending hardness is obvious: they are separated by something as strong as iron which the heat, the 'glow', of her passion could melt down if she still loved him. And then, in line 3, comes the first intimation of death and decay. Her breath, the indication of life, is mixed with the smell of mouldering foliage. The verb 'wittern' has many resonances: that of weathering and decomposing ('verwittern'), also of thundering and tempestuous raging ('gewittern'). Moreover, in its own right, the verb 'wittern' is often associated with animals and conjures up precisely the appropriate atmosphere of sexuality, primitive instinct and the chase. 'Versargt' ('coffins') has been carefully chosen not only for its stem 'Sarg' (coffin), but also for its propinquity to 'versagt' — her look falters, fails, 'says falsely', her eye drops and will not meet his, she feels guilty, momentarily. The fact that her glance 'fails' is for him the death-knell of their love — 'versargt' clearly has this meaning. Her hectic excuses pummel down onto the coffin of that love, just like earth tossed into an open grave. Their hands, having forgotten how they used to hold each other, crumble limply away — the mouldering foliage and the lifeless hands convey perfectly the idea of stale love and atrophied feelings. And then, in the last four lines, the girl flounces alluringly away. Deceit has taken possession of her whole body, of her every movement: she wants only to forget and bury her love for the man. She is free, whereas he is still very much her captive, still feels very attracted by her, by her swaying walk, by the hem of her dress. The fluttering of the hem parallels the indifferent dallying over the grave of their love. He is trapped — the lips bitten sore by passion and turned to ice, the breath, the glance, all still wield a fatal charm. Female sensuality is here depicted as insuperable. The work 'buhlt' ('woos') with all its connotations of wantonness and of frivolous courting, of lechery and caressing, conveys an appropriate impression of cheapness and meretricious temptation. 'Schlenkrig', a neologism, saves Stramm a lengthy verbal circumscription at just the moment when he is seeking to indicate the girl's swift departure. And 'drüber rüber'? The sound of feet moving away? Unlikely. A real or imagined sexual assault? Perhaps. A reference again to the dress caressing the body he longs to touch? Most likely.

According to Bozzetti (pp. 22–27 and 52), 'Untreu' belongs to the middle period of Stramm's work and was written in April or May 1914. Not its least surprising feature is the number of preliminary sketches (twenty-four) which Stramm made before choosing between three 'penultimate drafts' for his final version. During the course of the poem's genesis, its impersonality is heightened by the simple act of dispensing with almost all the first person possessive adjectives and pronouns which occur in the early sketches: verbs are used to replace adjectives and adverbs wherever possible. All colour adjectives disappear. Stramm's technique is one of painstaking compression, ellipsis, depersonalization, honing and rethinking. Only after twenty exploratory words and word-combinations does he decide on 'Laubwelk' in line 3. He explains his reasons in a letter dated 22 May 1914 to Walden, to whom he has sent two versions of the poem:

'Welkes Laub' ('withered foliage'), it is true, sounds softer and more melodic, but to my mind it is also less definite, whereas 'Laubwelk' ('leaf-wither') contains more of the sense of the aroma which is what I am after. It also solves the problem of having two consecutive words beginning with 'w' which I wanted to avoid precisely because I have deliberately used wherever possible the prefix 'ver' as a means of evoking decay and abandonment. And lastly the accumulation of 't's' followed by 'l' also awakens in me the idea of breath gliding, wafting past! All reasons then why I prefer the final version. (Radrizzani, pp. 426–27)

There is nothing very startling or original about this letter (the comment on 'ver' is particularly trite), except that it hardly corroborates Thomas Mann's description of Expressionist methods as heedlessly arbitrary or indeed Rilke's picture of the Expressionist poet. A shaping hand, a firm resolve and a meticulous mind, patient of the smallest nuance, are clearly at work throughout the preliminary sketches. Yet Stramm hates pre-meditation above all: '. . . all intention is misguided, all rationality is nonsense. A sin against the unconscious which alone has the strength and the power to shape, to become! Intention and rationality are stains indiscriminate aimless, tasteless, purposeless on a great house, the palace of the unconscious' (to Walden, 21 March 1915; Radrizzani p. 447). With this unconditional repudiation of intention and rationality *and* the highly conscious and carefully reasoned fastidiousness of the 'Laubwelk' letter with its 'because I have *deliberately* used . . .', Stramm echoes a fundamental paradox in the '*Sturm*lehre' and does nothing to resolve that paradox by writing in another letter to the Waldens, in connection with the poem 'Freudenhaus': 'Behind "sich" comes the abrupt unstressed syllable and "das Geschlecht" is a new strong accented syllable. I deliberately [again!] did not put it in a new line' (11 June 1914; Pörtner, p. 46).

Other conceits and stylistic ploys, typical of the 'Sturmlehre', are evident in 'Untreu': the poem, like all Stramm's poems, is in the present tense — use of the past would suggest that something could be objectively fixed, whereas Stramm and the Sturm theoreticians do not acknowledge a stable, rigid reality; the verbs (except 'hastet') are intransitive — transitive verbs are involved in relationships with, and come to a stop at, objects, whilst intransitive verbs are expressions of pure open-ended intensity; there is no rhyming — only one poem of Stramm's, 'Werttod', uses rhymes; a trochaic rhythm predominates and the unstressed syllables are reduced to negligible significance — there are very few dactyls or anapaests in Stramm's poetry or in that of the Sturm poets generally; the atomistic approach to language and the attention paid to acoustic, rhythmic and phonetic considerations are again typical of Sturm school precepts; the use of a substantivized infinitive as subject in the first three words of the poem is, Bozzetti contends (pp. 83–84), a means of creating pure intensity and of suspending the static character of being; a word like 'schlenkrig' fulfils a general demand amongst Walden and his colleagues for uniqueness and for the creation of new words — a new word at the moment of its creation is laden with an intensity of feeling, and, furthermore, adjectives in '-ig' reveal a substantial, fundamental quality, whereas present participles can serve only to describe the adventitious characteristics of things and invite the possibility of a direct object and, thus, of a dead stop. Poetry, according to Stramm and the others, is perpetual movement, and its dynamism is maintained by the creation of new words, the modification of old ones and the resolve not to settle at the inert verbal material available; Stramm's 'new' words are, nevertheless, always neighbours of the old ones. A word like 'glutverbissnen' — and such neologisms (with four exceptions) Stramm uses only once so that they retain all their pristine intensity — is not only an example of Stramm's general predilection for composite adjectives as a means of striking the exact nuance, but also typifies the Sturm school's determination to achieve the greatest possible compactness and concreteness, without resorting to lengthy clauses. The concreteness which a poem like 'Untreu' presents does not issue from descriptions of external reality. There is no time to describe the location or the girl, no time to provide background information on the affair: Stramm seeks to convey the supreme moment of betrayal *and* the realization that her allure works on, and is dynamic. The reality which the poem distils is the reality of a suffocating sense of loss and emptiness as the poet confronts the girl, sees her pause and then watches her sway past, as enticing as ever.

'Untreu', like all Stramm's poems, places being under the aspect of time. Even love cannot, love especially cannot, bring about a state removed from the effect of time. Love obeys a law of attraction and repulsion, it is played out between and at the two poles, it inevitably degenerates into conflict and rancour, it does not bring stability or lasting fulfilment. In Stramm's poetry, love, no less than war, is characterized by tentative advances, fierce skirmishes, little victories and heavy losses. 'Untreu', like all the poems of *Du*, presents itself as a love-poem, but never do we feel in it a sense of person addressing person. On the contrary, a rhetorical, one-sided reproachful tone is sustained throughout. The theme (betrayal and faded love conjured in images of ice, autumn and death) and the motifs (Eros, nature and death) all have an honourable and familiar literary tradition, and all are the common currency of some of Stramm's contemporaries. Stramm, the most successful practitioner and adapter of the '*Sturm*lehre', interlocks with that tradition *and* radically modifies it.

'There will be wars, the like of which have never been seen on earth':[26] even Nietzsche could not have foreseen the full horror of the holocaust which fell upon the world in 1914. English and German poets of the First World War felt landed with obsolete, inappropriate verbal means for rendering their experiences. All art was subjected to an immense strain:

> Rent or furled
> Are all Art's ensigns. Verse wails. Now begin
> Famines of thought and feeling.[27]

Owen's line 'Verse wails' is a strikingly twentieth-century line. In, for example, three famous nineteenth-century essays about poetry — Wordsworth's *Preface to the Second Edition of the Lyrical Ballads*, Hazlitt's *On Poetry in General* and Shelley's *A Defence of Poetry* — there is never a suggestion that poetry cannot and should not encompass *every* area of human experience. A profound confidence and joy pervade Hazlitt's essay: joy in the confidence that 'poetry is the language of the imagination and the passion . . . relating to whatever gives immediate pleasure or pain to the human mind'.[28] Even a poem like Wordsworth's 'Ode: Intimations of Immortality . . .', in which a degree of retrenchment concerning the poet's and poetry's scope might have been expected, ends on a celebratory, joyous note stressing the *in*clusive nature of poetry. And Shelley vouchsafed to poetry wide-ranging power and authority, firmly believing that poets should actively support humanitarian causes, work for political reform and point out both present evils and future directions. Moreover, much of the war-poetry which was produced in the early nineteenth century was marked by a similar jaunty confidence. Some time during the middle of the nineteenth century in England, that sublime confidence began to be undermined. A book such as Cecil Woodham-Smith's *The Great Hunger* (about the Irish famine) has the constant refrain of those who observed the famine: 'It cannot be described', 'The scenes which presented themselves were such as no tongue or pen can convey the slightest idea of . . .', 'Believe me, my dear Sir, the reality in most cases far exceeded description'. It is a truism of European literary history that, by the early years of this century, consciousness of language's inadequacy to encompass modern empirical reality had swelled into profound scepticism towards the traditional claims of language: hence the upsurge of interest in the study of linguistics and the extreme language-consciousness of such writers as Kraus, Wittgenstein, Husserl, Ebner and Cassirer.

Stramm shares this language-consciousness and the conviction of language's inadequacy. Such cries from the heart as 'I have no words' or 'The horror is such that

37

I am lost for words' or 'I am always short of words' or 'Where are words for the experience' recur in the letters (Pörtner, pp. 52–53, 47, 57, 47): *he* has not got the right words, the right words are not generally available, what is happening is too ghastly for words (though we recall Edgar's words in *King Lear*: 'The worst is not/ So long as we can say "This is the worst"' IV, i).

Stramm, like his colleagues on *Der Sturm*, is also convinced that a new start has to be made — away from the attitudes and language of much nineteenth-century (English and German) war-poetry which survived into the First World War. Evidence for the survival of earlier attitudes can be adduced from any of the numerous anthologies which appeared during and after the First World War. Ernst Volkmann's *Deutsche Dichtung im Weltkrieg 1914–18* (Leipzig, 1934) is an excellent example. The vast majority of the poets in it start with a ready-made set of conceptions, phrases, words and rhymes, and churn out their poems on a formula: Germany is 'chivalrous', her honour is 'inviolate', her spirit 'invulnerable', her enemies 'perjured' and branded with the 'mark of Cain', they must be 'mown down' (images of 'harvesting', 'scything', 'reaping' etc. proliferate'), Germany's mission is 'sacred', peace is too 'easy' and 'ego-fostering', as many 'sacrifices' as possible must be made, 'duty' is what matters, God defends the 'right'. Poetry to a formula is, of course, what medieval poets produced, and a number of the elements listed here apply to epic (for example, Carolingian) poetry, not all of it bad! But Stramm is intent on breaking away from this tradition and, more especially, from its pallid epigones: he scorns and despises the work of Richard Dehmel, one of the best represented poets in Volkmann's anthology.

Stramm wrote thirty-one war-poems: they are usually assembled under the title *Tropfblut*. In his letters he never comments on the rights and wrongs of the war. Indeed, with only two not very significant exceptions, it is impossible to find any remark of a remotely political nature in his correspondence. He had precisely that first-hand experience of trench warfare which nineteenth-century English poets lacked. His letters from the front reveal, in the same way as Ivor Gurney's (written from a different front)[29] do, a man on the very edge of sanity and knowing himself to be there. In his desperate endeavours to keep alive the life of the spirit he never mouths vast sentiments or indulges in chauvinistic attitudinizing. His poems are the snatched distillation of battle-field incidents. Wrenched from the haphazard slaughter around him, they are both a bastion against the onset of intimidating doubts and the notations of a mind under extreme strain. War he saw as his incontrovertible fate, as a cosmic event, a machination of the omnipotent nature of the 'Auswanderer' essay, rather than as a political event, the outcome of politicians' designs or blunders. War placed him in a state between despair and, occasionally, intoxication: despair, because of the wanton waste of life suffered by 'his boys' and because he dreaded not being granted sufficient time to write the poetry he sensed fermenting within him; intoxication, because war was 'a zone of intense life',[30] a node of dynamic energy and a touchstone of authentic existence after the fraudulent hiatus of peace.

Early in 1915 Josef Winckler wrote to Dehmel, suggesting that he, Dehmel, should be *the* German war-poet. Dehmel replies:

I'm supposed to play the war-poet. But, if you don't mind my saying so, that is your business! . . . In any case it's not my practice to turn an experience into poetry as long as I am still caught up in the middle of it. Just be patient for a few short years. What's more, even you can't write a psalm whilst thunder and lightning are raging all around you.[31]

Stramm takes up precisely the challenge which Dehmel refuses — the challenge of responding instantly to experience. Later would be too late. He is concerned to grasp what is after all a new experience or at least an old experience of startlingly new dimensions. He seeks to encompass, without mediation, the experience he knows at first hand of, for example, leading a patrol into possible ambush ('Patrouille'), standing watch ('Wache' and 'Wacht'), being fired upon ('Feuertaufe'), leading a charge ('Angriff' and 'Sturmangriff'), sitting round a camp-fire ('Frostfeuer'), watching shells explode in the air ('Schrapnell'), coming upon a grave near the front-line ('Krieggrab'), or looking out over the detritus and mouldering corpses of a battle-field ('Schlachtfeld'). The poem 'Zagen' ('Wavering') also has to do with the battle-field:

> Die Himmel hangen
> Schatten haschen Wolken
> Ängste
> Hüpfen
> Ducken
> Recken
> Schaufeln schaufeln
> Müde
> Stumpf
> Versträubt
> Die
> Gehre
> Gruft.

The skies hang. Shadows seize clouds. Fears Skip Duck Stretch Shovel shovel Tired Dull Resists The Covetous Grave.

The scene is set: an overcast sky, or rather, overcast skies. On all sides, the men at the front seem to be compressed flat, squeezed into the landscape, by the lowering sky. There is something minatory in that first line, the men below are threatened. So low is the sky that the onlooker sees shadowy figures of men apparently seeking the shelter of the clouds, or perhaps the clouds are clouds of smoke or gas into which the phantom soldiers race. 'Haschen' with its common connotation of children playing 'tag' adds to the grisly and surreal effect of the scene — someone is observing soldiers tentatively advance. The title word 'Zagen' is the infinitive, devoid of subject therefore, and is an example of one of Stramm's favourite techniques of drawing a particular and limited act (that of trembling, wavering) into the absolute. The use of the infinitive ensures that all outlines are blurred: everything becomes 'infinite', unchecked by subject or object, and dissolves in intensity. The four words after 'Ängste' are either infinitives used for the same purpose as 'Zagen' *or* the third person plural of verbs with 'Ängste' as their subject. In either case the meaning is clear: frightened men leaping up from the trenches, ducking, stretching, digging themselves in. Again, we have the ironic use of a verb associated with children —

39

'hüpfen' — and 'Recken' with its other common (substantival) meaning of 'heroes', follows close upon 'Ängste', fear-ridden men. This odd plural of an abstract noun is a characteristic conceit: it suggests diverse degrees of fear, both a personification of fear *and* the depersonalization of the frightened men. 'Recken', too, raises thoughts of the colloquial verb 'verrecken' which means 'to die like a dog', a by no means inappropriate resonance in a poem in which the protagonists seem no more than marionettes. Indeed there is something very uncanny about the impersonal, theatrical, Bergmannesque actions of the soldiers as they move across a scarred terrain beneath an oppressive sky. A kind of ghostly charade is played out before the spectator's eyes. 'Schaufeln' is beautifully onomatopoeic: repetition of it underlines the feverish urgency of the action. But what are the men digging? Trenches to protect themselves? Graves to offer sanctuary to their tired, benumbed bodies? Just as earlier in the poem the soldiers were dematerialized, impersonalized into shadows and then, as it were, reassembled as bundles of fear ('Ängste'), now these soldiers are reduced to two adjectives/adverbs, 'müde' and 'stumpf'. The verb 'versträubt' is singular. The picture, therefore, is of a mass of tired, enervated men resisting a death‑which, however, has its attractions. 'Gehr', a neologism, has all the sexual under-tones of 'begehren' ('to desire') and is formed directly from 'be-gehr-end'. This again is a typical ploy: the advantage to Stramm of 'gehr-' over '(be)gehr*end*' is that the former provides an essential, substantial quality, whereas the latter has some-thing merely descriptive, interpretative and adventitious about it. 'Gruft' is the usual word for 'family vault' and seems appropriate for a company of soldiers: it is also a poetic word for 'grave' and can mean any 'pit' or 'dark cavern'. Perhaps '$\frac{G\ ehre}{G\ ruft}$' (that is, '$\frac{G\ honour}{G\ calls}$') is another valid way of looking at the last two lines. 'Ver-sträuben' is a neologism: the usual verb is 'sich sträuben'. By dropping the reflexive pronoun (as he does earlier with 'recken' and 'ducken'), Stramm not only achieves the kind of abbreviation he is always seeking, but also allows the movement of 'sträuben' to become open-ended and not be delimited by reference to some known, actually present subject/object. The intransitive use ensures that the verb becomes a nucleus of uninhibited intensity. In the last six lines of the poem a conciliation with death takes place, or perhaps the men are too exhausted to resist death any more.

Many of the best examples of Expressionist art are in the medium of woodcuts or linotype engravings. The absence of colour, the simplification of planes and lines, the sharp contrasts, all minimize any nisus toward a reproduction of reality. Stramm's poetry gives the impression of a woodcut on a page, etched out black on white. This effect is accentuated by his habit of taking up a panoramic, bird's-eye view, the battle-field becomes a field of projection, the magnetic zone of a subjective vision. But it must be stressed that Stramm's method of taking up a panoramic view is *not* the same as what Jon Silkin calls Wilfred Owen's 'tendency to recollect', his 'preference for perspective and synopsis' which means that Owen's language 'suffers from the settled quality of the "spokesman"'.[32] On the contrary, and like Rosenberg's (to follow Silkin's comparison through), Stramm's war-poetry is sustained by a compact specificity. In 'Zagen' Stramm focuses attention on the fate of one platoon, thus following the example of a nineteenth-century French poet, Rimbaud, whose few war-poems 'work' because, in 'Le Dormeur du Val' for instance, the poet concentrates the agony of the battle-field into the fate of *one* soldier. Stramm does write about war in generalized, synoptic terms, stressing the annihilating loneliness of the *representative* soldiers and the irrationality of the course of events: yet his particular talent is for those poems which derive their strength and momentum from a terse selection of detail over a narrow corner of the battlefield — horses neighing, guns clattering, heavy eyelids, blood trickling, freezing limbs, rust on the move, and, every now and then, a heart-rending reference to a loved-one (a 'du') which, at the same time as widening the perspective and emotional range, serves to underline the strict economy of the poem's scenario. The detail of his poems has almost always to do with activities, rarely with objects. Stramm's poems *look* fragmentary and indeed offer only fragments of front-line experience, coherent fragments, but fragments nonetheless: we are at the opposite end of the spectrum from a poet like Werfel who not only craves for some totality of being, but also feels able to bring it about, to reconcile all opposites, to submerge all antagonisms in a maelstrom of feverish emotion and ultimately to unite man and world and God in an ecstasy of brotherly love. In 'Zagen' the referential objects, sky and clouds, are not background items, but part of the cryptic enumeration of activity and action — disparate, stranded, abandoned. Stramm reverses the usual procedure for objectifying states of mind: he goes a considerable way towards suppressing the world of the object. Some poems in *Tropfblut* consist almost entirely of verbs as Stramm strives to express the gesture of feelings; the tangible objects in his war-poems are very limited in number — rusty armour, a horse, shattered limbs, blood, and very little else.

The poem 'Zagen' is no exception. It represents an attempt to communicate directly the tentativeness of an advance and a look at death. The reader is rushed through the poem to the one piece of punctuation, the concluding full-stop. In the course of *Du* and *Tropfblut* Stramm gradually dispenses with all punctuation, ceasing to bother about legitimizing his poetry by having recourse to grammatical and syntactical rules. The sequence of mostly single words is meant to express an uninterrupted flowing action, and the links in the chain are intended to merge, not to serve a totting-up process of realistic background information. Intensity and tension are vital components of much Expressionist poetry. Stramm's method of introducing them into his poetry rests on many linguistic devices — unusual neologisms *and* the mining of traditional deposits around words, omission of pronouns, apparently 'wrong' grammar, catalexis and aphesis, anaphora and parallelism, compulsively rapid rhythm, orchestration of sounds and particles, an urgent rhetorical tone, an abundance of infinitives which read like imperatives, heavily accented and quickfire sentence units and the frequent use of hard consonants. All these unsettle the reader, dislocating his preconceptions and expectations, and creating an atmosphere of anxious movement and diffuse energy. A poem like 'Zagen' represents a worthy rejoinder to those critics like J. H. Johnston[33] who argue that the English First World War poets and, by implication, all First World War poets are so obsessed with the demoralizing conditions of modern warfare, are so close to their experience and so devoid of perspective that they cannot but produce unkempt verse. Stramm seeks to make a virtue of precisely that closeness and to found his poetry in single-minded loyalty to his experience. 'Zagen' and the other poems of *Tropfblut* also serve to allay doubts which Eliot raises in his 'A Note on War Poetry' (1942),[34] for Stramm, like Owen, *does* succeed in investing particular battle-field incidents with universal significance, distilling genuine insights and emotion from what Eliot disparagingly calls 'the merely individual' — but, unlike Owen's poetry, Stramm's is never self-consciously seeking to be representative and synoptic and hence never abstract. War is, Eliot maintains, hostile to life[35] and, consequently, recalcitrant to poetry, but Stramm shows that, whatever Eliot's strong reservations, war is not only an appropriate theme for poetry, but an especially rich source of poetic inspiration: 'War's damned interesting. It would be hard indeed [writes Ivor Gurney *not* in the falsely optimistic months of 1914, but halfway through 1916] to be deprived of all this artist's material now' (Hurd, p. 71). Stramm demonstrates that fragments of it can be ordered and articulated; the war which his small oeuvre encompasses is 'no mere discord of flags', not a sounding-board for nineteenth-century-style rhetoric and chauvinistic posturing but 'an infection of the common sky'.[36]

Examination of Stramm's work in the light of the general criticisms of Expressionism assembled in Chapter 2 leads to the following conclusions. In writing a poem, he adopts a slow, agglutinative approach, so that his poetry is simultaneously organic and constructed: daughter, editor/biographer, colleagues on *Der Sturm*, drafts of poems, personal letters — all bear testimony to the fastidiously tectonic character of his writing, which hardly accords with Rilke's picture of the Expressionist poet or with the argument of those many critics who, like Kurt Heynicke, assert that Stramm 'hurled words out' and that his poems were 'real language-explosions'.[37] As for 'responsibility to reality', it all depends, once again, what is meant by 'responsibility' and what is meant by 'reality'. According to the *Sturm* canon, the poet begins with an individual, concrete experience which is transmuted by the creative act and shorn of all subjective resonances: the original experience is so alienated that it becomes nothing more than a faint echo and is transformed into a new, autonomous, artistic reality which is accessible only to intuition and emotion. The right poetic word becomes an open sesame, the means of bursting through the bounds of empirical reality and uncovering layers beneath the surface. It is no part of the artist's task to imitate — 'this ape-like talent' is how Walden dismisses all mimetic aesthetic theory (*Erinnerungsbuch*, p. 26). Feeling is all that counts in the making of poetry, even in writing *about* it. In Stramm's letters, for example, it is always 'meinem Gefühl nach' ('according to my feeling'), 'meinem Empfinden nach' ('according to my way of feeling') or 'ich habe das Gefühl' ('I have the feeling . . .'). And yet Stramm, whilst sharing many of the assumptions and tenets of the 'Sturmlehre', builds on them, adapts them, thus distancing himself from its faithful practitioners who seek some rarefied ideal of art. The intense feeling which marks his poetry is always enlisted in the service of two recognizable, profound experiences and thus allows those experiences to reverberate through his poems — his experience of love and his experience of war. What makes his poetry uniquely moving (unique, that is, among the *Sturm* poets) is that he never sacrifices his apprehension of these experiences either for the sake of dramatizing his own grief and pain or in order to comply with the aesthetic expectations and demands of the

42

magazine which welcomed him. Not that the positive contribution made by *Der Sturm* to *his* success should be underrated.

Stramm is a minor master, an interesting miniaturist, a writer whose experiments with language represent one of the few successful attempts by Expressionist writers (despite their perfervid antitraditionalism) to change poetic forms radically. His thematic and emotional range is very narrow: man as a domestic animal, as a social being, as the lover of his fellows, as the shaper of his destiny, as a creature who can conceptualize and articulate, as the servant of his ideals, as someone who leaves his home to go to work or to vote, man as a crushed victim of social inequality — none of these has any place in Stramm's poetry. It is not that his poetry is any less social, less politically aware, than other writers' oeuvre, it is simply less. In *Du* his people, savaging and bypassing each other, almost always shut each other out, so that their confrontations, however intense, are hardly ever resolved. His critics do him a disservice by mentioning his work in the same breath as that of Mayakovsky or Ungaretti, Kafka, Dostoyevsky, Sartre, Camus, Beckett, Rilke, Faulkner and Joyce.[38] Stramm shares with some of these writers the characteristically twentieth-century obsession with existential loneliness and the concomitant themes of cosmic meaninglessness and lack of communication, and he shares with Joyce a pre-occupation with a certain kind of linguistic experimentation — but it is a question of scale and proportion. A more apt comparison would be with Trakl or, more recently, Pinter.

Similar reservations can be voiced about *Tropfblut*: Stramm's war-poems lack the wide sweep, the diversity and versatility of tone and content, and the explicitly compassionate involvement of, say, Owen, but they are dynamic cameos of articulated peril, a remarkable microcosm of front-line experiences. Like the poems of *Du* they are kinds of psychogram. Ivor Gurney's words of self-criticism and gentle self-approbation ring true for Stramm:

. . . the root of the matter is there, and scraps of pure beauty often surprise one; there is also a strong dramatic sense. Where it [a volume of his war-poetry] will fail to attract is that there is none, or hardly any of the devotion of self-sacrifice, the splendid readiness for death that one finds in Grenfell, Brooke, Nichols etc. (Letter of 27 July 1917 to Marion Scott; Hurd, pp. 81–82.)

It is not of these three that we think when we read Stramm, but of Gurney and Rosenberg and Jones. This comparison can best be illustrated by quoting Jon Silkin's brilliant characterization of Rosenberg's language as

more lived in than Owen's. Owen's language narrates or carries the ideas: Rosenberg's language is them, sensuously enacts them, and experiences them. So to this extent it shares some of the 'haeccity' (or thisness) of Jones's language. (Silkin, p. 52)

And of Stramm's, one might add. Here, if anywhere, Stramm 'tore down much that was rotten. He paved the way for the new' (*Erinnerungsbuch*, introduction). 'Paved the way'? In any significant sense? Some critics have over-estimated Stramm's influence. Mehring (himself very much part of the *Sturm* establishment) declares that Stramm 'produced the whole of the second generation of German Expressionist literature'.[39] Hering argues more soberly that Stramm's influence is felt even today as 'the anticipation of what we find in the modern literary avant-garde' (Adler/ White, p. 14). Perhaps. Stramm certainly had a considerable influence on the other members of the *Sturm* school and on modern Concrete poets: some critics have asserted, without demonstration and elaboration, that Stramm's work was taken up by Russian futurists (for example, David Burliuk, who joined *Der Sturm* in 1911, and Khlebnikov). Other critics deny Stramm any influence, insisting that his poetry follows a destructive path into a cul-de-sac — though even in a cul-de-sac 'genuine' important things can take place.[40]

A sense of proportion is lost if the claims which, for example, Livšic makes for Khlebnikov are then ventured on behalf of Stramm:

> The breath of the original word seared my face . . . the jungles of Dahl [compiler of the famous dictionary of the Russian language which contains many words not in general use] became familiar and cozy . . . the baring of roots was a real myth-making, an awakening of meanings dormant in the word, as well as the birth of new ones . . . he enlarged the capabilities of words to limits that formerly were not thought possible.[41]

Some commentators have claimed this, *all* this, for Stramm. What can be said rather less spectacularly about his work is that he fulfils the twin duties of the poet, as defined by T. S. Eliot in his 1945 essay 'The Social Function of Poetry' — 'to preserve, and to extend and improve his language'. Stramm 'preserving' his language? At the end of 1911 he does indeed set himself up as a trustee of the German language, he is keen to rid it of foreign words, he becomes interested in the work and aims of The German Language Union, and he grows concerned enough about the corruption and abuse of his mother tongue to write an essay partly on the subject in 1912.[42] This is one of the ways in which he interprets his particular 'responsibility' as a poet. Such concern represents the other side of Stramm, the poet of 'a few maimed syllables/dry as a twig', the writer whom one critic is pleased to dub that 'raving lunatic and language rapist'.[43]

NOTES

1   Eugenio Montale, 'Non chiederci la parola', *Ossi di seppia* (1939), quoted in: G. Singh, *Eugenio Montale: a Critical Study* (Yale, 1973), p. 30.
2   The principal source for this biographical material is *August Stramm: Das Werk*, edited by R. Radrizzani (Wiesbaden, 1963), pp. 405–51. All poems are quoted from this edition.
3   M. Esslin, *Pinter: a Study of his Plays* (London, 1973), p. 34.
4   See her introduction to: A. Stramm, *Dein Lächeln weint. Gesammelte Gedichte* (Wiesbaden, 1956).
5   I. Stramm, quoted in: C. R. B. Perkins, 'August Stramm's Poetry and Drama: a Reassessment' (M.A. thesis, University of Hull, 1972), pp. 17–18.
6   I. Stramm, *Dein Lächeln weint*, p. 15.
7   See his letter to the Waldens of 20 December 1914 in: N. Walden and L. Schreyer, *Der Sturm: Ein Erinnerungsbuch an Herwarth Walden und die Künstler aus dem Sturmkreis* (Baden-Baden, 1954), p. 85 (hereafter referred to as *Erinnerungsbuch*).
8   See his letter to his wife of 29 December 1914 in: *August Stramm. Kritische Essays und unveröffentlichtes Quellenmaterial aus dem Nachlaß des Dichters*, edited by J. D. Adler and J. J. White (Berlin, 1979), p. 132.

9 Letter to his wife of 22 September 1910; Adler/White, p. 131.
10 Letter to the Waldens of 25 February 1915 in: P. Pörtner, *Literatur-Revolution 1910–1925*, 2 vols (Darmstadt, 1960–61), I, 52.
11 'Hugh Selwyn Mauberley' (1920), in: E. Pound, *Collected Shorter Poems* (London, 1961), p. 220.
12 W. Rittich, *Kunsttheorie, Wortkunsttheorie und lyrische Wortkunst im 'Sturm'* (Greifswald, 1933), p. 55.
13 I. Stramm, *Dein Lächeln weint*, p. 9.
14 The phrase is Kurt Hiller's and is quoted in: Kolinsky, *Engagierter Expressionismus*, p. 119.
15 W. Emrich, *August Stramms 'Rudimentär': Zur Konzeption des Forum Theaters* [programme of Forum Theatre Production], edited by C. Rateuke (Berlin, 1973).
16 Published in *Euphorion*, 67 (1973), 205–11.
17 The phrases are Lothar Schreyer's, quoted in: A. Soergel, *Dichtung und Dichter der Zeit* (Leipzig, 1927), p. 598.
18 Vlatislav Hofmann writing in *Der Sturm* in December 1913. Quoted in: Elmar Bozzetti, 'Untersuchungen zu Lyrik und Drama August Stramms' (unpublished dissertation, University of Cologne, 1961), pp. 316–317.
19 W. H. Sokel, *The Writer in Extremis*, p. 112.
20 The phrases are Schreyer's. See Soergel, pp. 589–90.
21 These lines are from F. R. Behrens's 'Tannentod', quoted in: *Erinnerungsbuch*, p. 179.
22 H. Walden, quoted in: *Erinnerungsbuch*, p. 26.
23 As Döblin does in a letter to Walden of 21 September 1915; A. Döblin, *Briefe* (Olten and Freiburg im Breisgau, 1970), p. 76.
24 Herbert Cysarz, quoted in: E. Volkmann, *Deutsche Dichtung im Weltkrieg 1914–1918* (Leipzig, 1934), p. 312.
25 T. S. Eliot, 'The Three Voices of Poetry' (1953), in: *On Poetry and Poets* (London, 1956), p. 101.
26 'Warum ich ein Schicksal bin', *Ecce Homo*, in: *Nietzsche Werke*, VI/3,364.
27 W. Owen, '1914', *War Poems and Others*, edited by D. Hibbert (London, 1973), p. 58.
28 W. Hazlitt, *Lectures on the English Poets* (London, 1819), pp. 2–3.
29 See chapters 7 and 8 of Michael Hurd's *The Ordeal of Ivor Gurney* (Oxford, 1978).
30 F. T. Marinetti, quoted in: *Futurist Manifestos*, edited by U. Apollonio (London, 1973), p. 98.
31 Dated 28 April 1915, in: R. Dehmel, *Ausgewählte Briefe* (Berlin, 1923), p. 367.
32 *First World War Poetry*, edited by Jon Silkin (Harmondsworth, 1979), p. 31.
33 See his *English Poetry of the First World War* (Princeton, 1964).
34 T. S. Eliot, *Collected Poems 1909–62* (London, 1974), pp. 229–230.
35 See stanza 5 of Eliot's poem which begins: 'War is not a life . . .'.
36 Robert Graves, 'Recalling War', in: *Men Who March Away: Poems of the First World War*, edited by I. M. Parsons (London, 1965), p. 171.
37 K. Heynicke, 'Zum 100. Geburtstag von August Stramm', *Die Horen*, 94 (1974), 31.
38 See A. Arnold, *Die Literatur des Expressionismus* (Stuttgart, Berlin, Cologne and Mainz, 1966), p. 42.
39 W. Mehring, *Die verlorene Bibliothek* (Icking and Munich, 1964), p. 136.
40 Gustav Wangenheim, 'Klassischer Expressionismus', *Das Wort*, 3, Heft 3 (March 1938), 88.
41 Quoted in: V. Markov, *Russian Futurism* (London, 1968), p. 14.
42 Called 'Deutsche Titel', in: *Blätter für Post und Telegraphie*, 15 August 1912, and reprinted in Adler/White.
43 The abusive terms are Richard Specht's in his *Franz Werfel. Versuch einer Zeitspiegelung* (Berlin, Vienna and Leipzig, 1926), p. 170.

IV GEORG HEYM

Build your cities on Vesuvius! Send your ships
into unexplored seas! Live at war with your
peers and with yourselves![1]

Georg Heym was born on 30 October 1887 in Hirschberg, Silesia.[2] He grew up in a sombre atmosphere, compounded of his father's introverted piety and his mother's self-effacing reticence. As a public prosecutor, his father was required to attend many executions, and, partly as a result of witnessing these, had a nervous breakdown in 1899 and spent a year in a sanatorium. Between 1896 and 1905 Georg went to grammar schools in Gnesen, Poznan and Berlin. He left Berlin's Königlich Joachimsthalsches Gymasium at Easter 1905 in some disgrace — he had been involved in burning a school boat — and was, to quote his diary entry for 23 April 1905, 'banished' to a school in Neuruppin. This school was run on strictly regimented lines, discipline was enforced by a staff of patrolling teachers, supervised in their turn by a martinet headmaster, Dr Heinrich Begemann. A grim atmosphere of repression and conflict prevailed. The pupils sought to assert their independence of authority and to find a measure of personal freedom by forming clandestine groups, one of which, 'Rhinania', Heym soon joined. These clubs represented potential pockets of seething revolt which invariably took the shape of petty acts of indiscipline and drunken debauchery in an establishment where, by tradition, schoolboy pranks were treated as major criminal misdemeanours. Heym contributed poems to a VIth form magazine *Kreißende Sonnen*, the penultimate edition of which took up what was very much a subject of contemporary concern — the theme of suicide.[3] Once again, after frequent transgressions and reprimands, Heym left school under a shadow in March 1907. In May he began to study law, first at Würzburg and then Berlin. Throughout these years, until his death in 1912, he conducted a series of desultory romances which brought him and his partners nothing but distress and frustration. At the end of March 1910 he was introduced to the 'Neuer Club', and on 6 July he read some of his poems for the first time in public. After two terms at Jena University in 1910 he continued his law studies in Berlin. In February 1911 he was assigned to the district court at Berlin-Lichterfelde for practical experience, but was dismissed for destroying a land-registry deed. It was from this time, too, that his work for the magazine *Die Aktion* dates. In April his first volume of verse, *Der ewige Tag*, was published, and in the Summer he successfully applied for permission to gain further legal experience, this time at the district court in Wusterhausen an der Dosse. He was already, however, toying with the idea of giving up law and becoming an officer or dragoman. On the afternoon of 16 January 1912 he and his friend, Ernst Balcke, were drowned while skating on the Havel. Heym's body was recovered four days later 'frozen stiff and with cramped legs tucked tight into the body, the skates still on his feet, his hands raw with scratches and his features twisted out of shape' (D VI, 465). His body was laid first of all in the morgue of the suicides' cemetery at Schildhorn: his companions in death were the mutilated bodies of the suicides whose busy peregrinations had always been one of the major pre-occupations of his verse.

It had been a footloose and cheerless life, sustained by smallscale skirmishes with authority, by a series of particular antagonisms (for his parents, for their world, for his teachers, for all manifestations of authority, for the legal profession, for his fellow writers) and by a generalized torpid hatred, the same kind of hatred which another Expressionist poet, Johannes Becher, writing in 1937, recalls feeling — 'not a knowing, seeing hatred, but a dull self-consuming loathing which often contented itself with petty, cavilling little spites'.[4] Heym's life was rarely illuminated by great moments of happiness or success: he remained embattled, introverted, ill-starred, tenaciously self-destructive and consistently at odds with all potential sources of love and understanding. Auden's comment on *his* generation has a peculiar relevance to Georg Heym and to other Expressionist poets:

> While the disciplined love which alone
>   could have employed these engines
> Seemed far too difficult and dull, and when
>   hatred promised
> An immediate dividend, all of us hated.[5]

Apart from poetry, Heym wrote a small number of plays, some drama fragments and a few short stories. Karl Ludwig Schneider divides the poetry into two groups — those poems written between 1899 and 1909, and those written in the last two years of Heym's life. Only one volume of verse, *Der ewige Tag*, was published during Heym's lifetime: it consists of poems written between March 1910 and January 1911. Friends of the poet edited and published another collection, *Umbra vitae*, six months after his death, and in 1914 Balduin Möllhausen and A. R. Meyer published *Marathon*, a small collection of Heym's sonnets. Eight years later Pinthus and Erwin Loewenson brought out an edition of Heym's work consisting of the two principal earlier collections, seven short stories and some fifty hitherto unpublished poems which the editors considered to be the best of the 'Nachlaß' and which they grouped together under the title *Der Himmel Trauerspiel*. The pre-1910 poetry is, for the most part, undistinguished, derivative, and over-burdened with nineteenth-century detritus. Whilst Heym certainly wrote some poems (particularly after 1907) which are recognizably his own and which prefigure the urgent strength, the prolific imagining and the tight formal control of his post-1909 poetry, it is not until 1909 and the beginning of 1910 that he consistently finds his familiar voice and the appropriate means to encompass his obsessive visions.

47

'There is only the lonely man and his images.'[6]

'Je préfère les monstres de ma fantaisie
à la trivialité positive.'[7]

In his 'theory of modes' Northrop Frye asserts that 'fictions may be classified, not morally, but by the hero's power of action, which may be greater than ours, less, or roughly the same'.[8] The mode in which the hero's power of action is less than ours is the 'ironic where we have the sense of looking down on a scene of bondage, frustration, or absurdity'. Frye argues that irony issues from the low mimetic, it begins in realism and dispassionate observation, but then 'moves steadily towards myth, and dim outlines of sacrificial rituals and dying gods begin to reappear in it'. In this late phase in which it returns to myth, Frye notes, the ironic mode seizes upon 'demonic' imagery regardless of the 'world' it observes. Frye describes the domain of demonic imagery, 'the world that desire totally rejects', and erects an opposition between apocalyptic symbolism and 'the presentation . . . of the world of the nightmare and the scapegoat, of bondage and pain and confusion . . . the world . . . of perverted or wasted work, ruins and catacombs, instruments of torture and monuments of folly'. Not surprisingly in this context, Frye refers to Kafka and Joyce to support his argument. He might also have mentioned some of the Expressionist poets — Heym, Trakl and Klemm in particular, for their work belongs to his category of the 'ironic mode'. Heym, like Trakl and Klemm, begins from the premise that man's power of action is rigidly circumscribed and that his life is at the mercy of some hostile, unknown and unknowable spirit. Heym, for example, writes:

If the demon who let the world slip from his fingers could be caught, he should be chained up and flogged so that he can never cause such a disaster again.[9]

Created with gruesome arbitrariness by a demon-god, inhabited by hordes of more or less malevolent demons and ruled over by them, this is the world which Heym depicts in his poetry.

His *Der ewige Tag* represents a self-contained cosmos of proliferating images, a twilight world of pandemonium and phantasmagoria. It is a poetry of bloated corpses and faces grimacing in pain, of rivers crammed with the detritus of cities and the paraphernalia of the modern industrial world, where hostile forces prey on the vulnerable and the deprived. The towns and wintry landscapes of *Der ewige Tag* are peopled by the blind, by hectically alive suicides, the crippled, the dying, the dead, the plague-ridden, by circling prisoners, by mothers in agonizing childbirth, and licentious figures from the underworld. The typical furniture of a poem by Heym is a gallows, a skeletal tree offering shelter to a cluster of sinister birds, an isolated mill stranded in a huge plain. He depicts the heightened life of the dead (the obverse of the congealed existence of those 'living' here-below) in hospital corridors and wards, in penumbral churchyards, in the back-rooms of houses where maimed wretches cower and vampires lurk, in graves where worms are gnawing skulls, on ghostships drifting on lonely seas, and in soot-stained cities where man is dwarfed by his own inventions and edifices. It is in these cities above all that Heym locates the gruesome scenes which *are* his poems, for the city in Heym's poetry (as in much other Expressionist poetry) is an absolute datum of human experience, something approaching the natural condition of man, a maelstrom of energy and power demanding and receiving admiration and homage beyond good and evil. And there is in Heym's many poems about cities an explicit translation of metaphysical, indeed religious, vocabulary into the language of a demon-cult; instead of incense and sacrificial burnings, the smoke of factories and furnaces; instead of altar and crucifix, chimney-stack and crane; instead of the incandescent light of a religious revelation, the red glow of revolt and insurgence on the sky-line, and instead of a beneficent God, demons and spectres straddling and crushing cities.

In *Der ewige Tag* the theme of death recurs constantly. Heym portrays death not as an abstraction, but as an active and prehensile force:

> Die Straße kommt der Tod, der Schifferknecht.
> Um seine gelben Pferdezähne staut
> Des weißen Bartes spärliches Geflecht.
>
> Along the street comes death, the ferryman.
> About his yellow horses' teeth is caught up
> His white beard's sparse tangle.

And man, if he ever was, is no longer in control, no longer capable of subordinating the world by rationalization: man is fatalist and will-less; man is faceless victim, impotent before the blind ferocity of an anonymous power. He is depicted as for ever 'wriggling and scrabbling up and down the sides of a honeypot, like a pathetic fly' (PD II, 74). *Der ewige Tag* thus becomes a denial of the anthropocentric view of life, yet it would be wrong to give the impression that Heym's first volume of verse is weighed down by cumbrous personifications and abstractions. On the contrary, a great deal of its intensity and power derives from a meticulous attention to invariably gruesome detail: a child's waxen hand pokes out of a coffin, the crew of 'The Flying Dutchman' sit mummified at their oars whilst their hands take root in the rotten woodwork, a rat-chewed corpse drifts slowly downstream, niggers dig a grave, worms sing in a dead man's cranium, a priest is slaughtered as he administers the sacrament, the rigid legs and bloated bodies of dead horses litter the dawn on the day after a battle, huge spiders weave long threads from their bellies on hospital ceilings, a glow-worm appears on Ophelia's dead body, emaciated children grab at 'rubber-tube' breasts, a ravenous dog gulps withered grass ripped from the sand, and a cripple, clutching a castanet, dances a carmagnole. The resourcefulness of this kind of imagining, always rendered in striking detail and always serving the dark sides of life, provides impetus and dynamism in poems whose nameless demons and cosmic immensities soon begin to pall, however skilfully Heym uses them to regulate the perspective of his visions. And indeed he does preside over these teeming scenes with apparently complete control. In keeping with his view of contemporary life as 'a cheap diversion in a hideous fair-booth' (PD II, 175), his poetry is theatrical and melodramatic. He is the puppeteer, the manipulator of outsize stage-properties, enjoying the kind of mastery denied to all the figures in his poems: a kind of grotesque Naturalism is allied to strict formal, almost Classical, discipline.

One of the most remarkable aspects of Heym's poetry is its lack of anything resembling thought, a philosophy or an ethic. Oskar Loerke underlines this when, ten years after Heym's death, he writes that 'Heym's poems are devoid of ideas if by ideas of a poet one means the ability to look beyond one's own obsessions at the world'.[10] All we are given in a typical poem by Heym is the insistent accumulation of the visual and the concrete: image breeds image, vision is laid alongside vision, relative clauses pile up and jostle with paratactic constellations of chopped-up main clauses, there is no plot but only 'a series of loosely connected events or tableaux'.[11] Horrifying subject-matter is treated nonchalantly, actions are not motivated, no conclusions are reached, no commentary is offered, no interest is evinced in the analysis of the human mind, and no personal stances are adopted. Things are directly present and are not illustrations of thoughts or feelings or moods, there is a complete sublimation of private experiences in visions of timeless breadth, there is no sarcasm or explicit cynicism, nothing complex or elegiac, nothing restful or contemplative, none of the spiritual uplift of Whitman or even Verhaeren whose two early collections *Les Campagnes hallucinées* (1893) and *Les Villes tentaculaires* (1895) prefigure Heym's poetry in many significant ways. Instead, Heym's verse has a primitive, almost lapidary quality; it is mythopoeic and desolate; it has urgent sensual power and yet does not really move us; it stands four-square on the page and, to all appearances, eschews formal arbitrariness; its tone is hard and plangently monotonous, its rhythm is uncompromising. Everything is larger than life *and* firmly reined back by his allegiance to the rules of prosody.

Its very cumber of timeless cosmic events and the hugeness of its mises en scène, together with the grotesqueness of its protagonists and the universality of the human degradation which is its premise — all this makes it into an inherently apolitical poetry. Heym's response to his age in *Der ewige Tag* is 'pure' in the sense that he is not concerned to point to social abuses with a view to putting them right. He does not condemn bad social conditions or uncaring politicians. Believing that life itself is a perverse scandal, he does not underscore the scandal of differences between social classes, because in the world of *Der ewige Tag* all such differences are eliminated — all classes are equally wretched and sunk in a morass of irredeemable physical and moral squalor; eternal darkness (in spite of the title of the volume) engulfs everything. He focuses attention on the miserable existence of those people excluded from a full enjoyment of life as indeed he felt himself excluded by the tedium of life in Wilhelminian Germany. The litany of horror in the poem 'Die Vorstadt' ('The Suburbs') contains a reference to children playing in the excrement of the streets:

> In ihrem Viertel, in dem Gassenkot,
>
> . . .
>
> Es spielen Kinder, denen früh man brach
> Die Gliederchen. Sie springen an den Krücken
> Wie Flöhe weit und humpeln voll Entzücken
> Um einen Pfennig einem Fremden nach.

In their quarter of the town, in the excrement of the streets,
. . . There are children playing, their little limbs broken
At an early age. They leap great distances
On their crutches like fleas and joyously hobble
After a stranger for a penny.

But this is not a preamble to an indignant attack on the outrageously unhygienic social conditions of contemporary city suburbs, for there is nothing time-bound about the inventory of gruesome visions of which a poem like 'Die Vorstadt' is composed. And 'all' that the reference to the children's broken limbs arouses in the reader is horror at the arbitrariness of the parents' vicious act and of the *perennial*, apparently inevitable, conflict between children and parents. To depict him, as such Communist commentators as Leschnitzer and Kersten have done, as 'the apostle of a new humanism',[12] to describe him as 'the herald of democracy'[13] and 'a Zola of lyric poetry'[14] is to misinterpret grossly the evidence of *Der ewige Tag*, for Heym's poetry is not underpinned by ideological considerations or by a determination to institute some kind of altruistic crusade on behalf of the impoverished. Implied in his verse is, if not a criticism, then certainly an artist's, and above all a painter's, awareness of the threatening blackness of contemporary life, but that awareness and criticism are never made explicit. Any comment of a directly political nature is self-regarding and issues from intense personal frustration or from a craving for some, any, sort of action and excitement. The diary entry for 22 October 1910, for example, reads: 'I have some seven or eight poems almost ready, but the wretched, lousy Prussian state never lets me achieve anything'.

Heym's imagination, as fertile as it is, never engages in questions of cause and effect, or in the quest for remedies or any idea of mutuality. Karl Kraus's kind of proprietorial involvement in his age has little meaning for Heym except in one strictly delimited way: life in Berlin and in the provinces at the turn of the century served to trigger a plethora of bleak visions in a sensitive young man's mind. His poetry amounts to an expression of those visions. Beginning with a little run-up of empirical reality (Frye wrote that irony issued from 'the low mimetic' and 'began in realism'), his poems quickly erupt into a cumulus of surrealistic and grotesque images. In a poem such as 'Die Vorstadt', for example, the proletarian quarters of a city become a pretext for discharging his own visions and constructing his own mythic world, and yet all trace of the poet's overweening ego has been sublimated in the creative process. It is significant that the activists and the writers of *Vorwärts* thought little of Heym's work, condemning its determinism and passivity, though some Marxists were quick to praise what they construed as its essentially anti-bourgeois attitudes. Heym's is a fundamentally vitalistic reaction to his age and to historical events: his age he sees as stifling and tepid; history he regards as the realm of a malignant fate where the outstanding individual like Robespierre is hounded to death by an uncomprehending populace.

Critics almost without exception detect little development between *Der ewige Tag* and *Umbra vitae*. Heinz Rölleke, for example, stresses the 'immutability' of Heym's 'way of seeing' and of his 'artistic form'.[15] To a certain extent Rölleke is right. It is the same nightmare territory of death and war and lunacy, and the same figures stalk or are harried through it. The same penumbral gloom envelops the volume in an atmosphere of morbid excessiveness. The only signs of development, some critics concede, is a slight relaxation in Heym's fiercely willed form: Stadler, for example, writes of 'a more flexible and more subtly nuanced softness.'[16] But such concessions render scant justice to the elegiac cadences of 'Deine Wimpern, die langen' ('Your Lashes, your Long Lashes') or to the graceful, light 'Mit den fahrenden Schiffen' ('With the Moving Ships') or the gentle, mysterious 'Träumerei in Hellblau' ('Reverie in Light Blue'). In poems like these it is not so much a question of relaxation as of a radical change of voice and form. Other poems such as 'Fröhlichkeit' ('Cheerfulness') and 'Die Tänzerin in der Gemme' ('The Dancer in the Cameo') are reminiscent of Rilke's *Neue Gedichte*, and others again, like 'Der Nebelstädte winzige Wintersonne' ('The Fog-bound Towns' Tiny Winter-sun'), are at a considerable remove from the severely drilled quatrains of *Der ewige Tag*. The twenty-four-year-old poet who was to drown four weeks after writing 'Der Nebelstädte . . .' was beginning to demonstrate a willingness to blur harsh outlines and to imbue his poems with delicate mysteriousness. Once again we think of the example of the French poet Verhaeren who, surviving until 1916 when he, too, had a fatal accident, found a positive serenity and reconciliation with life in later volumes like *Les Rythmes souverains* (1910) after the austere pessimism of early collections.

In the two volumes *Der ewige Tag* and *Umbra vitae* Heym's visions and images grow to be the rule, displacing the normal condition. Indeed there is in them a certain tendency — a tendency which Leavis criticizes in Shelley (incidentally one of the 'gods' whom Heym revered) — namely, that of forgetting 'the status of the metaphor or simile that introduced the images' and of assuming 'an autonomy and a right to propagate, so that we lose . . . the perception or thought that was the ostensible raison d'être of imagery'.[17] A poem by Heym does not pivot on a central thought, there is no sequence of action, no hierarchy of images: they peel away in so many layers and, uncovered, reveal nothing at all. His own comment that 'his greatness is founded in his realization that there is little sequentiality. Most things lie on one plane. Everything is juxtaposed' (T III, 140), is an accurate appraisal. Heym's poetry is a paradigm of Keats's 'negative capability', the capability of being 'in uncertainties, mysteries, doubts, without any irritable reaching after fact and reason'.[18] Love, faith, praise, hope, fact, reason are *not* present in Heym's poetry, wrung out and achieved against the odds, as they are in, say, the work of a modern writer like Sylvia Plath, the moods and themes of whose poems are in many important respects close to Heym's. In *his* work, those forces which militate against the possibility of man's achieving grace and which render impotent and irrelevant the authority of man's reason hold the centre of the stage — unchallenged and apparently unchallengeable.

> Form! We are entering a volcanic region, the
> German danger-zone![19]
> Sound gives me an outline in flesh and bone.
> Form becomes a life-saver for me.
> Towards one light my sufferings are spent.[20]

The Expressionist poet's attitude to 'form' is profoundly ambiguous. In a lecture in 1917 Edschmid declares that 'after Stefan George it could no longer be forgotten that a great form was unavoidable for the work of art'.[21] Yet one year later he avers that 'we [Expressionist writers] . . . attach very little importance to formal considerations'.[22] With strident braggadocio, the Expressionist poet purports to despise any suggestion of formal restraint. In his introduction to *Menschheitsdämmerung* Pinthus asks: 'But can a poetry which gives shape to the suffering and passion, the aspirations and the longings of those years and which burst forth from a generation devoid of ideas and ideals — can this poetry have a pure, clear countenance? Is it not bound to be chaotic like the age . . .?' (p. 25). And elsewhere in the same introduction he writes of the Expressionist poet's craving to explode 'that hostile crust' (of form) and of a 'chaotic shattering of language'. As if illustrating and confirming Pinthus's observations, Becher describes his own method of writing poetry in the following terms:

Scorning all rules, crudely and consciously violating anything remotely systematic and ordered, and in an illegible scrawl which I had recently perfected, I wrote a poem called 'City of Damnation' in which any rhyme, even if it occurred fortuitously, was replaced by a plonking assonance — anything to remove all traces of traditional style . . .[23]

The sentiments voiced here are the common currency of Expressionist theoretical writing. And, paradoxically, the other side of the argument — in favour of some kind of formal concern and conservatism — is amply defended, sometimes tacitly, sometimes explicitly. It is as if Expressionist poets, lacking the courage of their terrorist instincts, constantly find themselves slithering back to traditional forms. Their poetic practice is equally confusing. Becher, having 'scorned all rules', has by 1952 come round to the opinion that, 'if passionately felt emotion is to be converted into a poem, the poet must be familiar with poetic forms, otherwise they will be exploded by feeling,'[24] *but* even in 1920 he is represented in *Menschheitsdämmerung* by 'Berlin', 'Der Wald' and 'Klänge aus Utopia' which demonstrate some kind of formal discipline to set against such emotionally peripatetic outgrowths as 'Hymne auf Rosa Luxemburg' and the interminable 'Mensch, stehe auf!' Becher also shares the Expressionist poet's nostalgia and reverence for one particular literary form, the sonnet: he praises it as protection and analgesic when poet and poem are threatened with collapse, as an austere symbol of order and as a means of controlling and organizing the proliferation of images which assail the poet's eye and mind.[25]

Critics have tended to ignore the Expressionist poet's practical and theoretical concern for form: *all* Expressionist poetry is seen and depicted as formless, wilfully unformed and scornful of traditional prosody. F. J. Schneider's 'Expressionism's ultimate aim is the total dissolution of all poetic forms that have ever been practised'[26] and Schirokauer's even more dogmatic 'In as far as poetry is form, it is not Expressionist'[27] are typical examples of this crude oversimplification. Robert Newton convincingly demolishes what he calls 'the aging burden that Expressionist poets abandoned the conventional elements of verse' (p. 39) and vouchsafes the following prudent conclusion:

Perhaps the most general and most necessary insight which has been thoroughly confirmed is that the traditional prosodic elements are still widely used [in Expressionism] as effective elements of form, often enough without innovation . . . (p. 219)

Newton continually invokes the name of Georg Heym to illustrate his argument, for Heym's poetry and the criticism of it represent the sustained moment in which the whole tangle of contradiction and paradox with regard to Expressionist form comes into focus . . . but remains unsolved.

Heym wrote one hundred and five sonnets in all: this amounts to about one seventh of his entire œuvre. Eight of these are drafts, five are first versions which he may well have wanted to alter, and five more are, in part, unrhymed. Of the remaining eighty-seven, thirty-three repeat in the second quatrain a rhyme from the first. The sonnet 'Die Stadt', for example, rhymes abba in the first quatrain, then caac: the tercets rhyme aaa/bbb, and remarkably each of the fourteen lines rhymes either on an 'a' or an 'ei' sound. In fact, fifty-two of the eighty-seven completed sonnets are more or less traditional examples of this literary form. This is a statistic which in itself says a great deal for Heym's concern with strict formal control and demonstrates the absurdity of Heselhaus's claim that Heym's poetry somehow represents 'a shattering of conventional form'.[28] It is also a statistic which sits uncomfortably with what we know about Heym. We have it on his own word that 'poetic images steam out of my ears' (diary entry, 20 December 1910; T III, 154), and on the word of one of his biographers and best friends, Erwin Loewenson, that 'every word gushed out from him in an uncontrolled, stuttering, naive explosion', and that, 'living only for the moment, he was a Vesuvius of his unconscious'.[29] Few literary commentators, few of the people who knew Heym, match Loewenson's rapturous language, but very few contradict the purport of his remarks. In the man the startling dichotomy — teeming with life, an aggressive maverick and freebooter, and yet dedicated to death and dying; in the poet the equally bewildering conflict — assailed by visions and yet compelled to shape them: 'To have imagination is easy. But how difficult it is to mould the images conjured by imagination' (diary entry, 20 September 1908, T III, 118). And that shaping is marked by the greatest possible degree of strenuousness and care. Heym felt a powerful urge to expend inordinate effort on detail, to render what was apparently an all but overwhelming Dionysian onrush of inspiration subservient to an Apollonian will-to-form in a way which would have pleased, did please, Rainer Maria Rilke. The categories Dionysian/Apollonian are not used fortuitously here: they are peculiarly appropriate for Georg Heym and have frequently been invoked by critics of his work. Raabe, for example, reports that, when Heym joined 'Das Neopathetische Cabaret', its members believed that he was 'the post-rational Dionysus'[30] for whom they were all longing. Another critic, Wolfgang Paulsen, sees Heym as completely under the sway of his visions,[31] as if the poet were no more than host to a visitation from a kind of latter-day *furor teutonicus*. Given his particular character attributes and the way in which he was 'inspired', Heym might justifiably have been expected to write like such fellow Expressionist poets as Becher or Leonhard. Instead he regularly commits himself to the sonnet, the paradigmatic Apollonian form, which had been constantly developed over the centuries by poets ever since Fra Guittone d'Arezzo had limited it to fourteen lines in the thirteenth century.

A boy with a record of persistent indiscipline and rebelliousness bowing to a literary form, the principal characteristics of which are control and superimposed orderliness? It does not make much sense, and critics have been tempted to make sense of it by concluding that Heym's apparently ineluctable will-to-form issues from a fervent hope that shaping means subjugating — Heym, the argument goes, consigns his feverish visions to the beautiful architecture of the sonnet in order to master them and thus achieve, perhaps, at least a short-lived relief. Such an argument has worthy enough precedents: Wordsworth, for example, makes precisely this claim for the sonnet in his account of the pleasure and solace which it has granted him.[32] Hans Stieber is one amongst many critics who subscribe to the view that Heym needed and, in fact, welcomed the bounds set by the sonnet form, 'banishing as it were his visions into sonnets for fear of disintegrating himself'.[33] Heym's diaries and letters, disappointingly empty of comments on literary matters, reveal no hint that he shared this view. According to Stieber and those who think like him, Heym resorts to the sonnet form for the very reasons and at the very times Goethe chafes under its restraint '— when the spirits stir with immense vigour'.[34] Thus, Heym regards the sonnet as some kind of protective caul for the poet when he finds himself confronted by spiritual or mental chaos, a means of making sense of what he finds in everyday life intractable for one reason or another, so that the sonnet form takes on prophylactic powers, and poems become a series of strategies for containing emotional pressures too severe for direct confrontation. Other critics assert that Heym clings to traditional forms like the sonnet because only thus can he banish the evil and the chaos which he sees all around him and which he feels bound to introduce as major motifs into his poetry. The sonnet thus becomes a means of exorcizing demons. Again this sounds convincing enough, but there is no evidence to suggest that Heym brought such expectations to his writing. What evidence there is points in another direction — that he 'used' poetry, and his talent for it, for essentially mercenary and mundane ends: to win fame, and thus, he hoped, to win girls. His eye is always cocked towards posterity and its judgement of his verse, and, when in his diary he is pleading for a cure for his malady, his thoughts do *not* turn instantly to art:

I do not know what sort of illness is sitting inside me. Where is the remedy to cure all illnesses . . . I know of one cure, but I cannot pick the herb. That is fame, the applause of a thousand-headed throng . . . (20 July 1909; T III, 128)

Indeed, Heym's diaries and letters give the impression that he would have much rather been participating in 'a great revolution, a Hellenic war, anything at all, a trek across Africa, something different from everyday routine' (T III, 128) than wrestling with sonnets in boring old Berlin. Art in any case fails him — 'I think that poetry very soon becomes a silly occupation, for it is a pathetic surrogate for action and for life' (7 December 1910; T III, 153).

For him the sonnet was primarily a convenient literary form. It may also have been a means of controlling his own demons or, less likely, a means of exorcizing

E

other people's or the world's, but it is not, as such critics as Kohlschmidt have argued, a symbol of his political views[35] (which did not move beyond the naive and extremely superficial) and certainly not an excrescence of a belief in the value of form for form's sake in lived life and poetry. In fact, Heym simply does not make the connection which critics so frequently make for him — the connection between the overwhelming nature of his visions and nightmares on the one hand and his loyalty to strict formal control on the other. It is as if critics, having dubbed all Expressionist poetry formless and incoherent, have to rationalize Heym's carefully chiselled verse by finding more or less ingenious psychological explanations for it. Thanks to the efforts of K. L. Schneider we now know, often to the day, when Heym wrote his poems. We also have his diary which Mautz, author of a full-length study of the poet, describes as 'the key to all Heym's work'.[36] In September 1911, four months before his death, Heym wrote thirty-seven poems, one of which is a sonnet. These thirty-seven poems are an extremely variegated crop. Some rhyme, some do not; some are very long, some very short; some are stanzaic, some are not; one has five syllables per line, another ten; and there are all kinds of variations within each individual poem. They are the work of a poet who is maturing and experimenting. If the equation 'poet inundated with visions of death and destruction and overwhelmed by gloom means flight to the refuge of the sonnet', then surely, given all the sundry experiments which Heym makes in September 1911 and turning the equation round, the month of September should be comparatively blissful and trouble-free. It is not. He despairs at the way all his girl-friends are abandoning him (3 September), he writes 'I have waged a heroic struggle. But suddenly I feel as if I cannot go on any more' (4 September), and, one day later, 'But sometimes I cannot go on'. A week goes by and the situation has not improved: 'My head is like a hollow ball. I'm not sleeping any more . . . at the moment I'm at rock-bottom again. And that girl did love me after all, my God'. On 13 September he inserts the astonishingly prescient quatrain into his diary:

> Mund und Augen sind ihm zugefroren
> Selbst des Abgrunds Tiefe ist vergessen
> Und ihm ist als hätt er nichts verloren,
> Aber auch als hätt er nichts besessen.

> His mouth and eyes are frozen shut
> Even the depths of Hell are forgotten
> And he feels as if he has lost nothing,
> But also as if he has never possessed any-
> thing.

Two days later he writes: 'It could perhaps be said that my poetry provides the best evidence of a metaphysical country which thrusts its black peninsulas far into our fleeting lives . . . My God — this banal age is stifling me and my stagnating enthusiasm.' Neither the tone nor the content of the entries changes during the last fortnight of the month. Abandoned by his girl-friends, rebelling against his flaccid time and place (and doubting the value of that rebellion), besieged by feelings of deep gloom and guilt-ridden self-pity, toying with thoughts of suicide, he is and remains in a desperate state. But he does not turn to the frame of a sonnet to shore up his crumbling world. On the contrary, his last entry for September is an acrimonious leave-taking from, and denigration of, formal precision: 'The iambus is a lie . . . "transparent, square-shaped" is a constraint on thinking. I have gone back in a great curve to where I once began . . . forced rhyme is a blasphemy, I am back again with my very first poems '— and those 'very first poems' are a hotchpotch of formal experiments, some are strictly reined in, others run fast and loose. A pattern emerges, the pattern of the rebel manqué, of the essentially Dionysian man too frightened to yield to his instincts and continually straining to invoke Apollonian control, and ending by regretting it. He would have liked to be an out-and-out rebel in his dealings with his family, but he amazed his friends by his passivity towards his father and by his readiness to live with his parents in Berlin. He liked to play Casanova, yet he was gauche and chronically shy: at school he had had a persistent, embarrassing stutter which his fellow-pupils imitated by yelling 'Gra-gra-gra-grabbe' whenever he walked into the room, thus reinforcing the intense self-consciousness which he never lost. He inveighed constantly against the tepidity and ennui of middle-class existence in pre-war Germany, and yet launched himself on the classical middle-class life-style of grammar school — university — law. Admiring Rimbaud and hankering after similar adventures, the nearest Heym got to foreign climes was when he began attending seminars in the Arabian-Moroccan class of the School for Oriental Studies at Berlin University. And literature? It is the same pattern of a fairly, but not too, relaxed start, then harshly checked impulses and emotions, subsequently regrets and greater relaxation and abstraction. Heym craves three things — fame, love, excitement — and it is probably the craving for excitement which gives his poetry its greatest impetus. In one of those powerfully autobiographical prose pieces, entitled 'Eine Fratze', which are so characteristic of his œuvre he writes that 'our sickness is boundless boredom. Our sickness consists in living in the evening of the world's life-span, an evening which became so sticky that the reek of its decay is barely tolerable' (PD II, 173). He feels profoundly insecure, yet he appears to derive a kind of perverse pride and self-satisfaction from his ability to hold out: 'I tottered and was shaken by the wind. I was only a man. But I was not knocked down.' Fifteen years later, touching upon some of the categories which arise in any discussion of Georg Heym, the problem of form and his countrymen's attitude to it, Graf Hermann Keyserling ventures an interesting generalization about the Germany of *his* day when he writes:

The German needs external discipline to counterbalance his inner freedom. A Dresden bookseller once said to me: 'At one time when the king was still here, I would come home from work and look into the lit-up windows of the castle and would feel secure in the thought that even after a day's work he's doing something which you don't understand. Nowadays I don't feel secure. I need a tight-fitting coat to feel at ease in myself'.[37]

Although Heym's poetry issues from a deep feeling of insecurity, he did not consciously seek a 'tight-fitting coat' in literature and did not have frequent recourse to classical and traditional forms in the hope that he would find such a garment.

So why sonnets? In the four grammar schools which he attended between 1896 and 1907 Heym received a heavy classical education. Very few critics have pointed to the possible connection between Heym's staid education and his poetry, though Carl Seelig, one of Heym's earliest biographers, reports that at school Heym could hold conversations in Latin hexameters.[38] The sonnet is the form which might be chosen by a poet supremely confident in his handling of prosody *or* by one who is not very certain of his means of expression. The former, like Wordsworth, enjoys testing his skill against the sonnet's demands, the latter is grateful for the bounds which the sonnet sets him — in a quite definite way, the sonnet saves him trouble. His many experiments in his early poetry indicate that Heym was feeling his way amongst formal possibilities, though he never breaks loose after the fashion of Becher or, on occasions, Werfel. When Heym is more certain of himself—certain of himself in literary terms, as a poet — he has less frequent recourse to the sonnet: of his last one hundred and ninety poems only seven are sonnets. The suggestion is then that he wrote sonnets because they, as examples of rigid verse forms, were what he knew best. Granted neither Wordsworth's longevity nor the precociously confident versatility of his 'hero', Keats, Heym was just emerging from his self-imposed and ingrained limits when the fatal accident occurred in January 1912. He began by needing the sonnet not in order to dispel or discipline bogeymen, but simply to accommodate his visions; in doing that, he was turning to a configuration familiar to him from many lessons at school. He ended by occasionally returning to it. It is necessary to harp upon Heym's recourse to the sonnet not only because critics of his work constantly focus their attention upon this aspect of his poetry, but also because they rarely move beyond gross simplifications and generalizations — in the same way as Expressionist form as a whole is dealt with cursorily and superficially. Mönch, in his study of the sonnet, detects a relationship between the sonnet and drama, pointing out how everything in a sonnet builds up to the final explosion enshrined in the second tercet.[39] Heym, himself a playwright, was no doubt aware of such potentialities, and regarded the sonnet as another means of generating tension and intensity, two crucial categories in all Expressionist art. Instead, therefore, of resorting to possible neuro-pathological or psychological causes, the reader of his poetry might do better to rely on literary explanations of the paradoxical case of Georg Heym, to settle for something along the lines of Adorno's interpretation of Expressionist attitudes to form:

All traditional forms which Expressionism rages its way through become so many sources of friction . . . Hurling its energies against innumerable obstacles, it never finds the way into its self, it directs itself against the world.[40]

'The self against the world'? That is certainly the confrontation upon which Heym, like so many of his generation, founds his life. And the sonnet as 'a source of friction'? Heym's 'Berlin II' provides an excellent opportunity to test the validity of Adorno's general observation. This poem may appear too slight to be dignified with lengthy analysis, but then such a reservation holds for most of Heym's poems if they are taken in isolation from the mass of his œuvre, perhaps even for poems like 'Der Krieg' rendered so familiar by anthologists and too long anyway for interpretation here. The undoubted power of Heym's poetry resides in its sustained consistency of tone and image. 'Berlin II' is, nevertheless, a wholly typical and respectable example of Heym's work, useful in underlining its strength and pointing to its essential limitations.

> Woe to her that is filthy and polluted, to the
> oppressing city! . . . she trusted not in the Lord;
> she drew not near to her God . . .her prophets
> are light and treacherous persons . . .[41]

> . . . I sing my most exultant paean to you, you
> great, you roaring cities! | Corrupted by
> you. My way lost in you. Seduced by you.[42]

The urbanization of our culture, in England, Europe and most spectacularly in the United States, has been the major sociological phenomenon of this century. But the city, seen in terms of its corrupting influence, has been a perennial theme in poetry and prose. Writing two hundred years ago, William Cowper depicts the city as a hotbed of filth and vice:

> Thither flow,
> As to a common and most noisome sew'r,
> The dregs and feculence of ev'ry land.
> In cities foul example on most minds
> Begets its likeness. Rank abundance breeds
> In gross and pamper'd cities sloth and lust,
> And wantonness and gluttonous excess.[43]

Raymond Williams, in his *The Country and the City* (London, 1973), shows how even in the days of Quintilian and Juvenal the contrast between town and country life was a stock thesis. Williams takes us via Blake, Wordsworth, Dickens, Gissing, Wells, and Hardy nearer to the present day and such writers as Huxley and Orwell. Most of these are prose-writers, and it is of James Thomson (particularly his *The Doom of a City*, written in 1857, and *The City of Dreadful Night*, written between 1870 and 1873) and of T. S. Eliot that we think when we seek for illuminating parallels with Georg Heym. Urbanization in Germany came later than in England, but its impact on man's consciousness was no less great. Heym's immediate predecessors are the Naturalist writers at the end of the nineteenth century. In the biblical quotation at the head of this section the city is a renegade, it has betrayed God. That is not surprising, for 'God made the country, and man made the town'.[44] And it also seems a natural development that, over the years, urban scenes have become scenes of cruelty and inhumanity so that Shelley can write: 'Hell is a city much like London — | A populous and smoky city',[45] whilst in our own century Eliot's depiction of city life in 'Little Gidding' merges with a frightening picture of purgatory. In the work of Proust, Joyce, Kafka, Musil, Döblin, and Broch — to give obvious examples — the city casts a thick shadow across characters and events alike. Expressionist writers, too, seize upon the city as a theme: their treatment of it is characterized by unrealistic detail, lacking, for instance, the subtle complexities and ambiguities of Blake's visions and the sense of possibility and optimism of some of Wells's work. Nor do Expressionist writers set up any opposition between rural and city life. In Heym, as in parts of Eliot and Thomson, man is isolated, anonymous, rootless, insecure, godless in 'a great gloomy city, webbed and meshed . . . by the spinnings of a huge poisonous spider'.[46]

From the age of thirteen Heym lived a considerable part of his life in Berlin, a metropolis for which a visitor from abroad like his English contemporary Charles Sorley, demonstrating the kind of open-minded and unselfconscious nature so typical of *his* generation in England and so untypical of the embattled attitudes of many of the German Expressionist poets, felt ecstatic admiration:

All through the night the city was equally alive and humming, with happy people . . . Natural, bourgeois, unaffected Hedonism seems to be the prevailing note: Hedonism of the very best kind, which depends on universality not on contrast for its fulfilment.[47]

Heym hated this hedonism and the garish optimism which he believed served only to conceal imminent and universal catastrophe, and whilst his fellow poets at the 'Neuer Club' were swept along by the feverish excitement of the capital, Heym was excluded, or excluded himself, from it:

Anything which ran counter to the vision was truly repugnant to Heym. That includes the superficial optimism, the sterile 'polka jollity' of the shallow recreational activities in Berlin, the music which seeped from the Metropol Theatre onto the street . . . the nearer we got to August 1914, the more furiously, the more exquisitely the intellectual turmoil of Berlin seized us. None of us had anticipated the war the way he had. Not in political terms — he knew nothing about politics! — but he saw it as a poetic vision bearing down on him.[48]

Characteristically, Heym does not make explicit his sense of impending doom or his distaste for the heedless sybaritism of the capital. The eight 'Berlin-Gedichte', written between 6 April and 25 December 1910, are, however, freighted with apocalyptic menace. In the course of the cycle, Berlin becomes 'a place of disaffection': 'tumid apathy . . . eructation of unhealthy souls . . . inoperancy of the world of spirit . . .'[49] — all Eliot's categories and epithets apply with striking relevance.

'Berlin I' is a mixture of impressionistic sense effects and naturalistic loyalty to detail: the poet lies on the edge of the road and looks over at the distant city bathed in the rays of the setting sun. 'Berlin III', another sonnet, is a description of a scene from a train waiting outside a main station and then eventually, in the tercets, disgorging its passengers — again it is evening. 'Berlin IV', consisting only of two quatrains, depicts an afternoon siesta scene on Berlin's streets: it has been raining, haze rises from the pavements as the sun comes out and the city enters a lazy, postprandial period. 'Berlin V', again two quatrains, seems to be a prologue to 'Berlin IV': the rain beats down, the clouds race, the trees sway, and with the comparison of the umbrellas in front of the railway station to 'a black swarm of great rats' the poem takes on a more minatory and dynamic aspect — the siesta of 'Berlin IV' erupts into frenzy. 'Berlin VI', entitled 'Vorortsbahnhof' ('Suburban Station'), shifts the perspective back to a vantage point outside the city and is a description of railway lines, of carriage doors opening, of passengers boarding the train which then disappears into the evening — we are reminded once again of the lives being played out alongside the railway when Heym refers our attention to the balconies and the people, dimly seen, eating there. 'Berlin VII', called 'Laubenfest' ('Garden Party'), is an impressionistic study of a kind of harvest festival celebration: Chinese lanterns, music, fireworks, dancing, violin-playing, and clouds looking like pink-finned dolphins; by now the visionary has virtually ousted the actually seen, the whole spectacle is diffused into a series of snatched-up details, people remain vague and generalized, the abstract and the enigmatic take over. There is a mysterious violinist, a flock of children, but the little old woman of the first version does not survive into the last. 'Berlin VIII' is written four months later and transports us to authentic Heym territory — chimneys weighed down by a heavy wintry sky, bare trees, fences, sheds, icy rails along which a goods-train drags its weary way, and then suddenly a churchyard for the poor. Here the dead are watching 'the red decline' as the sun sets: they savour the demise of the day, they knit in time to the Marseillaise, caps of soot on their naked temples. The abstract quality of 'Berlin VII' is accentuated here with the introduction of ever more exotic, quasi-medieval, Bergmannesque images. From 'Berlin I' to 'Berlin VIII' the line of development runs like this — the impressionistic-cum-naturalistic yields to the visionary, the 'actual' assumes a more and more attenuated role, until finally we enter a fantastic Baroque world where the dead, feigning pathetic rebellion, witness and cheer the destruction of the universe.

In the eight 'Berlin-Gedichte' we have six sonnets and two poems consisting of two quatrains each. The sonnets all have the same shape — two quatrains and two tercets — and, taken chronologically, permutate the following rhyme-schemes: abba, baab, cdc, dcd/abba, acca, ded, ede/abba, cddc, efe, fef/abba, abba, cde, cde/ abba, cbbc, ded, fef/abba, cddc, efe, fef. The poems, consisting only of two quatrains, rhyme abba, cddc, and abab, cdcd. Manifestly, heedful thought and controlled shaping have gone into this cycle of eight poems, all of which are five- foot iambics with ten or eleven syllables. None is wholly realistic, none is wholly impressionistic. The objects which characteristically squeeze out human beings in Heym's poems — the 'little mother in the flowered dress' of the first draft of 'Berlin VII' gives way in the final draft to an anonymous, mysterious series of couples — are felt to be hostile and overbearing. The trains which meander so frequently in and out of Heym's poetry — in three of the eight 'Berlin' poems they play an important part — are vouchsafed more dynamism than his people who are reduced to the role of helpless spectator and wholly passive witness. The action of at least six of the eight poems unfolds in an evening setting: the word 'Abend' appears six times, the word 'Nacht' once. And so we catch Berlin invariably in penumbral, dusty gloom. Three times it is described as a 'world city', thus linking its fate, its destruction which the dead watch with such glee in 'Berlin VIII', with all the world's cities. All are doomed. There is no hint of pity for the city's fate or for the urban inhabitants' grim lives, yet Heym, though he may have been the political naif H. E. Jacob makes him out to be, certainly had at least an artist's awareness of the degrading conditions in which city dwellers and particularly railway commuters live. Ronald Salter is right to regard Heym as a neutral observer and reporter, as a painter manqué rather than as a would-be reformer:[50] for Salter and other critics, lines such as 'We saw in the cramped space | Numberless throngs of people crushed together' or 'Masses of humanity shove | Still white with chalk and yellow . . .' contain no social comment and merely demonstrate 'Heym's optical flair' and 'the sculptural quality of his imaginative powers' (Salter, pp. 7–9). Seen from this point of view, 'Berlin II' (and the other seven 'Berlin' poems) becomes the configuration of an artist's impressions of particular, very limited, aspects of the city which serves as a lightning conductor for Heym's visionary powers:

> Beteerte Fässer rollten von den Schwellen
> Der dunklen Speicher auf die hohen Kähne.
> Die Schlepper zogen an. Des Rauches Mähne
> Hing rußig nieder auf die öligen Wellen.
>
> Zwei Dampfer kamen mit Musikkapellen.
> Den Schornstein kappten sie am Brückenbogen.
> Rauch, Ruß, Gestank lag auf den schmutzigen Wogen
> Der Gerbereien mit den braunen Fellen.
>
> In allen Brücken, drunter uns die Zille
> Hindurchgebracht, ertönten die Signale
> Gleichwie in Trommeln wachsend in der Stille.
>
> Wir ließen los und trieben im Kanale
> An Gärten langsam hin. In dem Idylle
> Sahn wir der Riesenschlote Nachtfanale.

Tarred barrels rolled from the thresholds | Of dark warehouses onto the high boats. | The tugs pulled tight. The smoke's mane | Hung down sooty onto the oily waves.
Two steamers came with music bands. | They lopped their chimney on the arch of the bridge. | Smoke, soot, stench lay on the dirty waves | Of the tanneries with the brown skins. |
In all the bridges beneath which the barge | Brought us, the signals resounded | Ever louder in the silence, just as in drums. |
We cast off and drifted on the canal | Slowly past gardens. In the idyll | We saw the nocturnal torches of the gigantic chimneys.

All the 'things' of this poem have a demonizing and mythological impetus behind them. The very first image contains factors which portend sinister happenings. 'Tarred' barrels are black barrels which roll from 'dark' warehouses. 'Dark' and 'tarred' reinforce each other and escalate in that metaphorical blackness peculiar to Heym. The same blackness, retreat of a malignant fate, occurs in connection with 'warehouses' in the poem 'Die Tote im Wasser' ('The Dead Girl in the Water') where masts jut out 'black as clinker' and the water 'stares dead at decaying, crumbling warehouses'. The 'high rafts' can only be black 'tarred' freight barges similar to the 'black rafts' in the poem 'Sehnsucht nach Paris' ('Yearning for Paris'). Furthermore, black is evoked by 'smoke', 'soot' and 'oily': all these repetitions ('tarred', 'dark', 'oily', 'smoke', 'sooty', 'smoke', 'soot') are not pleonasms as some critics suggest, but have the same expressive function as the persistent accumulation of certain colour metaphors in 'Die Tote im Wasser' (white) or 'Der Krieg' ('The War' — black) or 'Die Irren III' ('The Madmen III' — red). They point the way to the 'Nachtfanale' of the final tercet. A strange kinship is forged between the initial and concluding lines of the poem, between the ostensibly naturalistic images and the visionary, metaphorical last line. The dimensions of real objects are exaggerated: the 'high rafts' seem outsize because, in actual fact, Heym is referring to the flat-bottomed Spree barges; the metaphor 'the smoke's mane' distends an easily imaginable mane into that of an enormous animal; the drums with which the bridges are compared are also huge. Such comparisons serve to lend, indirectly, an appearance of enormity to objects — in this case, smoke and bridges. The chimneys, too, are 'gigantic stacks'. The whole picture of the industrial landscape is composed of grotesque, demonic elements. Salter demonstrates that the 'object' of a Heym poem is invariably something visible, that Heym operates like a painter because he creates from a fixed standpoint, maintaining one perspective and working within a range of vision demarcated strictly by optic logic. Salter selects van Gogh as the crucial influence on Heym's visual and visionary training. We know that Heym read van Gogh's letters and indeed felt a special affinity with the painter,[51] so that statements of personal methods from the painter's letters assume particular significance in any understanding of Heym's poetic techniques:

Instead of reproducing precisely what I see in front of me I use colour in a high-handed way. Above all, I am out to achieve strong expression . . . I begin by painting a man just as he is, as faithfully as possible, but that is only the beginning. The picture is by no means finished yet. Now I begin to use colour arbitrarily. I exaggerate the fairness of the hair . . . behind the head — instead of the ordinary wall of the room — I paint infinity.[52]

Poet and painter share common methods and aims in their treatment of empirical reality (beginning with it and then abruptly moving beyond it), their wilful attitude to material and model and their search for strong effects. They also demonstrate the same readiness to accentuate and exaggerate, the same pointing-up of a 'background of infinity' and hence a similar end-result of elusive mysteriousness, which, for example in 'Berlin II', informs the final image of 'the gigantic chimneys' nocturnal torches'. The reader of Heym's poetry is invited, or left, to picture what is going on — the implication is that such a picturing procedure (on the part of poet and reader) will yield more significance than could be provoked by a kind of 'atmosphere' poem or by bare analytical statement.

In the second quatrain of 'Berlin II' two steamers with 'music bands' are introduced to confront the tugs trailing the mane of smoke. The very expression 'kappen' ('lop') for the way the steamers' chimneys are apparently sliced off by the arch of the bridge is a metaphorical negation of all that the steamers and the bands represent: gaiety, carelessness, the idyllic joys of a day's trip on the river. The bridges themselves represent the industrial landscape. And whereas the steamers are 'beheaded' by the city's bridges, the chimneys of the factories tower up in the final image over the idyllic scene which the steamers traverse. Each time, the idyll ('music bands' in the fifth line, 'gardens' in the thirteenth) is undermined by a succeeding image ('bridge-arch', 'gigantic chimneys'), with the result that it is cordonned by phenomena from the encroaching, stifling world of industry. In the last two lines of the second quatrain we find an ostensibly naturalistic reproduction of a piece of industrial scenery, and yet once again there is a shift beyond naturalistic description. The repetitious enumeration 'Smoke, soot, stench . . . dirty', the accumulation of ugly detritus from industry, serves a more subtle purpose than an apparently identical device in, say, Dehmel's poem 'Der Wunschgeist' where the poet simply reels off those items which go to make up Berlin's sky-line.[53] Heym has other designs for his kind of naturalistic descriptions. The main clue comes from his use of the 'tanneries' and 'brown pelts'. Although he means us to understand dead skins when he uses the word 'Fellen', both that word and the word 'brown' remind us of *living* animals or, at any rate, of animals that were once alive. The 'brown pelts', made into leather in the tanneries, help to underline the viciousness of the mass industrial procedure of turning living things into dead, saleable objects. And the fact that 'Fellen' has as its rhyme-word 'Kapellen' ('bands') draws our attention to Heym's purpose here — the images following upon 'steamers . . . with music bands' are in vivid contrast to the music which is being played on the steamers, and the point of contrast is to reveal the meretricious futility and ingenuousness of the music merely by listing, unrhetorically, items of a repellent, sinister kind. The next image (in the first tercet) reinforces this contrast by opposing 'signals which resound on all the bridges' to the naive heedlessness of the bands on the steamers. These signals which issue from unmentioned ships' sirens become generalized alarm-signals. They ring out in silence which is not really a silence, for all the preceding images conjure up noise (from the band, the tanneries, industry generally). It is an unreal, paradoxical silence, because nothing but alarm-signals can be heard in it. The menace of this silence is metaphorically accentuated by the comparison Heym draws between 'all the bridges' and enormous drums, as if the signals were resounding in something hollow. 'Barrels', 'warehouses' and 'high rafts' have already prepared the reader for the idea of hollowness. Like 'the pack of dogs baying in the hollow' in the poem 'Die Städte' ('The Towns'), these alarm-signals proclaim catastrophe, the catastrophe which is just about to befall a world that is fundamentally hollow beneath its surface of hectic activity.

In the final tercet the whole process of transmuting reality into something alien and mythic attains its climax. In the image of 'the gigantic chimneys' nocturnal torches' there is no question of celebrating or transfiguring the size of the industrial scene, as some critics maintain. On the contrary, Heym is intent on discovering the intrinsically subversive nature of everything which appears in that scene where, in Baudelaire's words, 'le spectre en plein jour raccroche le passant'.[54] 'Fanale' are incendiary torches, beacons which signify revolt, war, revolution. The war-god in 'Der Krieg' brandishes a fire-torch, and in 'Sehnsucht nach Paris' the 'bloodily' rising sun is compared with a 'Sturm-fanal' in memory of the French Revolution. In Heym's poetry 'night' betokens catastrophe and destruction. It is the nocturnal cities which are destroyed by conflagrations in many of his poems. H. E. Jacob (pp. 18–19) has already described the vacuity and sickliness of the Berliners' pursuit of pleasure, and particularly of the canned music provided for them. Heym for his part in 'Berlin II' intimates the same spuriousness in their recreations, and the final tercet depicts the illusory and ephemeral quality of the idyll, the city's treacherously seductive lure which yields to the menace embodied in the closing image: the 'nocturnal torches' receive as the final rhyming word special stress and herald those fires of destruction which in Heym's mythologizing city-poems mean the end of the urban world. The 'Fanale' and their metaphorical equivalent, the huge chimney-stacks, have the same characteristic of ominous, physical dominance. Contrasted with the 'Idyll' they are not only *not* picturesque, they constitute a threat to the 'Idyll' itself. The poem reveals, step by step, the mythic and minatory character of the elements which go to make up Heym's selected scene from empirical reality. It focuses attention on phenomena where that mythic character manifests itself and contrasts them with the deceptive façade of an apparently frivolous boating trip. The tercets bring to the fore all that is intimated in the naturalistic descriptions of the quatrains — the presence of a blindly compelling power working in and through the objects, a power which by 'Berlin VIII' has wrought its havoc and has only the dead from the local cemetery as its witnesses as it exerts 'many a potent evil influence, | Each adding poison to the poisoned air; | Infections of unutterable sadness, | Infections of incalculable madness, | Infections of incurable despair'.[55]

Bernhard Blume has shown[56] how in the lyric poetry of the eighteenth century a communal boating trip involving lovers or friends symbolized a feeling of profound integration amongst the group, a release from the everyday world of humdrum chores, and the utopia of a party atmosphere in an idyllic and timeless landscape. The two quatrains of 'Berlin II' contain no hint of such an outing. It is not until the first tercet that we realize that everything is being viewed from the vantage-point of a boat. The 'uns' of the first tercet remain anonymous and casually indefinite, nor is the boat independent. It is pulled by a barge — 'we cast off' and drifted on slowly. There is mention of 'gardens', but only incidentally, in the flat part of the rhythmic structure. The presence of the city overshadows everything else: there is no suggestion that the gardens represent potential asylum. And the boat, instead of taking the group of friends away from the industrial world of the city, appears to plunge them ever more deeply into it. The things of the poem play a much greater part than the faceless people ('steamers with bands', 'us'), thus underscoring the essential point: the city is what man has made without God, and this microcosm of a world which man has thus created is an alien, all-powerful, menacing place. Man is not at home in it, nor can he find a home in it. The degree and kind of alienation which permeates Blake's view of the city of London and which finds overt expression in Wordsworth's *Prelude*[57] is strongly implied in Heym's 'Berlin' cycle.

Taking up Adorno's phrase 'source of friction', the reader does not have the impression of any tendency on the poet's part to push his material around to fill out a complex and demanding form. On the contrary, Heym seems to have found the sonnet a congenial literary refuge. Formally the poet is in control. Indeed one of the earliest reviewers of 'Berlin II' finds it too strictly regimented, asserting that 'discipline snatches up the rhythm', that we are frogmarched through the lines as if they are 'a suite of parallel rooms' and are compelled to wait 'for the door-curtain of the rhyme to rise'[58] so that we can enter the next line. Jacob's criticism can be countered by reference to the poem's fairly flowing and relaxing enjambment — only *fairly* flowing because the enjambment at the end of the densely alliterative iambic line is blocked by compulsively heavy rhyming and because there is a sharp break after 'signals' in the second line of the first tercet. There is nothing *ad hoc* or arbitrary in terms of Rilke's criticism of Expressionism about the poem: it is constructed on the traditional basis of thesis-antithesis, it bodies forth the evolution of one thought, 'one poetically apprehended fact',[59] and it follows, in a competent way, a conventional rhyme scheme — competent, with two exceptions: in the last line of the second quatrain, Heym relies on the false extra syllable in 'Gerbereien' ($\stackrel{\smile}{}\!-\!\stackrel{\smile}{}$) where the true value is $\stackrel{\smile}{}\!-$, and, in the penultimate line of the poem, 'Idylle' looks, and sounds, like a feminine noun, that is 'in der Idylle', which he cannot possible want, whereas it *is* the dative +e (*metri causa*) of the neuter 'das Idyll'. Such prosodic offences are by no means rare in Heym's poetry: they catch and distract the eye, and precisely because the organization of his poems is taut, little indulgences and failures quite to fulfil all the rigours of a recognizable form are disturbing.

Heym varies the rhythm in his sonnets: there is a vast difference between the flowing cadences of 'Berlin II' and the staccato and abrupt rhythm of, say, 'Louis Capet' or 'Robespierre'. Not that he has the versatility and confidence of a poet like T. S. Eliot with whom an anonymous critic in *The Times Literary Supplement* of 28 October 1960 (p. 694) compares him and who in the third part of *The Waste Land*, writing on a very similar subject to Heym in 'Berlin II', erupts suddenly into 'The Song of the Three Thames-daughters':

> The river sweats
> Oil and tar
> The barges drift
> With the turning tide
> Red sails
> Wide
> To leeward, swing on the heavy spar.

In his unwillingness or inability to imitate such bold rhythmic experiments, Heym is illustrating a point that can be made generally about German poetry — that it is not often rhythmically interesting or adventurous — and, more specifically, about Expressionist poetry — that, in spite of its stridently proclaimed anti-traditionalism, it makes very little contribution to any development of prosodic techniques. Again and again, consciously or unconsciously, Heym settles for rigid and conventional literary moulds and patterns. In committing himself to formal discipline, Heym shares in the paradox inherent in the creation of poetry, for that creation is spontaneous and free *and*, simultaneously, fiercely controlled by the conscious judgement of the poet. It is not a question of either/or, but both: each demands its opposite, poetry is like a magnet in that, whatever Expressionist theoreticians believed and their critics maintained, it cannot exist without both poles. Looking back in 1955 to the Expressionist era, Benn imagines what the poets of that era would have wanted to become if, like him, they had survived the 1914–18 war. He writes in terms of the Apollo-Dionysus dialectic:

The Expressionist poet desires discipline because he was the most chaotic one of all; and none of them, painter, musician, poet wants that myth to end in any other way than with Dionysus coming to rest at the feet of the clear-sighted Delphic God.[60]

Heym for his part hardly wavered in his support for the god of order.

> We sought in harsh brutality for the light,
> Which is meant to show us our way ahead,
> And are amazed that it is darker than ever.
> We ourselves called forth the packs of grey Furies,
> Which are now chasing through the skies of our homeland,
> Scattering horror —[61]

Georg Heym, dead by January 1912, and National Socialism? It sounds far-fetched, but it is a link which critics often assert. The assertion invariably takes one of two different forms. It is argued, on the one hand, that, given his cast of mind, his political ingenuousness and his particular appetites and frustrations, Heym would have found the National Socialist party a very attractive proposition. Kurt Hiller, who had been very much part of the Expressionist scene in his younger days, avers in a 1960 lecture that 'it is clear from parts of Heym's letters and diaries that this fate, along with others, lay in his prematurely shattered urn'.[62] It requires, Hiller implies, no great stretch of the imagination to visualize Georg Heym, with very little adjustment of his fundamental outlook on life, following that particular path, at the extreme end of which stood Arnolt Bronnen who, in the 1930s, slithered with a macabre inevitability into the National Socialist camp and revelled in what he found there. Heym and Bronnen do, after all, share the same envenomed attitude to the world of their fathers, a similar amoral pursuit of pleasure and stimulation, a kinship with the irrational and the perverse, and a fascination for *Caligari*-style nightmare and viciousness. Or, on the other hand, critics underline the anticipatory aspect of Heym's visions: Uhlig, for example, in his analysis of Heym's poem 'Die Gefangenen' (I and II), writes of 'concentration camps',[63] Sokel claims that the Nazis 'transmuted Heym's visions into social reality' (p. 2), and Sengle, discussing Expressionism in general terms, concludes that 'the much lauded visions of horror contribute to the intellectual causes of the catastrophes which filled the first half of the twentieth century'.[64]

Ernst Keller in his *Nationalismus und Literatur* (Berne and Munich, 1970) knits together both strands. He sees Heym as a paradigmatic example of 'the spreading unease in technological civilisation' (p. 232) and focuses attention on the poet's intrinsic hostility to authority and moral sanctions, his establishment of an evil God at the centre of creation, his stigmatization of all rational thought processes, his repudiation of civilized and traditional values, his lust for destruction, his cult of heroism, his love of festivals and ritual, and his temperamental affinity with the ideals of the *Wandervogel* movement. Keller underscores the oddness of the only vision of a social order which Heym purveys — a priest state in which veneration of heroes is one aim, worship of nature another.

Perhaps, instead of indulging in unprofitable speculation about Heym's 'inevit-able' enlistment in the National Socialist party, we can best approach the idea of a connection between his work (and Expressionism as a whole) and National Social-ism by regarding his poetry and prose as *one* among diverse 'intellectual structures which make it only too comprehensible how easily this German mind was bound to succumb to the temptation of totalitarianism' (Keller, cover). To all that Keller interprets in Heym's work as symptomatic of those aspects of literary and intellectual life which helped to deliver Germany into the arms of the National Socialists can be added others of Heym's convictions and prepossessions: 'the combination of an unpolitical abstention from state affairs with an equally unpolitical worship of power',[65] a craving for excitement (note his diary entry for 17 June 1910 where he writes: 'Why doesn't someone just do something out of the ordinary even if it's only cutting the balloon-man's string . . . Why doesn't someone murder the Kaiser or the Tsar?'), an uncritical cultivation of the instinctual and elemental, a loathing for everything lukewarm, a simmering anti-semitism, an implicit repudiation of the reasonable and decent, generous and tolerant, and a corresponding addiction to the bestial and excessive. For those who want to find them, there are in Heym's poems visions of a murderous, chaotic future: and underpinning those poems are many of the attitudes which, twenty years after his death, turned ghastly vision into even ghastlier reality. By 1922 these attitudes have become the common currency of Weimar's musical, literary, and artistic life. In his detailed depiction of that society in *The Weimar Chronicle — Prelude to Hitler*[66] Alex de Jonge draws up a list of the characteristic features of the age, a list with which Heym's life has already made us familiar: 'a sinister willingness to search for and worship strange gods', 'occasional flashes of perverted violence and vileness that are almost beyond description', 'thirst for some kind of intoxication', 'demand for unheard of pleasures', 'call of the irrational', 'radicalism and rejection of a rotten old world', 'attraction of the radical alternative', 'moral ambiguity and aimlessness' etc . . . And, in a quite remarkable way, Heym prefigures Erich Kästner's Fabian, the young anti-hero and product of the Berlin of the Weimar Republic:[67] Heym and his fictional counterpart live out a similar ill-starred existence, sharing the same paralysing fatalism, drifting passivity, joyless amorality and purposelessness, and even the same death by drowning. An awful sense of cruel arbitrariness pervades both lives.

And Heym's poetry to one side of the political nexus? If he was more than 'a slender talent', 'a strong promise', he certainly did not initiate a T. S. Eliot-style revolution in German poetry. His work is heavily dependent, for its particular themes and for its general response to life, on Grabbe, Rimbaud, Baudelaire, Büchner, Verhaeren, Kleist, and Nietzsche. Promising nothing, his poetry is the obverse of the work of other contemporary German writers like Toller, who seeks to reorganize society along definite political lines, or Schickele who places his hopes for mankind on the intrinsic qualities of the human soul, or Werfel who believes that all conflicts and hostilities can be submerged and resolved in a welter of ecstatic love. Heym's poetry derives its power, and ultimately its limitations, from a tenacious commitment to the black, bleak sides of life (as we saw even in the comparatively low-key 'Berlin' poems) and from his ability to cast his visions into tautly structured verse. Of 'man without God . . . driven this way and that, and finding no place for lodgement and germination', of 'waste and void. And darkness on the face of the deep . . .',[68] of all this, Heym's poetry renders a full account, but it offers nothing at all on the other side of life where there may be found 'the lifting light, Light/Light /The visible reminder of Invisible Light' (Eliot, p. 165). We cannot expect theological discriminations from him. In many of his 'city' poems he picks up the story of Sodom and Gomorrah *after* they have been destroyed by God's vengeance, but *not* (by Heym's account) purged of evil men and evil ways: corpses and rodents, diseases and demons are paraded before us in long undiscriminating sequences. Heym saw with almost incomparable breadth many of the manifestations of actual and potential evil of his day. But he did not see *through* them after the manner of an earlier rebel, Georg Büchner, whose name he frequently invokes. Heym has no criticism of similar depth to offer: a large part of his report, for all its vivid imagining, is not profoundly penetrating or, rather, is penetrating only along a very narrow spectrum. The kind of reservations which the Romantic poet Tieck had voiced a century before about Grabbe's plays are directly appropriate to Heym's poetry. Having praised individual lines for their 'authentic poetic power', Tieck wonders how Grabbe, another of Heym's heroes, will find sustenance on 'his trek through the desert' now that he has lost, at such an early age, 'genuine poetic optimism and vitality', and then Tieck adds: 'Precisely because your work is so gruesome it destroys all belief in itself and thus cancels itself out'.[69] The powerful self-destructive element in Georg Heym's life is mirrored in his work, where the insistent accumulation of horror ends, if not in 'destroying all belief in itself', then in delimiting the value, and diminishing the interest, of his writing. The poetry of Sylvia Plath offers an illuminating analogy. Her work, too, blends profoundly experienced horror and almost icy formal control. Like Heym, she is appalled by the anonymous force which she senses inside herself and outside: 'I am terrified by this dark thing | That sleeps in me; | All day I feel its soft, feathery turnings, its malignity'.[70] She knows that life is unremittingly bleak, that Heaven is evacuated and dimmed, that all promises of salvation are illusory, that 'the far fields' will perhaps let her through, but only 'to a heaven | Starless and fatherless, a dark water' ('Sheep in Fog', p. 13). She, too, is all but overwhelmed by a sense of desperate loneliness, her life is a quest for love: 'I am inhabited by a cry. | Nightly it flaps out | Looking, with its hooks, for something to love' ('Elm', p. 26). But if, as with Heym, her poetry is despairing and destructive, it is also generous, tender, sardonic, indignant, not sealed against the world of people and things. Sustained by a personal anguish which is *not* submerged beneath the images of horror, it moves beyond the darkness and wins through to an implication of that 'something to love'. Moreover, she has a kind of fierce critical self-awareness which is not to be found in Heym — 'wrapped up in yourself like a spool, | Trailing your dark as owls do' ('You're', p. 57).

In conclusion it might be helpful to elaborate on the anticipatory aspect of Heym's work and suggest a link between his work and that of Franz Kafka: there is a remarkable prefiguring of *Der Prozeß* in 'Eine Fratze', but, in more general terms, a disabling sense of guilt and will-lessness and an identical resort to judicial terms and images as a means of sanctioning apparently arbitrary acts of sadistic cruelty can be found in Heym's œuvre and the novel which Kafka began in 1914. Yet whilst Kafka's world prefigures Nazism as a prediction subtly informed with criticism and warning, Heym's work (which is also about Hell, and Heym knows it is Hell) is an undifferentiated rendering of Hell. This is the burden of the attempted contrast with Eliot. It is not just that Eliot has, in thematic terms, something positive, something life-enhancing to offer: Eliot's religious faith and the confidence which it brought him are totally alien to Heym. Nor do we demand that writers should seek to balance the positive and the negative, but there should be some sense of differentiation inherent in the work's relationship with its thematic material. There is little of this sense in Heym's poetry. Instead, there is a kind of controlled and insouciant voluptuousness about his poetry's relationship with evil and sin and disease: where Sylvia Plath writes of 'malignity', Heym's metaphor for man's place in the universe — 'scrabbling up and down the sides of a honeypot' — ends with man slipping inexorably 'down into sin, into *sweetness*' (PD II, 74). The example of Thomas Mann's Adrian Leverkühn comes to mind. A composer, a poet, is *not* a politician, a musician's or poet's life and work are *not* the same as the historical life and activity of a nation, and yet the intellectual and linguistic conditions out of which a work of art emerges and which it helps to mould are a factor in the imaginative and cultural life of a nation — and can and do feed into politics. It is at this point in any assessment of Heym's work that Thomas Mann's phrase 'responsibility to reality' comes into sharp focus.

NOTES

1 Nietzsche, *Die fröhliche Wissenschaft*; *Werke*, V/2, 206–07.
2 For biographical information see: G. Heym, *Dichtungen und Schriften*, 6 vols (Hamburg and Munich, 1960–), VI (*Dokumente zu seinem Leben und Werk*, 1968), 627–35. Frequent reference will also be made to the other published volumes of this edition: I (*Lyrik*, 1964), II (*Prosa und Dramen*, 1962), III (*Tagebücher*, 1960). The editor for all volumes is K. L. Schneider; with volume VI he had the assistance of Gerhard Burckhardt. The abbreviations for these volumes are: LI, PD II, T III, D VI, followed by page numbers in arabic.
3 Between 1880 and 1900 there was an almost epidemic outbreak of suicides among secondary school pupils in Germany — in those twenty years it is reported that 1152 students took their own lives. See: R. Hessen, 'Zur Hygiene des Schülerselbstmords', *Die Neue Rundschau* (September 1911), p. 1295.
4 J. R. Becher, *Internationale Literatur. Deutsche Blätter*, Heft 4 (Moscow, 1937), 91 f.
5 W. H. Auden, 'The Malverns', poem XVII in *Look Stranger!*, quoted in: A. T. Tolley, *The Poetry of the Thirties* (London, 1975), p. 155.
6 G. Benn, 'Zur Problematik des Dichterischen' (1930); *Gesammelte Werke*, I, 82.
7 C. Baudelaire, *Curiosités esthétiques* (Paris, 1923), p. 273.
8 For this paragraph I have drawn on 'Historical Criticism: Theory of Modes', the first chapter of Frye's *Anatomy of Criticism* (1957; reprinted Princeton, 1971).
9 Entry for the 'end of December 1909'; T III, 134.
10 Quoted in: H. Denkler, *Gedichte der 'Menschheitsdämmerung'* (Munich, 1971), p. 52.
11 R. P. Newton, *Form in the 'Menschheitsdämmerung'*, p. 169.
12 F. Leschnitzer, 'Georg Heym als Novellist', *Das Wort*, 2, Heft 10 (1937), 29.
13 K. Kersten, 'Strömungen der expressionistischen Periode', *Das Wort*, 3, Heft 3 (1938), 79.
14 A. Watzke, in: *Die schöne Literatur*, 13 January 1912, col. 23.
15 H. Rölleke, 'Georg Heym', *Expressionismus als Literatur*, edited by W. Rothe (Berne and Munich, 1969), p. 356.
16 E. Stadler, 'Georg Heym: Umbra vitae. Nachgelassene Gedichte', *Cahiers Alsaciens*, 1 (1912), 319–20.
17 F. Leavis, *Revaluation* (London, 1936), p. 206.
18 *The Letters of John Keats* (Oxford, 1935), p. 72.
19 G. Benn, 'Rede auf Stefan George' (1934); *Gesammelte Werke*, I (1959), 473.
20 J. Guillén, 'Hacia el poema', *Cántico* (Buenos Aires, 1973), p. 263.
21 Quoted by P. Raabe, *Expressionismus. Der Kampf um eine literarische Bewegung* (Munich, 1965), p. 93.

22 'Über den Expressionismus in der Literatur und die neue Dichtung', *Tribüne der Kunst und Zeit*, No. 1 (Berlin, 1920), 11.
23 J. R. Becher, *Abschied* (Berlin and Weimar, 1970), p. 356.
24 J. R. Becher, *Bemühungen*, in: *Gesammelte Werke*, 18 vols (Berlin and Weimar, 1966–81), XIV, (1972), 52.
25 See J. R. Becher, 'Das Sonett', *Gedichte 1942–1948*; *Gesammelte Werke*, V (1967), 230.
26 F. J. Schneider, *Der expressive Mensch und die deutsche Lyrik der Gegenwart* (Stuttgart, 1927), p. 114.
27 A. Schirokauer, 'Expressionismus der Lyrik' (1924), in: *Germanistische Studien* (Hamburg, 1957), p. 37.
28 C. Heselhaus, *Deutsche Lyrik der Moderne* (Düsseldorf, 1961), p. 190.
29 E. Loewenson, *Georg Heym oder Vom Geist des Schicksals* (Hamburg and Munich, 1962), pp. 8–9 and p. 18.
30 This phrase is Ernst Blass's and is quoted in: P. Raabe, *Expressionismus. Aufzeichnungen und Erinnerungen der Zeitgenossen* (Olten and Freiburg im Breisgau, 1956), p. 38.
31 W. Paulsen, *Expressionismus und Aktivismus* (Berne and Leipzig, 1935), p. 132.
32 See his 1807 poem 'Nuns fret not'.
33 H. Stieber, 'Frühverstorbene nach 1910' (dissertation, University of Munich, 1955), p. 194.
34 See his poem 'Das Sonett', in: *Sämtliche Gedichte. Gedenkausgabe der Werke*, edited by E. Beutler, 24 vols (Zurich, 1948–54), I, 445.
35 See W. Kohlschmidt, 'Der deutsche Frühexpressionismus im Werke Georg Heyms and Georg Trakls', *Orbis Litterarum*, 9 (1954), 15.
36 K. Mautz, *Mythologie und Gesellschaft im Expressionismus. Die Dichtung Georg Heyms* (Frankfurt a.M. and Bonn, 1961), p. 55.
37 Graf Hermann Keyserling, *Das Spektrum Europas* (Heidelberg, 1928), p. 145.
38 C. Seelig, *Georg Heym. Gesammelte Gedichte* (Zurich, 1947), p. 208.
39 W. Mönch, *Das Sonett, Gestalt und Geschichte* (Heidelberg, 1955), p. 37. Mönch, oddly, mentions Heym only once in this study.
40 T. W. Adorno, 'Expressionismus und künstlerische Wahrhaftigkeit'; *Gesammelte Schriften*, 22 vols (Frankfurt a.M., 1971–), XI (1974), 609.
41 Zephaniah 3. 1–4.
42 J. R. Becher, 'De Profundis III', quoted in: *Lyrik des Expressionismus*, edited by S. Vietta (Tübingen, 1976), pp. 65–66.
nic43 W. Cowper, 'The Task', *Cowper's Poems*, edited by H. I'A. Fausset (London, 1966), p. 323.
44 Cowper, 'The Task', line 749, p. 324.
45 Opening lines of the third part of *Peter Bell the Third*.
46 G. Gissing, *Introduction to Bleak House*, quoted in: Raymond Williams, p. 224.
47 A letter of 2 June 1914 to the Master of Marlborough in: *The Letters of Charles Sorley* (Cambridge, 1919), p. 181.
48 H. E. Jacob, quoted in: P. Raabe, *Expressionismus, Aufzeichnungen . . .*, pp. 18–19.
49 The phrases are all from Section 3 of 'Burnt Norton' in *Four Quartets*.
50 R. Salter, *Georg Heyms Lyrik. Ein Vergleich von Wortkunst und Bildkunst* (Munich, 1972).
51 See Heym's letter of 2 September 1910 to John Wolfsohn; T III, 205.
52 V. van Gogh, *Briefe* (Berlin, 1906), p. 43.
53 R. Dehmel, *Gesammelte Werke*, 3 vols (Berlin, 1913), I, 63.
54 C. Baudelaire, 'Les Sept Vieillards', *Les Fleurs du mal*, edited by M. A. Ruff (Paris, 1957), p. 244. Baudelaire, unlike Heym, does not mind moving to words like 'spectre' beyond, and without imagery-support from, the actual.
55 J. Thomson, 'The City of Dreadful Night', in: *Poems and Some Letters of James Thomson*, edited by A. Ridler (London, 1963), pp. 196–97.
56 'Die Kahlfahrt. Ein Beitrag zur Motivgeschichte des achtzehnten Jahrhunderts', *Euphorion*, 51 (1957), 355–84.
57 I am thinking of such lines (in the seventh book) as: 'And all the ballast of familiar life, | The present, and the past; hope, fear; all stays, | All laws of acting, thinking, speaking man | Went from us, neither knowing me, nor known.'
58 H. E. Jacob, quoted in: G. Heym, D VI, 67–68.
59 Theodore Watt, quoted in: W. Sharp, *Sonnets of this Century* (London and Newcastle upon Tyne, 1886), p. lxiii.
60 G. Benn, *Lyrik des expressionistischen Jahrzehnts* (Wiesbaden, 1955), pp. 18–19.
61 H. Carossa, *Ungleiche Welten*, pp. 672–73.
62 Quoted in: P. Raabe, *Expressionismus, Aufzeichnungen . . .*, p. 32.

F

63 H. Uhlig, 'Vom Ästhetizismus zum Expressionismus', in: *Expressionismus. Gestalten einer literarischen Bewegung*, edited by H. Friedmann and O. Mann (Heidelberg, 1956), p. 102.

64 'Wunschbild Land und Schreckbild Stadt. Zu einem zentralen Thema der neueren deutschen Literatur', *Studium Generale*, Heft 10 (1963), 628.

65 K. D. Bracher, W. Sauer and G. Schulz, *Die nationalsozialistische Machtergreifung* (Cologne and Oplanden, 1960), p. 2.

66 (New York and London, 1978). See especially Chapter 10, 'The Spirit of Weimar'.

67 A Berlin which by 1931 Kästner/Fabian describes as follows: '. . . Berlin has for a long time resembled a madhouse. In the East crime resides, in the centre fraud, in the North poverty, in the West lechery, and in all points of the compass, death and decay', *Fabian* (1931); *Gesammelte Schriften*, 7 vols (Cologne, 1959), II, 81.

68 T. S. Eliot, 'Choruses from "The Rock", 1934', in: *The Complete Poems and Plays of T. S. Eliot* (London, 1975), p. 160.

69 Letter to C. D. Grabbe of 6 December 1822, in: C. D. Grabbe, *Werke und Briefe*, 6 vols (Emsdetten, 1960–73), V (1970), 49–50.

70 S. Plath, 'Elm', *Ariel* (London, 1979), p. 26. All subsequent quotations are taken from *Ariel*.

V FRANZ WERFEL

At worst, one is in motion; and at best,
Reaching no absolute, in which to rest,
One is always nearer by not keeping still. [1]

All things are imbued with just one
consideration,
Just one word, an eternal: hence from here! [2]

Franz Werfel was born in Prague in 1890. He died fifty-five years later in Beverly Hills. In the summer of 1912 he obtained the post of reader at the Kurt Wolff Verlag in Leipzig, but, after less than two years, was called up and sent to the Russian front. From 1917 onwards he worked in the 'Kriegspressequartier' in Vienna where he met Alma Mahler, his future wife. Between 1918 and 1925 he treated Vienna as his base, but made frequent sorties to Alma's estate in Breitenstein and paid regular visits to Prague. In 1924 he was in Venice, the following year in Egypt and Palestine (which he visited again in 1929), in 1927 he was on the Italian Riviera and, a year later, in France. By March 1931 Alma and he had moved to a sumptuous house in Vienna. He continued to travel widely and frequently, on holidays and lecture-tours. Santa Margherita, Venice, Milan, Locarno, Paris and Capri were some of the places he visited alone or with Alma between 1933 and 1938. When German troops marched into Austria in March 1938, the Werfels fled to Paris and then to Sanary-sur-mer. In June 1940, after the defeat of France, they set off on a tortuous journey to America where they landed on 13 October. Slightly less than five years later Werfel suffered a heart attack from which he died.

It had been a restless life, marked by passionate allegiances, extraordinary volatility and fervent personal engagement. The continual migrations and the abrupt involvements were in part forced by circumstances, in part willed. It was as if Werfel *had* to be borne along on some intellectual current or other and was bound to be recruited by a cause which offered a refuge to his apparently inexhaustible enthusiasm and emotionality, not *any* cause, for he had only very shortlived sympathy for Communism and none for National Socialism. Public stances were suddenly adopted and passionately defended, and always with an eye cocked to an eagerly waiting audience. On the evidence of his wife's autobiography Werfel had an unstable disposition and conducted his life at the maximum pitch of intensity, investing the trivia of everyday living with weighty significance and indiscriminately pursuing adventure and novelty in a constant endeavour to live out his own tenet: 'God measures only the more violent heart-beat' (WLW, 267). His life is representative of the whole Expressionist generation, for, like almost all his contemporaries, he came from a social class which he despised and strove to abandon. But he then found himself rootless. In his 1929 novel *Barbara oder die Frömmigkeit*, in which he seeks to render an account of his past, he offers through the character of the protagonist Ferdinand many insights into his own attitudes:

Ferdinand's specific weight was less than that of all other people. He had no country, no class of his own. He stood completely on the outside, he was unimaginably free. And that was precisely the reason why he lived so fiercely.[3]

In his resolve to fill this 'unimaginable freedom' with as much hectic purpose and personal commitment as possible, Werfel again typifies his generation.

He was a fluent and versatile writer. He won early and wide fame with four collections of poetry: *Der Weltfreund* (1911), *Wir sind* (1913), *Einander* (1915) and *Der Gerichtstag* (written 1915–17, published 1919). There were other, later volumes of poetry: *Beschwörungen* (1922), a volume of collected poems in 1927, *Schlaf und Erwachen* (1935), *Gedichte* (1938) and *Gedichte 1908–45* (1946). After 1920, though, Werfel focused his main attention on plays — the best known of which are *Der Spiegelmensch* (1921), *Juarez und Maximilian* (1924) and *Paulus unter den Juden* (1926) — and on novels such as *Verdi, Roman der Oper* (1923), *Barbara oder die Frömmigkeit*, *Die vierzig Tage des Musa Dagh* (1933), *Das Lied von Bernadette* (1941) and *Stern der Ungeborenen* (1945). It is upon his first four volumes of verse that his reputation as 'the greatest Expressionist poet'[4] rests.

> 'To be a poet' — that was something religious,
> a bestowal of grace beyond anything man
> might will for himself, a special way of
> life . . .[5]

> From the heavens the new poet descends
> To earthly and greater deeds.
> . . . Girdled by his vibrant spirit
> The earth builds itself up and is fulfilled.[6]

The writing and reading of poetry are both social acts; they take place in the context of history and the preconceptions of generations. Even in denying preconceptions and challenging traditions, poetry is engaged with a historical and social context. 'Dichter' had long held an exalted position in Germany, a uniquely exalted position according to one nineteenth-century observer, Mme de Staël:

. . . tragedies and novels are accorded greater significance in Germany than in any country. They are taken quite seriously, and reading such and such a work or seeing such and such a play can influence the course of one's life. What the Germans admire as art they seek to introduce into their real life. Werther has caused more suicides than the most beautiful woman in the world; and poetry, philosophy, in short the ideal often wield greater power over the Germans than nature and even the passions. The Germans often need the mediating influence of poetry in order to love or to understand.[7]

And the Expressionist writers in the second decade of this century did nothing to qualify the theoretical powers vested in poets and claimed for poetry by poets and others. They saw themselves, and were glad to be seen, as the spiritual leaders of the age, as 'treasure-seekers, heralds of a new mythology, as discoverers of men, conquerors of the world . . .'.[8] Spiritual values were, they believed and claimed, the especial charge of the artist and no longer to be consigned to the trust of family, church, court, state, government, aristocracy or university — manifestations of power which Werfel in his messianic zeal is determined to destroy:

So the powerful one takes refuge in your institutions, your disciplinary authorities, committees, statutes and decrees!

But I want to smash your institutions, set fire to your disciplinary authorities, smoke out your committees, lash you away from your statutes and decrees. ('Der Mächtige', 1915–17; WLW, 265)

The best autobiographies of the period — Carossa's *Ungleiche Welten*, Arnold Brecht's *Aus nächster Nähe: Lebenserinnerungen 1884–1927*, Zuckmayer's *Als wärs ein Stück von mir* and Stefan Zweig's *Die Welt von gestern* — together with the letters, diaries and reminiscences of such *politicians* as Harry Graf Kessler and Walther Rathenau bear ample testimony to the atmosphere of intense expectation in which such poets as Werfel grew up and lived. Carossa, for example, relates how in the Germany of the 1930s 'every genuine artistic configuration' was voraciously snapped up as 'pure sustenance, an irreplaceable comfort'[9] by those suffering at the hands of the Nazis, and Zweig, writing about the Vienna which he knew as a boy in the 1890s, describes the awe in which all art and artists were held at that time. Surveying the immediate pre-war years, he writes:

People still heeded the written word, they waited for it . . . and so it was by no means wasted effort for a poet, a writer to speak at that time because people's ears and souls had not yet been inundated by the relentless prattle of the radio wave-bands; on the contrary, the spontaneous utterance of a great poet was a thousand times more effective than all the official speeches of the statesmen which, as everyone knew, were tactically and politically adapted to immediate needs and at best contained only half the truth.[10]

'A thousand times more effective than all the official speeches of the statesmen' — seeking to take possession of their readers body and soul, the Expressionist poets hoped and aimed to have precisely *that* degree of influence and thus helped to shape and fuel their readers' expectations of them. According to Kessler, it was an essential part of the Expressionist writer's creed to seek 'publicity . . . and [exert] influence on broad masses',[11] and at least the activists amongst the Expressionist poets saw it as a god-given duty to extend that influence to include the world of politics: Rubiner significantly calls two of his earliest articles for *Die Aktion* 'The Poet intervenes in Politics' and 'Painters build Barricades'. Making global claims for their art, Expressionist writers had no intention of ignoring the political realm: there especially, they raised all kinds of expectations. Almost explicit in Zweig's review of the pre-war years is the assumption that the poet's word is somehow purer, more valuable, more honest, and certainly less expedient than that of the professional politician. What was true of Zweig's fin-de-siècle Vienna and the Germany of the 1930s which

Carossa depicts applied equally to Werfel's Leipzig and Prague, to Berlin, Munich and the other cities in which Expressionism flourished. Moreover, because official Weimar politics seemed so colourless and drab by comparison, and because the upper and middle classes had lost much of their public influence, all moral authority, indeed all talent, flowed through exclusively cultural channels.

Werfel shared the traditional German confidence in the authority of the poet's word and willingly subscribed to the contemporary ludicrous public over-estimation of the poet's power. He was sustained by what in more sober years he called 'the brazen self-deification of artists' (*Barbara*, p. 133), the specifically Expressionist arrogance of believing that poetry will improve and redeem the world — having once destroyed it:[12]

All poetry represents a transformation, the transformation of reality into rightness, the transformation of sinfulness into redemption, the transformation of the world into prehistory (into paradise). (ibid, p. 95)

Any hint of burgeoning humility is summarily stifled beneath typically all-embracing, *exclusive* claims:

The new poet will know that his poem is not some sentence structure in a book, but a part, a fragile, inexpressibly delicate drop of his great, all-merciful, sympathetic, universally committed life, a flash of lightning from his heart in which alone the quaking world has a direct apprehension of itself.[13]

Like all Expressionist work, his poetry and prose are written from a grossly simplified, dogmatic point of view, assumed rather than established, proclaimed rather than debated, and not in tension with any convincingly propounded alternative attitude. In his poetry 'wir' and 'ich' can be taken freely as autobiographical signs, for there is with him a striking continuity between poetry and prose, between the 'ich'/'wir' of poetry/prose and his own standpoint. Again like other Expressionist writers he has no use for that whole range of experience which lies between pure sensation and universal truth. He was not one of the 'false activists': indeed, he repeatedly affirms that the world of poetry is separate from the world of politics. He wants no part of sordid political in-fighting: when, in the 1912 play *Die Versuchung*, the devil seeks to seduce the poet (Werfel in thin disguise) with promises of active participation in a revolutionary cause, the poet exclaims: 'No, no, your fight against dynasties, parliaments, stupidity, crime is not my fight.'[14] There is always present the implicit suggestion that the world of poetry, which Werfel informs with a heavy religious or, rather, religiose atmosphere, is not only divorced from, but superior to, the domain of public and political virtues. Indeed, that suggestion is subsequently made explicit in Werfel's 1932 speech 'Können wir ohne Gottesglauben leben?' where he opposes 'the world of the great question' (man's true concern, he maintains) to 'the world of the drab answer' (that is, the world of political interests). Yet, throughout his career, having assumed the roles of prophet and messiah ('I am the Revelation'; *Die Versuchung*, p. 40) he constantly strays into the political world, assuming public stances and engaging in public debate. He was one of the first to join the Red Guard in Vienna in 1918 where he harangued the mob from benches in the Ringstraße, responding, as it were, to those revolutionaries who saw, and had been encouraged to see, a link between radical politics and radical art: 'Expressionists! You have the reputation of having done much to prepare for the revolution . . . be not only Expressionist artists, but Expressionist human beings!'[15] Throughout the 1920s and 1930s he gave lectures and made speeches in which he claimed to be taking issue with the burning political questions of the day and in which, incidentally, he regularly derided all democratic institutions, all political parties, all manifestations of the modern industrial world, preferring the categories 'above' and 'below' to the tedious political designations 'left' and 'right'. In 1937, invited by the 'Organisation de Coopération Intellectuelle de la Société des Nations à Paris' to speak on the subject of 'The Future of Literature', he proposed that the League of Nations should establish a 'World Academy of Poets and Thinkers', a 'supranational body' to oversee the moral welfare of nations and 'to raise the prestige of serious literature' untainted by politics and 'its perfervid propaganda'.[16]

It is obvious from this project that, in spite of much facile post-1920 *mea culpa* about the wild, arrogant days of his Expressionist youth, he perpetuates his earlier conviction that 'poets and thinkers' are not only the sole custodians of all spiritual values, but (even, or rather, especially, in 1937) mankind's only potential saviour. This had been heady stuff in the years 1910–1920, and it had been rapturously received. By 1937 it had begun to pall, and many of his audience at the congress in Paris, more interested in finding practical ways of offering resistance to Fascism, rejected his speech as fatalistic and escapist. On the evidence of his speeches in the 1930s and of much of his literary output during those years (with one or two exceptions, notably *Die vierzig Tage des Musa Dagh* and the 1938–39 novel *Cella oder die Überwinder*), Werfel too demonstrates that, however vigorously he repudiates his membership of the Expressionist movement from about 1920 onwards, he remains an Expressionist writer all his life in the important respect that his attempts to take issue with, and to come to terms creatively with, political events and social problems rarely shifted beyond purely personal, heavily idealistic concerns. He seemed oblivious of all practical considerations, regarding self-criticism merely as another way of advertising the violent contortions of his tyrannical ego, and apparently blind to the potentially vast influence which his words might be having on an impressionable audience. The Expressionist poets lived in a state of mutual dependence with their readers: with innumerable publications and proclamations they responded to the expectations which they themselves had been instrumental in raising, whilst many of their readers accepted uncritically the mass of verbiage that was thrust upon them from many different directions. The historical context is vital here, for Expressionism was only one of the components of an intensely confusing and confused scene. Musil, who never tired of mocking Werfel and the vast popularity which Werfel enjoyed, has perhaps been most successful in documenting the confusion of the times in his celebrated litany of opposing obsessions and moods: '. . . and the superman was loved, and the subhuman was loved . . .'.[17] Werfel, in the introduction to *Zwischen oben und unten* (1944), recounts how he was educated 'in the spirit of humanitarian autonomy and confidence in human progress, in the blissfully naive belief that the world would be improved by science, in deeply sceptical repudiation of metaphysical, religious or mystical thinking and feeling and in the most fatal confusion of freedom with moral anarchy' — all of which he subsumes under the phrase 'that mental haze'.

This ideological farrago occurred at a time when a great expectation was placed in the efficacy of idealism, literature, culture, words. Expressionism was one of the forces which added to the confusion by flustering and drowning the voice of reason whenever and wherever that voice was raised — it is significant that Kafka rejects Expressionist poetry in general and Becher's and Werfel's poetry in particular, maintaining that the teeming words are a barrier to sense:

I do not understand Becher's poems. There is such a din and hotchpotch of words here that one cannot get away from oneself. The words do not become a bridge, instead they are a high insurmountable wall . . . The words do not condense into language.[18]

A microcosm of this anarchic period of German history is the literary café, which the Viennese writer, Alfred Polgar, in his description of the Café Central calls a kind of 'surrogate universe' and 'organization for disorganization'[19] Here Werfel and other Expressionist poets whiled away many days and nights. The clientèle of these cafés could bask in glorious unaccountability, their confidence in poets' ability to shape politicians' decisions *not* modified by their real impotence: the air buzzed with grandiose plans and promises and 'the dull thunder of approximate words'.[20] Werfel's own depiction emphasizes the bewildering pandemonium and stultifying atmosphere of the place:

> Ein Summen, Surren, ungeheures Sieden
> Erfüllte mich und Traum wie Kesselsud.
>
> Eh noch der Sinn sich selber unterschieden,
> Stand ich in einem scheußlich strengen Chor.
> In Kreisen donnernd, die einander mieden,
>
> Nach allen Seiten vor und hoch empor,
> Unendlich durcheinander, kreisten, höhnten
> Schwarz Fliegenvölker ans verlorne Ohr.
>
> ('Das Café der Leeren', 1917; WLW, 228)

A humming, a buzzing, a huge seething | And a dream like the boiling of a cauldron filled me. | Before even the meaning had disengaged itself | I was standing in a hideously austere chorus. | Thundering in circles which avoided each other, | In all directions, forwards and high aloft/, In infinite confusion, gyrating, jeering | People like swarms of black flies beat against my distraught ear.

In such 'cafés of empty people' all sorts of theoretical iconoclasm could be mooted and global projects proclaimed, with no hostages being offered to life as it was being lived by the vast majority of people in pre-war Europe and with no commitment made in practical terms. Max Weber has continually warned of the blatantly uncompromising nature of this kind of fierce moral and philosophical purpose, and its inevitable conflict with mature political considerations — all is subordinated, he argues in his correspondence and in such essays as 'Politik als Beruf', to the realization of an ideal, and all is justified by reference to some spiritual or intellectual sanction. Weber's was precisely the kind of voice for moderation and rationality which was submerged by the cacophony of, amongst others, the Expressionist writers.

More than once in the 1920s and 1930s Werfel endeavours to depict the smoke-filled atmosphere of the coffee-houses, where his early Expressionist poems had fascinated and thrilled his audiences.[21] Here Werfel held the floor. An evocation of the coffee-house atmosphere which forms the opening paragraph of the 1939 short story *Weißenstein, der Weltverbesserer* is very powerful, because any sense of nostalgia which clings to Werfel's earlier depictions yields to the kind of incisive historical awareness that is rare in Werfel's work:

Europe 1911! Golden sunset glow of an age whose most pressing concerns seem idyllic to us today . . . the world enthused over a new opera, a bold book, a radical artistic intuition . . . for the time being those gloomy psychoses which these days we call 'political ideologies' only filled the distinctive dishevelled heads of individual dreamers, fools and amateur apostles. The social and national messiahs, in full undisturbed possession of their defects, still lived in doss-houses and not the Empire's chancelleries. You could meet them in the musty haunts of would-be petit bourgeois politicians or, best of all, in the literary cafés. These cafés in Paris, Vienna, Berlin — they were mockingly referred to as Café Megalomania — were not only the hotbeds of alternating artistic fashions, but more than that: they were among the intellectual witches' kitchens preparing a future horror which has now become a present reality.[22]

In this extract many important points come into focus — the euphoric pre-war days, the universal interest in culture, the haphazard interchange between those who, since the halcyon pre-war days, played at politics on the side-lines and those who became professional politicians, the self-regarding arrogance of the coffee-house messiahs, an implicit scorn for them and for those who are now practising 'political ideologies' in the 'Empire's chancelleries', the vital role played by the cafés as a rallying point for the latest artistic fashions and as seedbeds of future catastrophe. Six years later, in his sprawling futuristic and Utopian novel *Stern der Ungeborenen* which also contains much retrospective comment, Werfel echoes these sentiments of evident remorse in his elliptical, but more directly personal statement: 'After all, we all did our bit'[23] [in unleashing the horror of the Second World War].

There is much evidence for believing that Werfel's powerful personality dominated the literary cafés in Leipzig and Prague. For a time at least, he captivated such discriminating critics as Kraus, Kafka, Rilke and Thomas Mann. Hesse, Buber, Brod and Lasker-Schüler, amongst many lesser names, are on record with declarations of unqualified admiration for the infectious spontaneity of the early volumes of verse. To them and many others he is *the* spiritual leader of the age, *the* voice and conscience of his time. For Fritz von Unruh he has 'a strength which feeds thousands',[24] and, according to Alfred Kurella, the young generation regards him as its preceptor and paragon: 'A generation of young people looks up to you, hoping for shimmering solutions, hoping for the assurance of future splendours from you'.[25] And when, almost twenty years later, a National Socialist thesis-writer seeks to repudiate Expressionism and to dissociate National Socialism from certain elements in it (*not* from its irrationalism which, she argues, has much in common with National

Socialist irrationalism), it is the egocentric, passive, muddled, religiose (her epithets) work of Franz Werfel which she chooses and bothers to demolish, partly because it proves an easy target and partly because she knows that, as an influential force, Werfel is worth shooting down.[26] Kraus, too, spends a great deal of polemical energy endeavouring to undermine a reputation which, to his utter chagrin, he realizes he has helped to build by printing some of Werfel's early poems in the pages of *Die Fackel*. In an article entitled 'Ich und das Ichbin' Kraus quotes a wildly enthusiastic assessment of Werfel's work — 'He has been celebrated. Hundreds of essays have been written about him. Politicians and aesthetes quote his verse, noble ladies place his poems on their bedside table and in melancholy moments read them. For this young poet caresses their feelings . . .' — and then goes to great pains to denigrate both the reviewer and Werfel. It becomes clear from this article and from an earlier philippic ('Dorten')[27] that Kraus's disillusionment with Werfel issues from a conviction that Werfel has abused and exploited the responsibility which was the inevitable concomitant of his fame and that he has compromised his talent for the sake of that fame. Worst of all in Kraus's eyes, Werfel's sloppy use of language has led to a fatal confusion of values — in both reader *and* Werfel himself. This means that already by 1918 Kraus looks upon Werfel as a dangerous charlatan. Kafka's eventual disenchantment with the poet is founded in similar reservations, whilst Musil never faltered in his belief that Werfel was a morally corrupt, and morally corrupting, writer. Within a few years the dangers and the influences for debilitating corruption have taken on a stark political reality: Erich Kästner, in an introduction added in 1950 to his novel *Fabian*, 'written about twenty-five years before', has the benefit of hindsight when he refers to the ready audience given in the 1920s to 'fairground mountebanks and drummers extolling their mustard plasters and poisonous patent solutions and to Pied Pipers whom we followed into the abyss . . .' (p. 10). Something very like this, after all, is the substance of Werfel's own subsequent professions of mea culpa.

> I have not fully fathomed | What I have
> entangled in my singing. ('Friede', 1922;
> WLW, 376)
> We must not allow ourselves to be confused.
> That would be the greatest catastrophe . . .
> (*Cella oder die Überwinder*, (1938–9) in:
> *Erzählungen*, III, 90)
> . . . and in a tumult of shrill voices the demons
> burst their fetters. (*Zwischen oben und unten*,
> (1944); p. 310)

Der Weltfreund (1911), Werfel's first volume of verse, took the literary cafés of Prague by storm, and no wonder, for it is sustained by a fervent yea-saying to the whole of creation and is shot through with a euphoric and contagious feeling of omnipotence. Its deliriously proclaimed message is one of love for everybody and everything. It spoke to and for a whole generation:

This joy in loving [to be found in *Der Weltfreund*], now playful, now blissful, corresponded exactly to our own attitude to the world at that time, ready as we were in our youthful enthusiasm to make a new start, to conquer the world through love, and certain that the world was bound to open up to kindness. So *Der Weltfreund* became our beloved prayer-book and its poet quite naturally was acknowledged and publicized as our apostle.[28]

Der Weltfreund amounts to an ecstatic affirmation of the things of the world and, less frequently, a declaration of love for all the people in the world. The poet, borne along on a current of barely mastered passion, is impatient to do good, to give the world the benefit of his all-embracing love:

> Tausend gute Taten will ich tun!
> Ich fühle schon,
> Wie mich alles liebt,
> Weil ich alles liebe!
> Hinström ich voll Erkenntniswonne!
> Du mein letztes, süßestes,
> Klarstes, reinstes, schlichtestes Gefühl!
> Wohlwollen!
> Tausend gute Taten will ich tun!

I want to do a thousand good deeds! | Already I feel | How everything loves me | Because I love everything! | I flow along in the delicious knowledge of it! | You my latest, sweetest, | Clearest, purest, simplest feeling! | Benevolence! | I want to do a thousand good deeds!

He looks longingly towards childhood as the state which represents a person's most intense contact with the world, he invests trivial items with the highest possible degree of poetic ardour so that inanimate objects visibly respond to his love for them, he opens his arms wide to receive them, he takes upon himself the world's suffering, indeed he welcomes it because that suffering serves to consolidate the cosmic harmony and, more important to him, does not disturb *his* harmonious relationship with the world.[29]

He tears aside the thin veil of worldly phenomena behind which there begins a reality of a higher order and opens up the boundless vista of an ardently imagined world which the force of his love has willed into existence. He is overwhelmed by the joy of being alive and being in the world:

> Ich will mich auf den Rasen niedersetzen
> Und mit der Erde in den Abend fahren.
> O Erde, Abend, Glück, oh auf der Welt sein!
>
> (WLW, 51)

I want to sit myself down on the grass | And accompany the earth into the evening. | O earth, evening, happiness, oh being in the world!

Even death is only a means which the soul has contrived to merge with the universe, and the poet thrills at being a mere human being before the vastness of the world and of God.

He does not remain a mere human being for long. The subjective spirit is seated on an absolute throne, wilful and barely controlled, as the poet revels in the power which his overweening ego arrogates to itself. He defies those who would mock him, for he has experienced everything, has suffered all kinds of degradation, he has sacrificed himself to save the world, and that alone, he maintains, makes him uniquely qualified to offer himself to the world in a climactic gesture of irresistible loving:

> So gehöre ich Dir und allen!
> Wolle mir, bitte, nicht widerstehn!
> Oh, könnte es einmal geschehn,
> Daß wir uns, Bruder, in die Arme fallen!
>
> (WLW, 63)

So I belong to you and to everyone! | Please do not resist me! | Oh, if only it could happen one day | That we fall into each other's arms, brother!

And any potential protest from the voice of reason is swiftly submerged in the welter of hysterical, all-embracing love:

> Schon klärt sich Zeichen und Wunder,
> Denn die Fessel des Verstandes fiel,
> Und mein Geist ist eine einzige
> Riesenempfindung.
>
> (WLW, 48)

Symbol and miracle are already being clarified, | For the shackle of reason fell, | And my spirit is one single | Giant feeling.

All is feeling, and feeling is all.

His love of the world is undiscriminating and uncritical: the only moral categories he acknowledges are those of 'openness' and 'closedness'. His master-plan for mankind — his 'friendship for the world' — is vitalistic, irrational and thoroughly amoral. Everything that is, receives his unconditional blessing and his unstinting love; he welcomes evil because on evil he can whet his good; intensity becomes a value in itself, and so he longs for manifestations of intensity, for catastrophe and tempest, for slaughter and grand finale. He has only one reservation about his project: it might not work *for him*. It might not serve the purpose for which he has evolved it — to rescue *him* from loneliness. As always happens with Werfel, a personal shortfall is distended into a mass deficiency and an affair of cosmic proportions. Pouring his love upon the world, he has reduced himself to a husk:

> Mein Mittelpunkt hat keine Kraft.
> Nichts reißt er mehr in mich herein.
> Von allem bin ich hingerafft
> Zu tausendfach zerstäubtem Sein.
>
> (WLW, 54)

My centre has no strength. | It no longer draws anything into me. | I am snatched along by everything | To a thousandfold atomized being.

Now he longs for a close relationship with his fellow-men. He has done his good deeds only, it seems, to avoid personal loneliness. What started out as an altruistic panacea for the benefit of man and things becomes a series of ostentatious heart- barings and self-regarding effusions. The poet becomes not a philanthropist, but a prima donna.

Der Weltfreund is a bewildering pot-pourri of styles and influences. The voices of Whitman, Stadler, Rilke, Heym, Laforgue and Klopstock resound heavily in many of the poems. Metre, lengths of line, stanzaic construction, rhyming, alliteration — all often seem a matter of chance and personal whim. The berceuse effect of the rhythm of one poem contrasts abcuptly with the strident rhetoric of the next. Sentimental sillabub jostles with shrill declaration of intent, self-indulgent nostalgia with blissfully optimistic project. The loose form of many poems and the frequent enumeration of optical and acoustic sense data are impressionistic: on the other hand, a poem such as 'Pompe funèbre' is almost naturalistic in its predilection for carefully delineated and unattractive detail. 'Dampferfahrt im Vorfrühling', the long rhyming couplets of which are not divided into stanzas, is informed with an animating and free-wheeling sense of dynamic urgency, whilst the sonnets in the volume are almost as strictly reined back as those of Georg Heym. Werfel's characteristic voice is the hymnic, and in this respect, as in the haphazard line which he favours and which seems best suited to accommodate his extravasating ardour, his poetry is very reminiscent of Klopstock's. Werfel is often praised for his versatility, but it can be his worst enemy because it seems to lead him into ever greater braggadocio and to extend the fundamental dissipation of creative energy. There is about the volume a determination to bully individual poems arbitrarily into deeper resonance and to invest them with massive but unearned significance, together with a gross, consciously cultivated naïvety which becomes wincingly mawkish and has no astringency of mind to balance it or tone down its excesses. Each feeling is allowed to receive an apocalyptic heightening and comes direct to the page.

Two years after *Der Weltfreund*, Werfel published his second volume of poetry, *Wir sind*. In a postscript to the first edition he writes:

We . . . forget all too quickly the unthinkable, mighty words: We are. I believe that everything noble in man, kindness, joy, exultation, pain, loneliness, the ideal can issue forth only from this eternal, impenetrable, mighty consciousness of existence. (WLW, 137)

It is difficult to make much of this or to disentangle a coherent ductus of argument either from what claims to be discursive prose in the postscript or from the poetry in the volume. It seems, though, that the poet has assigned himself the task of awakening in people and things the 'consciousness of existence' which is enshrined in the exultant and thaumaturgical 'Wir sind!' ('We are!') and of involving people and things in the unadulterated joy of being alive:

> Daß wir hier stehn und sitzen
> Wer kann's beklommen fassen?!
> Doch über allen Worten
> Verkünd' ich, Mensch, wir sind!!
>
> (WLW, 108)

That we are standing and sitting here | Who can grasp it with a heavy heart?! | Yet above all words | I proclaim, brother: we are!!

Being alive is in itself a value: being intensely alive is a greater value. For example, in the poem 'Der Entschwindende', the poet's longing 'to stretch out uninhibitedly on green grass . . . to flow with fervent breath from pasture and benighted cottage into infinity' (WLW, 88–89) is hallowed by its own overwhelming intensity and brooks no further qualification. Even the age-old, poisonous hostility between father and son dissolves in a climactic, unspoken moment of mutually fierce emotion, and inanimate objects spring to life as the poet arouses in them a consciousness of their participation in wondrous existence.

This volume is, then, a paean to boundless, indiscriminate love and to the creative power of feeling. The poet turns his attention particularly to the deprived and the under-privileged, to the diseased and to social pariahs, seeking to embrace them all in his community of love and fervent feeling. He selects lesbians, prostitutes, the poor, anyone not shackled by social convention and morality, anyone as 'open' as he, for he is 'open' to everyone and 'at home' everywhere. But there are times when the poet's state of euphoric omnipotence is clouded, when he feels inhibited by the fearful weight of an original guilt and by the sensation of being walled-in, cut off from other people:

> Mein, mein und mein! Und immer diese Wand!
> Warum bin ich nicht durch die Welt gespannt,
> Allfühlend gleicherzeit in Tier und Bäumen,
> In Knecht und Ofen, Mensch und Gegenstand?!
>
> (WLW, 95)

My, my and my! And always this wall! | Why am I not stretched out through the world, | All feeling at the same time in animal and trees, | In servant, and stove, human being and object?!

He seeks out torture, because the pain of torture can release redeeming, ecstatic feeling, and the ecstatic feeling of love in particular can break down walls, can melt the calloused hardness of a vindictive heart. Love is all-important, he must love as much as he can, whatever he can, for only then will he attain to a transcendental existence:

> Erst wer sich jauchzend bot
> Der Schande und der Not
> Und zehnfach jedem Tod,
> Im heiligsten Verzicht,
> Vor Liebe ihm zerbricht
> Sein irdisch Angesicht!
>
> (WLW, 115–16)

Only anyone who offered himself exultantly | To ignominy and distress | And tenfold to every death | In most sacred renunciation | Will find his earthly face | Crumbling with love.

And the poet makes the discovery that where earthly life is at its most impoverished and defective, the true world of the spirit is most likely to reveal itself. Humiliated and lowly and suffering people seem called to represent higher humanity *and* to arouse the best, the 'consciousness of existence' in others. Maids, the poor and

84

humble, even an opera-singer whose voice suddenly fails in mid-aria, are closer to God.

This evangel of indiscriminate love offers at times a grossly trivializing view of the world. It is anchored to a belief in the absolute equality of all manifestations of life and issues into the kind of wickedly perverse nonsense of the couplet 'In murdering and embracing, | Human grace [is to be found]' (WLW, 107) or the highly dubious morality of the dramatic poem 'Das Opfer' where revenge and murderous intent and the sacrifice of a dog combine to make an odd, tasteless poem. Hatred, war, vengeance, crime of any kind are transferred from a moral to a physically determined and value-free order of things. It is not a huge step from emphasizing that God reveals Himself even or, rather, especially in prostitutes, muck, criminals, in 'every tatter of paper' to recommending that we should humiliate ourselves whenever possible and commit the foulest deeds as a sure way of winning God's love. Rhetorical devices and frequent apostrophe carry points in such a way that poems are falsified, because they fail to contain the complex balance which would make them ring true, that bringing into fertile tension, and retaining in tension, of contrasts or opposites. Tension there certainly is, but it is a tension which arises directly from the poet's overwrought language and from his hectoring assaults on the reader's ear. Although in *Der Weltfreund* the poet had written ecstatically about 'doing a good deed', that good deed remains stubbornly undefined and ultimately amounts to little more than an empty trumpet-call. In the same way, nothing transcendent is creatively conjured or imagined, with the result that the poet settles for a wholly immanent view of the world and absolutizes life. Once again rationality is swiftly repudiated — in both the postscript and 'Das Opfer'. A collectively conscious and emotionally warming 'Wir sind' leaves no room for a rationalistic 'Cogito, ergo sum' or even for a romantic 'Sentio, ergo sum' — though, as we have seen, feeling is an integral part of the process towards the longed-for 'consciousness of existence'.

The overriding impression of the cycle is of insubstantiality. The poet in his radical subjectivism is not confronted by any countervailing force, God is just a projection of the poet's imagination, the lather of feeling which the poet works up detaches itself more and more from physical, tangible objects and becomes an end in itself. The people in whom he has been summoned to arouse the spirit of 'Wir sind' never take on recognizable shape, there is no nature or landscape or townscape, the abstract and fiercely impassioned prevail in 'an untidiness of emotional debauchery',[30] the tone is consistently rhetorical and flatulent, and all is cast in a multitude of varying forms which prove, however, to be more disciplined than those in *Der Weltfreund*. There are occasions when the verse is 'hardly fastened and hangs suspended over the abysses like frail footbridges'.[31] On such occasions it reads like shards of prose, but on others the flow of the line is smooth and the poet's control clearly discernible. Yet the whole volume seeks its justification in a kind of bogus transcendence which the poet has manufactured from the fervour of his ecstatic love. The world, as it is presented in *Wir sind*, is seen from his own strictly personalized perspective and becomes merely the expression of his egotistic cravings and ambitions, the arena where *his* plans and his scheme of values are paraded before the reader. It is surely such verse as this that Hermann Hesse has in mind when he introduces modern German poetry to readers of *The Criterion* in the early 1920s:

With most of these young men, their breaking loose and enlargement go no further than a perception of their personality, and the assertion and proclamation of the rights of that personality. Beyond this, there is nothing but obscurity and aimlessness. [32]

The ethos of all-embracing love is sustained neither by humanistic nor theistic beliefs and issues into moral anarchy. And into farce — at one point in the volume, a school-satchel, too, is moved to join in the chorus: 'We all are, all are here!' (WLW, 76)

Einander (written between 1913 and 1915, and published in 1915) is about redemption — the redemption of God by man. Man is always the focal point of Werfel's concern, and man's soul is, according to Werfel, the original source of the divine spirit. Not only the true world, 'real reality', the spiritual world in which Werfel never ceases to believe, the world behind the 'thin veil' of the deceptive phenomena of our empirical reality, but also God Himself will be born in man:

> Mit dem Schreiten der Menschen tritt
> Gottes Anmut und Wandel aus allen Herzen und Toren.
> Lächeln, Atem und Schritt
> Sind mehr als des Lichtes, des Windes, der Sterne Bahn.
> Die Welt fängt im Menschen an.
>
> (WLW, 142)

With men's walking, go | God's graces and ways out of all hearts and gates | . Smiling, breathing and walking | Are more than the path of light, wind and stars. | The world begins with man.

God needs man, the Saviour needs to be saved — 'Child, just as I redeemed you with my blood, | So do I wait, crying, for you to redeem me' (WLW, 193). And once man has redeemed God, He will become part of that community which must first be created by the spirit born in man's soul. Man is God's orchestra, and the deity is to issue forth from the melody of the human heart. We are 'nothing but song' (WLW, 146).

Yet the relationship between man and God is one of mutual dependence. In his pessimistic moments the poet's view of man is melancholy. Man, immured in his own ego, needs God, for loneliness, homelessness and a bitter sense of alienation are the abiding experiences of man's life on earth. Men are strangers to each other, nothing binds them, everything eludes their grasp:

> Was wir halten, ist nicht mehr zu halten,
> Und am Ende bleibt uns nichts als Weinen . . .
> Fremde sind wir auf der Erde Alle,
> Und es stirbt, womit wir uns verbinden.
>
> (WLW, 170)

What we hold is no longer to be held, | And in the end there is nothing left but weeping . . . | We are all strangers on earth, | And what binds us together is in the process of dying.

It is not fortuitous that for one section of *Einander* Werfel uses as a motto the German Romantic poet Novalis's 'Where are we going? Always homewards' (WLW, 171). Man finds solace neither in his self nor in other people. A cold wall separates him from his fellows, and it is his lot on earth to be hastened ever onwards, to be his own persecutor.

The shadow of the war falls heavily across *Einander* and colours Werfel's view of life. The world, he asserts, has succumbed to the forces of evil, is vanity and lie, has fallen from God's grace. A curse is deeply engrained in all creation, and God is to blame. He is to blame above all for creating words. Words are at best futile, at worst deceitful. The contemporary age is characterized by tirades of 'false words': the war in which man is now embroiled burst upon the world amidst just such a tirade of lies and inane speeches. Werfel always derides and repudiates any order or category which emanates from man's thinking capacity, anything which separates or makes differences or creates distance — words, the state, convention, laws, rationality and science. With the aid of the spirit he wants to destroy them:

> Komm, Sintflut der Seele, Schmerz, endloser Strahl!
> Zertrümmre die Pfähle, den Damm und das Tal!
>
> > (WLW, 165)

Come, floodwater of the soul, pain, eternal beam of light! | Smash the stakes, the dam and the valley!

He inveighs against his tawdry age, rejects all manifestations of authority, and calls for annihilation, sacrifice and revolution.

There are more peaceful ways of achieving grace for this sinful, word-infested world. Music represents the mystical movement of the spirit and is stronger than death, stronger than words, because it is stronger than anything. Revolution, activism of any kind, is *not* the answer. Old favourites re-emerge and offer greater prospect of success — passion for its own sake, deep emotionality, inwardness as the pre-condition of mystic events, and Franciscanism. Above all, there is man, humble man, who willingly demeans himself and takes all sin upon himself, welcoming it. That magnanimous gesture tears him asunder and thus destroys all that is fixed in him, preparing him for salvation. Similarly, in 'Jesus und der Äser-Weg', Jesus revels in filth and muck, filling his hair with carrion, girding himself with a hundred corpses, because the divine spirit reveals itself above all in festering decay and disease. God gave man life to test him, man must love, and in turn give himself to, all aspects of life, especially the repellent and the defective. Only thus will he break down the barriers between himself and his fellows and resuscitate the divine spirit which has been suffocated beneath the welter of 'false words'. Man is God's last chance, man offers God the prospect of redeeming and making good His imperfect creation.

Because Werfel does not postulate a transcendental God, his doctrine of redemption ultimately becomes a self-deification; because he equates the divine spirit with human feeling and love, ecstatic feeling is recommended for its own sake, and love for all manifestations of life is as undiscriminating as in *Der Weltfreund* and *Wir sind*.

G

The radical subjectivism does not issue into self-criticism: never for a moment does the poet scruple about the effect of *his* words (which are bound to be false and chimerical because *all* words are false, or so he argues), though he is ready to imply in such poems as 'Die Wortemacher des Krieges' and 'Der Krieg' a connection between the contemporary politician's predilection for hectoring torrents of words and the outbreak of war. Self-doubt comes fifteen years later, with *Barbara oder die Frömmigkeit*. Only then do questions of cause and effect (with regard to his own work) and of personal responsibility begin to occupy his mind. Only then is impassioned advocacy accompanied by insight and moderation.

In mid-November 1918, a year after Werfel's fourth volume of poetry *Der Gerichtstag* was completed, Max Weber writes:

And I'm afraid that if it turns out that belief can indeed move mountains but cannot restore ruined finances and lack of capital, the disappointment after all that has already been taken away from people will be unbearable, especially for many of the most ardent believers, and will make them inwardly bankrupt.[33]

After the high hopes and strenuous believing of the early volumes, *Der Gerichtstag* is indeed pervaded by a feeling of inner bankruptcy as the poet surveys the rubble of his shattered expectations. The tone of the volume oscillates violently between the acidly sarcastic and the self-effacingly contrite, the militantly defiant and the cringingly servile, but its characteristic voice is a vigorously sustained stridency, what Nietzsche in his repudiation of Romanticism calls 'die falsche Verstärkung' ('false intensification').[34] Many of the categories which underpin Nietzsche's broadside against Romanticism and 'the Romantic attitude of modern man' are conspicuously relevant to the tone and content of Werfel's most Expressionist collection of verse: Nietzsche's assertion that 'this constant espressivo [of Romanticism] is not a sign of strength, but of a feeling of deficiency', his castigation of Romanticism's 'joyful indulgence in the all-embracing and the massive' (Musarion edition, XIX, 231) and its cult of unbridled feeling, his inventory 'noble indignation', 'sanctification through passion' and 'support for the oppressed and the disadvantaged'[35] as distinctive traits of that Romanticism which he sees developing inevitably into nihilism — all this is distilled in *Der Gerichtstag*, as if Werfel had intended to illustrate the accuracy of Nietzsche's predictions about the pernicious influence of Romanticism on twentieth-century thought. Werfel, himself, seven years after the publication of *Der Gerichtstag*, selects as a principal cause for contemporary moral anarchy that part of modern art which most clearly betrays the influence of Romanticism:

Romantic modern art with all its emblems, good and bad, is publicly arraigned as an accomplice in the chaos of values: intense feeling and vertiginous emotionalism, idealism and arrogant estrangement from life, refinement and neurotic coquetry, a belief in beauty and aestheticism, social zeal and social duplicity. Fanaticism has entered upon that inheritance.[36]

'Chaos of values' — the process of overturning traditional values begun in the three earlier volumes reaches its climax in *Der Gerichtstag*. The poet's worst fears have been realized, his vast projects lie in the dust, and he lashes out at a series of by now familiar targets: at words for betraying his every thought and for 'lying away heaven' (1915–17; WLW, 291), at God for burdening man with words and with the agony of living in this world, at this world for being such a disparate and multifarious place when he longs above all for oneness, at himself for 'hurling lies into the world' (WLW, 300) and for failing so conspicuously in all his plans, at consciousness and intention which (he argues) block insight, at law and all institutionalized manifestations of authority ('I have come, I come, to dismantle the law'; (WLW, 261) which he sees as causing the repellent 'rustle of twoness' (WLW, 284). He prefers total chaos to the survival of the older order, and, in an open letter to Kurt Hiller written at the same time as *Der Gerichtstag* and entitled 'Die christliche Sendung', he declares that the only appropriate political attitude for a Christian is 'anarchism'. Bitterness and a feeling of helplessness seethe in almost every poem of *Der Gerichtstag*. He has no opinion of himself, of his fellowmen, of God, of the world. In his furious repudiations and outbursts of self-disgust he resorts more and more to pathological metaphors and similes for expressions of his hatred and choler: his soul is a suppurating ulcer, he suffers badly from halitosis, and the world is nothing but 'God's angina, plague, pus' (WLW, 298). This is the level of poetic metaphor on which most of *Der Gerichtstag* is played out. He is ashamed of the adventitious, mendacious nature of the poet's words and of being part of doomed humanity. We are, he proclaims, superannuated, slaves, wretched for all eternity. And he who 'lied truth' amounts to no more than a splinter, an echo, 'stuck on a spit between a pair of needles' (WLW, 299).

Out of all this vituperation and venomous self-flagellation an inverted morality, a perverse system of values emerges, founded above all in a dread of the lukewarm: 'I fear my impotent soul, my silent heart, the undesperate | glance, frivolity, the so-so, the futile | shrug of the shoulders' (WLW, 287). According to the code of this 'morality', those who do evil passionately are hallowed, imperfection is a guaranteed way to salvation, and those who have brought glory upon themselves by living intensely on earth *away from* God's institutions and in direct conflict with His commandments are certain to find their ultimate rest with Him (see the poem 'Die Leidenschaftlichen'). Ambiguity and paradox adhere to Werfel's depiction of evil and evil men, for he does very little in this volume to render them unattractive. On the contrary: intensely done evil is not only a necessary prelude to good, but also a value in itself, the 'simply evil ones' no less that 'the simply good' are blest' (WLW, 289), the women 'who avenged themselves with vitriol' in 'Die Leidenschaftlichen' are worthier of admittance to God's right hand than the merely 'truthful and just' people, and the worst name the poet can call himself is 'lukewarm murderer' (WLW, 301–02). His particular crime, he maintains, is that he has not loved passionately enough: tepid loving, he implies, is inferior to passionate murdering. He has settled for half-heartedness and moderation, he has been chary of excess and vastness:

> Mein Gott, wie viele Liebe ließ ich aus,
> Nicht kalt, nicht heiß durchmessend Weg und Haus . . .
> Und ich, ein Mörder ungeheurer Güten,
> Geh meinen Kreis, den lauen Ort zu hüten.
>
> (WLW, 249)

My God, how much love I released, | Neither coldly nor passionately traversing path and house . . . | And I, a murderer of huge kindnesses, | Walk my round, guarding the lukewarm place.

To correct, and compensate for, the defective nature of his living and loving, the poet now demonstrates the strength of his commitment to passionateness by yelling a paean to carrion and rotting flesh, and, in a fit of vitalist frenzy, he declares that he would plunge 'into any fire' and revel in the greater pain and that he would go singing merrily to his damnation. The solitary, the criminal, the child, the murderer, the suicide, the sick, the sinner, the ugly, the social pariah, the terrorist — all are hustled indiscriminately together as candidates with an equal right to a place in Heaven. Despite the many assaults he has undergone during the course of *Der Gerichtstag*, man and man alone is summoned in the last poem as the potential saviour.

The poet appears in a variety of roles — as judge, prosecutor, plaintiff, fiery gospeller and, much less frequently than before, as the propounder of new doctrines of salvation. God, too, appears. He becomes for Werfel a postulate arising not from the contemplation of the best of all possible worlds nor from a Kantian consciousness of the moral law, but very definitely from a consciousness of sin: He is by turns an absolute God, the Judge of the Israelitic prophets and the Apocalypse, and a pure spiritual being who has nothing to do with the fallen world. Mara, the 'Mittagsgöttin' ('the goddess of the noon') in the fourth book of *Der Gerichtstag*, is a pagan goddess of fertility *and* a Madonna-figure proclaiming fervent belief and love. Bread, wine, body and blood appear both as pagan-vitalistic emblems and as Christian symbols. No synthesis is achieved between all these disparate stances and interpretations, the poetic transformation of deep doubts and hectic struggles and heavy defeats remains incomplete, and the general impression is one of querulous incoherence. The volume is littered with bits and pieces of the work of, amongst others, Strindberg, Dostoyevsky, Kierkegaard, Freud, Whitman, Nietzsche, Tauler and Böhme, and is built precariously on what Kraus calls a 'quicksand of hysteria'.[37] The world of empirical reality is wholly submerged, no explicit issue is taken with war in particular or generalized terms, although many of the poems were written in the trenches and sent direct from there to Kurt Wolff, and not for a moment is Werfel capable of grasping the intrinsic contradiction of, on the one hand, implying a condemnation of war for preventing his project of universal brotherhood from being fulfilled and, on the other hand, of calling in belligerent tones for the smashing of all established tradition and authority. After all, the war was surely providing the kind and degree of anarchy which, in content and form, the poetry of *Der Gerichtstag* constantly invokes.

Its versification and rhythm become mere servants of wilful ideas and platform vehemences, the lines of verse roll onwards heavily and arbitrarily, the 'moral' attitudes become bullying assertions as the poet gives free rein to his rancour, all the time substantiating Rilke's description of the Expressionist poet as 'dieser explosiv gewordene Innenmensch . . .'. The calculated violence is exactly matched with the brutalizing of the language, rhyme and rhythm, and again and again the formal indiscipline parallels the kind of political and social anarchy which the poet demands in his verse. Scorn for God's commandments and for man's institutions is barely contained as the poet's bafflement and defiance slop over into haphazard bombast. He uses language as an instrument of offensive aggression, choosing coarse textures and lurid images, and whilst the aim is to express disillusion and anger, the effect is to diminish sensibility. The poems, constructed out of the scrap and fragments of the poet's seething emotions, are allowed to proliferate across the page as he vents his disgust for a world which, now it is at war, offers daily proof of the utter failure of his grand designs for his fellow-men. The verbal torsions have become, it seems, the only way of communicating thwarted ethical imperatives and a baffled hunger for salvation, and are emblems both for his profound sense of failure and his continuing determination to destroy all that stands in the way of the establishment of his own code of 'morality'. Very occasionally, and certainly not often enough to take on credible or firm contours, a purpose and a hope dawn — there will, the poet maintains in the poem 'Wir nicht', be redemption, but not *for us*. In rescuing from the holocaust of the First World War a slender, but ardent, hope of salvation at some future date, in yet again placing all *his* hopes in immanent panaceas, Werfel provides an early foretaste of that open-ended, heavily religiose and neo-Romantic longing which sustains the poetry of Kurt Heynicke, the subject of the next chapter.

> But (he points to her forehead and eyes) there, there, what lies behind there? . . . Know each other? We would have to break open our skulls. [38]

'Veni creator spiritus' is one of Werfel's finest poems and is representative of the hymnic, rhapsodic mode, an important part of his work. It serves to demonstrate that he is capable of something other than the subversive, at times terrorist, at other times 'spoilt child', bluster of the vast majority of the poems in *Der Gerichtstag*. Quotations have already been taken freely from *that* kind of poetry in an attempt to substantiate the argument of this book, and there seems no point either in dignifying (at least by implication) a bad poem by subjecting it to lengthy analysis and gratuitously assuming that it must have a rational explanation or indulging in wholesale demolition. 'Veni creator spiritus' is typical of a whole swathe of Expressionist poetry: it is a celebratory hymn with heavy baroque resonances. Indeed it owes something to Hrabanus Maurus's ninth-century 'Pfingstlied' which begins 'Du, heilger Schöpfer-Geist, erschein . . .'[39]

> Komm heiliger Geist du, schöpferisch!
> Den Marmor unsrer Form zerbrich!
> Daß nicht mehr Mauer krank und hart
> Den Brunnen dieser Welt umstarrt,
> Daß wir gemeinsam und nach oben
> Wie Flammen in einander toben!
>
> Tauch auf aus unsern Flächen wund
> Delphin von aller Wesen Grund,
> Alt allgemein und heiliger Fisch!
> Komm reiner Geist du, schöpferisch,

Nach dem wir ewig uns entfalten,
Kristallgesetz der Weltgestalten!

Wie sind wir alle Fremde doch!
Wie unterm letzten Hemde noch
Die Schattengreise im Spital
Sich hassen bis zum letzten Mal,
Und jeder, eh' er ostwärts mündet,
Allein sein Abendlicht entzündet,

So sind wir eitel eingespannt,
Und hocken bös an unserm Rand,
Und morden uns an jedem Tisch.
Komm heiliger Geist du, schöpferisch
Aus uns empor mit tausend Flügen!
Zerbrich das Eis in unsern Zügen!

Daß tränenhaft und gut und gut
Aufsiede die entzückte Flut,
Daß nicht mehr fern und unerreicht
Ein Wesen um das andre schleicht,
Daß jauchzend wir in Blick, Hand, Mund und Haaren,
Und in uns selbst dein Attribut erfahren!

Daß, wer dem Bruder in die Arme fällt,
Dein tiefes Schlagen süß am Herzen hält,
Daß, wer des armen Hundes Schaun empfängt,
Von deinem weisen Blicke wird beschenkt,
Daß alle wir in Küssens Überflüssen
Nur deine reine heilige Lippe küssen!

('Veni creator spiritus', 1913–15; WLW, 153–54)

Come, Holy Ghost, creative spirit! | Crumble the marble of our form! | So that a sick and hard wall | May no longer stare round the well of this world, | So that together and upwards | We may storm into one another like flames!
Rise from our chafed surfaces | Dolphin from the basis of all being, | Ancient, universal and sacred fish! | Come, you pure, creative spirit, | Towards whom we eternally unfold, | Crystal law of worldly forms!
How we are all strangers! | As beneath their last shirt | The shadowy old men in hospital | Hate one another to the last, | And each, before he flows eastwards, | Lights his evening candle alone, |
Thus are we harnessed together in vain | And squat maliciously on our edge, | And murder one another at every table. | Come, Holy Ghost, creative spirit, | Rise up out of us in a thousand flights! | Crumble the ice in our features!
So that tearful and well and well | The enraptured flood may seethe up, | So that one being no longer | Creeps around the other distant and unreached, | So that jubilantly in look, hand, mouth and hair, | And in ourselves we recognize your qualities!
So that whoever falls into a brother's arms, | May lovingly hold your deep heartbeat to his breast, | So that whoever intercepts the poor dog's glance | May be presented with your wise look, | So that we all in a surfeit of kisses | May only kiss your pure, holy lips!

The theme of the poem is clear: the holy spirit is enjoined to shatter the rigidity of 'our form' so that we can conquer our feeling of isolation, our vanity, our hatred, and offer ourselves to the dynamic power of the 'spirit'. 'Form' in this poem, as in many other poems by Werfel, represents a kind of existential barrier, the limitations, the bonds, the isolation of individuality: it is a separating surface, yet 'Veni creator spiritus' expresses the ardent hope that this surface can still be breached. Brought up in the jealous little enclaves of German-Jewish Prague society, Werfel writes from bitter personal experience of the barriers between man and man. In 'Veni creator spiritus' two worlds stand opposite each other — a world of movement, intensity, dynamism, fluidity, inwardness, purity and love and a world of hidebound rigidity, intractability, restriction, sickness, hostility and vanity. The poem's momentum and the sense of anxious urgency which pervades it derive from the clash of the two worlds. Maurus's 'Pfingstlied', on the other hand, begins from the assumption of a joyful partnership between the 'holy creator-spirit' and man, and stays loyal to that partnership.

In the first stanza of Werfel's poem, the 'holy spirit' is invoked — 'Geist' for Werfel, as for all Expressionist poets, is an all-purpose incantation, and, whilst it is *never* associated with man's reasoning faculties, it does appear in a host of other guises in Werfel's work — as the transcendental, God, soul, conscience, feeling, and the very essence of man. In this poem, the phrase 'holy spirit' clearly has strong religious overtones: the spirit's creative attributes are stressed by the marooning of the word 'schöpferisch' at the end of the first line, a conceit popular with seventeenth- and eighteenth-century religious poets and with medieval Latin hymnists. The nouns 'Marmor' and 'Härte', the epithets 'krank' and 'hart', the verb 'umstarrt' with its connotations of rigidity and torpor, all underline the extent to which we are imprisoned in our own individuality:

> Ichbin ist um mich. Ich bin eingeschlossen,
> Und Unentrinnbar ist der zweite Name der Welt.
>
> ('Adam', 1914; WLW, 156)

I-am is all around me. I am shut in, | and Inescapable is the world's second name.

With the word 'Brunnen' in the fourth line Werfel echoes Maurus's 'Comforter is the name we like to call you . . . You fresh well, bright fire', and the opposition between the fluidity of the world of the spirit and the rigidity of man's disparate existence is set up. In Maurus's hymn, attention is focused undeviatingly on the 'holy creator-spirit', but in Werfel's poem interest shifts in line 5 from the 'holy spirit' to man and to the positive purpose of the invocation of the spirit. By destroying the walls which separate man from man, the 'holy spirit', it is hoped, will enable us to live communally, to merge with one another in an ecstasy of love and trust. The dynamic verb 'toben' emphasizes the urgency of the poet's appeal: the walls of individuality have refused to crumble at the 'Weltfreund's' trumpet-call. The twofold use of the word 'daß' demonstrates the poet's present determination to conjure the spirit, to beseech it to hear his plea.

It becomes clear from the second stanza that the 'nach oben' ('upwards') of the previous line is something of a subterfuge: although we have just been enjoined to merge 'together and upwards', the spirit itself dwells not in some transcendental abode, but within man, at 'the basis of all being'. Werfel's syncretic view of religion is illustrated by his identification of the spirit with the dolphin, which, in Greek and Roman mythology, symbolized the gods' domination over the sea and their protection of mariners, and in early Christian art represented water and was a symbol for Christ. In line 4 of the second stanza, the spirit, now not only holy, but 'pure', is once more summoned, for we shall evolve for all eternity according to *its* canons. 'Sich entfalten' is a crucial verb in this context: it conjures precisely the right sense of breaking out, of emerging from the cocoon of our own egos. In the last line the spirit is called 'crystal law'. 'Crystal' is an odd word here because, like 'marble', it connotes hardness and intractability. Werfel is using it for its suggestion of purity and transparency, in contrast to opaque marble.

In the third stanza, the poet directs his attention entirely upon man's life on earth. We are all strangers to each other, we hate each other with the kind of embittered mutual hatred which skeletal old men on the point of dying in hospitals feel. 'Münden' in the penultimate line evokes the sense of fluidity and water again (as in 'Mündung' — estuary) and of speaking (as in 'Mund' — mouth). 'Flows eastwards' — a metaphor for praying? for dying? The impression of the last line is one of overriding loneliness, aloneness, when the end of the day, the end of life draws near. Something of the Expressionist writer's perennially envenomed scorn for his elders is evident in this image of old men 'beneath their last shirt' fuelling their rancour to the bitter end. In stanza four, there is further comment on our severely restricted lives. We are yoked in, we 'squat maliciously' on the very rims of our selves and can get no further, no nearer to our fellowmen *or* to the core of our own being. We are caught up in a round of hostility, even murder. Again, more desperately, the poet implores the spirit to rise up 'from within us' and to smash the 'ice in our features', to break down the cold walls which segregate us from each other.

'Tearful', 'seethe up', 'flood' — once again, in the fifth stanza, the poet resorts to images connoting fluidity. Tears have a special meaning for Werfel not only as welcome signs of deep emotion, but as emblems of the divine spirit. At its behest, the barriers of individuality which hem us in are meant to dissolve in a flood of tears, and we should then establish mutual contact instead of circling round each other in suspicious hostility. We shall rejoice as our whole being is imbued with the divine spirit. The poet, repeating the message of *Der Weltfreund*, pleads that, when man loves man as his brother, when man is released from the cell of his individuality and shows himself capable of giving *and* receiving love, the spirit should welcome man to his side and deem him worthy of a 'wise look'. His final plea is that in the blissful rapture of mutual love we should kiss only the spirit's 'pure holy lip': the phrase 'in Küssens Überflüssen' (. . . 'overflowing') underlines once again the opposition between fluidity and ossification upon which the poem is constructed.

Like much of Werfel's poetry, this poem has its mawkish and syntactically careless moments — the impure rhyming of the first two lines, the logjam of nouns which shatter the rhythm in the fifth line of the penultimate stanza and which set up echoes of 'Now thank we all our God . . .', the feeble reiteration of 'gut' in that same stanza, the sentimental stuff about the dog and the frightful assibilation of 'Küssens Überflüssen', a clumsy parody of the medieval poet's frequent resort to internal rhyming. Moreover, it is difficult to see what ('Kristallgesetz) der Weltge-

94

stalten' in stanza two might be doing other than providing a rhyme for the keyword 'entfalten', and the insertion of 'Haaren' at the end of the fifth stanza strikes a ludicrous note. Werfel's poetry constantly raises such doubts about his poetic and moral integrity, as the trivial and (we are led to believe) the crucially significant, the parochial and the cosmic are flung breathlessly together. There is something tasteless and deeply inappropriate about the image of the old men in the hospital in a poem whose title arouses expectations of solemnity and piety, especially as the image slithers into unclarity: such 'old men' belong rather to Rilke's early collections or to Georg Heym's grotesque visions. And the need in line 3 of the fourth stanza for a rhyme for 'schöpferisch' generates the clumsily harsh and again inappropriately mundane 'Und morden uns an jedem Tisch', which stands in wan contrast to the vivid imagining of the two lines which precede it.

These anomalies and examples of doubtful taste notwithstanding, Werfel has taken over the traditional form of a Latin hymn and filled it, in general successfully, with a characteristically Expressionist theme. The intrinsic confidence of Maurus's hymn is sustained by a firm belief in the holy Trinity, whereas Werfel's poem, pervaded by a sense of strident instability, places man's salvation in man himself. The medieval hymnist prays ardently and humbly to a transcendental God, Werfel in true Expressionist fashion pesters and invokes a spirit who, it turns out, resides in man — but man, alienated from his fellows and from his innate humanity, marooned in his self-contained isolation, does not know it. Hence, 'Veni creator spiritus' becomes another example of the Expressionist yearning for escape from the old, discredited ways and for emergence into a new life. The plea goes up for the destruction of barriers, frontiers and walls as the poet sketches in a reality ripe for *and* needing destruction. In the process a great deal of religiose enthusiasm is generated and left floating free. In some of his poems Werfel makes a virtue and a value of aimlessness:

> Was ich such, ist nicht zu finden,
> Was mich lockt, ist nicht zu greifen.
> Ungebunden, nicht zu binden,
> Muß ich lungern, will ich schweifen.
> Andre, die vor Zielangst schnaufen,
> Hoffen eins nur: Anzukommen.
> Doch *mein* Teil ist: Laufen laufen.
> Zweck und Ziel kann mir nicht frommen.
> ('Vagabund der Städte, 1928–34; WLW, 441)

What I am looking for is not to be found, | What entices me is not to be seized: | Unbound, not to be bound, | I have to lounge about, I want to roam. | Others panting with fear-ridden purpose | Hope for one thing only: to arrive. | But it is *my* lot: To run run. | Purpose and aim cannot benefit me.

The Expressionist poet, lacking the 'certainty in God' of medieval mystics, seeks to make good the deficiency, or at least to camouflage it, by snatching the reader up and bearing him away in a flood of pleas to the spirit. In headily metaphysical language, man's fate is placed in man's hands, yet man with all his murderous intent and sultry hatreds seems an improbable source of the 'divine spirit'.

Throughout 'Veni creator spiritus', the speaker is in an agitated state, but his agitation is controlled: the balance between what Werfel calls 'highest pressure' and 'greatest circumspection'[40] is just about maintained, albeit artificially at times, and it is above all this sense of control, of a 'salutary antagonism' which makes the poem superior to most of Werfel's other work. The rhyming and fairly regular line-length and rhythm speak for *some* reflection, *some* filing. The theme of the poem, the clash around which it revolves, ensures that a certain pressure is sustained, whilst the reader is thrust along by various other sources of escalating tension and intensity: the reliance on verbs which are semantically percussive and intrinsically dynamic; an abundance of imperatives, exclamations, interjections and vocatives; the constant tone of fervent entreaty; the forced images which dislocate our attention and compel us to strenuous efforts at interpretation. Yet, whereas in *Der Gerichtstag* the call for fluidity and for the destruction of walls and barriers between individuals is mirrored precisely in the anarchic form of the poems, in 'Veni creator spiritus' that same call is harnessed to, and contained in, a traditional poetic framework.

The opposition 'fluidity-hardness' recurs throughout Werfel's work, and he unfailingly declares himself for flux and dynamism. By his 1929 novel *Barbara oder die Frömmigkeit* he has widened the scope of his appeal for the destruction of barriers and, making explicit what his poetry has always implied, includes in that appeal the world of contemporary politics. The Austrian monarchy is thus repudiated as 'something fossilized in convention' (*Barbara*, p. 335), the institution of the Church is derided as 'the eternally rigid' (p. 417) and mockingly compared with 'the eternally fluent' (1918) Revolution, and the Revolution itself is uncritically praised because during it 'the eternally rigid had come into flux, the innate hard-heartedness of possession had dissolved into effervescent greed . . . the cold horny conscience of the old world had been made to yield' (p. 540). If the poems of *Der Gerichtstag* are interpreted as reflecting in their unkempt form the longed-for condition of dynamic flux in the public, political realm, 'Veni creator spiritus' can be regarded as an early, controlled exposition of what becomes an abiding theme in Werfel's work. The directionless fervour which it releases is subsequently channelled into actual historical events and phenomena: his participation in the 1918 Revolution and his later endeavours in the 1920s and 1930s to take issue with contemporary political problems are characterized by a recourse to the same vertiginous exhortations and metaphors and the same 'moral' categories which have evolved from his pre-1920 Expressionist work.

Conclusions

> . . . man seeking good, | doing evil.[41]
> Nor will my poems do good only, they will do
> just as much evil, perhaps more . . .[42]

It is an ineluctable part of man's nature, Werfel maintains, to be confused, to be riven by conflicting tendencies:

Weh uns, wir heißen: Hinundher!
Und unsre Mutter: Mindermehr!
Hier Linksherum, dort Rechtsherum
Heißt unser Stadt und Königtum.
('Notwendigkeit', 1915–17; WLW, 257)

Woe to us, our name is: To-and-fro! | And our mother [is]: Less-more! | Round the left here, round the right there | Is the name of our town and kingdom.

The poet's mind, too, teems with alternatives:

Denn mein eigner Sinn ist voll Entweder
Und voll Oder, voll Sowohl=Alsauch,
Stören und verstören kann mich jeder.
('Gebet in der Dämmerung', 1935; WLW, 448)

For my own mind is full of either | And full of or, full of both-and, | Anyone can disturb and upset me.

And yet, in spite of the self-pity inherent in some of these lines, the Expressionist poet is not averse to the idea of confusion, for written into his poetic theory and practice is the tendency to mirror the chaos of experience without overcoming it, to re-create wholesale and not necessarily to clarify emotions, and to conjure feelings without, sometimes, bringing us nearer to understanding them. Georg Heym is the exception among Expressionist writers in explicitly regretting his state of constant mental turbulence: 'I, a lacerated sea, always tempestuous, I the mirror of the outside world, just as savage and chaotic as the world' (Heym, TIII, 164), whereas J. R. Becher positively welcomes confusion and all poems which sow confusion. Reacting to a book of Dehmel's poetry he writes:

The more obscurely, the more incomprehensibly a passage read, the more inclined I was to regard it as the ultimate revelation. It seemed to me that the essence of a poem resided precisely in obscuring the clear and the lucid, in making the distinct and the visible blurred and invisible, in replacing what has been stabilized with what is precarious. In this book I found an unsuspected confirmation of my own state of confusion, life revealed itself to me as eternal confusion. (*Abschied*, p. 222)

This is a remarkable, and remarkably clear, statement of the Expressionist poet's credo. In all of it, Werfel, implicitly in all his poetry, explicitly in *Der Gerichtstag*, acquiesces. In so doing he runs sharply counter to what his contemporary, T. S. Eliot, defines as the purpose of art:

For it is ultimately the function of art, in imposing a credible order upon ordinary reality, and thereby eliciting some perception of an order *in* reality, to bring us to a condition of serenity, stillness, and reconciliation.[43]

Starkly highlighted in these two quotations from Becher and Eliot are the vastly different expectations which two poets — one a paradigmatic Expressionist poet, the other an indisputably great twentieth-century writer with deep roots in Classical literature — bring to art in general and their own poetry in particular.

Like the other Expressionist poets Werfel wrote in intensely confused times. Moral, religious and political conflicts eddied and swirled in his mind, he played more or less passive host to a hotchpotch of semi- or totally digested influences, and whatever he wrote issued from the temporary hegemony of any one of a series of -isms or beliefs or private passions. He was irresponsible and haphazard in his reactions and attitudes to the political and social realities of the day, and yet, in a quite definite sense, he was timely, he did have his finger on the pulse, responding to, and thus fuelling, moods and trends. His work compounded the already hectically muddled time, widening ever more the disjunction between thinking and action which, for example, Musil depicts in *Der Mann ohne Eigenschaften* as symptomatic of the age. A major consequence of the confusion which is mirrored in his poetry can be suggested if his work is seen against the background of the rise of National Socialism in the 1920s: he is not so much a positive or active force for evil, but an enfeebling and, perhaps, corrupting influence on the few forces for good, one of those 'many false prophets', of whom the Bible speaks, who 'strengthen the hands of evil-doers, that none doth return from his wickedness' (Matthew 24.11) and 'who shall deceive many' (Jeremiah 23.14). By 1920 'snared in an evil time' (Ecclesiastes 9.12), he is disillusioned and resigned. He has no aims, moral, political, poetic, and no purpose. In a poem written some time between 1915 and 1917 and which again has intensely personal resonances, he declares what he has 'achieved' and what lies in store: 'In front of you is marshland, behind you is quarry!' (WLW, 306). Compare him with those who do have a home, do know what they want and where they are going. A political realist like the Becher of the 1920s, who has left his Expressionist obfuscations behind him, is writing in 1926: 'We do not venerate literature, we are not such hopelessly word-obsessed believers in literature that we cannot see what natural limitations literature has'.[44] And 'real' revolutionaries like Erich Mühsam are full of scorn for 'an aestheticism which preened itself on reducing the great problems of mankind to a resounding word and a voluptuous sigh'.[45] Or there are political pragmatists like Goebbels's Michael who is very sure of himself. He may be rootless, but he is determined to survive, for he has a calling: 'We human beings are indeed homeless on earth . . . we young people will not perish as long as we believe in our mission' (*Michael*, p. 33). As he writes his diary and uses such nebulous (Expressionist) terms as 'mission', Michael is already imagining the realization of that mission, convinced of his strength and entitlement to carry it through. As the Expressionist poet writes his poetry and bandies words like 'mission', 'spirit', 'humanity', he hears only the buzzing noise they make in his brain ('. . . loudest of all I heard the blood in my ears, | And I staggered along | Amongst shards of sound and coloured debris': 'Barkarole der Finsternis', 1923; WLW, 325) and thrills at the thought of 'if only I could . . .'. National Socialist propaganda is not wanting in heady metaphors and inchoate rant, but once the political structures of Nazism are present, uncommitted exultation cannot be accepted. In a letter to Goebbels in 1930, Hitler declares that the National Socialist party will never be 'ein Debattier-Klub wurzelloser Literaten oder chaotischer Salon-Bolschewisten'.[46] Already in *Mein Kampf* he had made reference to the subversive consequences of directionless religiosity (though the National Socialists were quick to exploit those consequences whilst it suited them): 'Without clearly delimited faith, religiosity with its unclarity and multiplicity of form would not only be worthless for human

life, but would probably contribute to general disintegration'.[47] *Michael* is freighted
with purpose and clearsightedness, *Der Weltfreund* effervesces with wild hopes and
dark dreams because the poet is interested only in 'the soul's every side-track,
obscurity . . .' ('Brief an einen Staatsmann', p. 92). The difference between Michael
and the author of *Der Weltfreund* is succinctly distilled in the words of the narrator in
Werfel's novel *Der veruntreute Himmel*: 'You have a stable belief and I have a confused
belief'.[48]

Writing in 1920, Brecht rejects Toller's *Die Wandlung* (1919) for its idealistic and
abstract depiction of man: 'Man as object, as slogan, instead of man as human being.
Man considered apart, as the singular of mankind — his cause rests in feeble
hands'.[49] Werfel did nothing to strengthen man's cause: perhaps it can even be
argued, as indeed he does in various retrospective comments in the late 1930s and
early 1940s, that he and the other Expressionist writers were more than a debilitating
influence and that he, with them, 'did his bit' (see p. 79 above) by creating in quite
definite ways the kind of atmosphere in which National Socialism or a movement
like it might flourish. In what ways? By subverting all authority and overturning
traditional moral values, thus contributing to what one historian calls 'the pervasive
uncertainty about opinions and truths which gives the face of the age an unmistak-
able pre-totalitarian look';[50] by repudiating the validity and value of anything
contained and 'fertig' and thus leaving available and unhoused considerable passion
and intensity of feeling, 'a secret treasure of enormous might';[51] by preferring the
dark, the mysterious, the daemonic, the subconscious, to anything clear-cut,
straightforward and transparent, thus incidentally anticipating Heidegger's notorious Loyalty Oath of March 1933 with its recommendation that the German people
in a spirit of heedless adventure should *not* seek to 'shut itself away from the horror
of the untamed and the confusion of the dark'; by subscribing uncritically to the
vitalist philosophy that danger and passion are preferable to the mundane, the
practical and the tepid; by automatically reaching for 'the radical alternative'[52] as
soon as traditional, gradual methods fail, at the same time implicitly denigrating
moderation and mutual debate; by reposing unconditional faith in an immanent
salvation, paradoxically couched in frantically otherworldly terms and removed
from the framework of any urgent ethical perspective; by fostering a kind of
Promethean arrogance which placed the poet outside the law and outside time — in
all these ways, Expressionism contributed to the upsurge of a political movement
which also based its appeal on irrationalism and emotionalism. Promising the world
and then failing to redeem that promise, Expressionist writers plunged into a
numbing sense of passivity and inner collapse, and, as Weber and other commentators predicted, encouraged the same feelings of helplessness and rootlessness in their
readers. Already in an early (1915) story and with quite startling insight, Werfel had
prefigured what was to become his own dilemma and that of his fellow Expressionist poets in terms of 'a young man, someone or other, who could not be equal to the
full measure of his awesome calling, as passive as a wheel which does not know
which way to roll'.[53] Moreover, Expressionist writers abused language,[54] distended
and brutalized it, blurred its edges, did not let it relax in its lower reaches. Logic and
precision yielded to declamatory tirades. With Werfel, for example, it is not 'sich

aufhellen' (brighten up), but 'sich verklären' (be transfigured); not 'hinaufgehen' (go up), but 'emporgerissen werden' (be torn aloft); not 'öffnen' (open), but 'aufreißen' (rip open); not 'werfen' (throw), but 'schmeißen' (hurl); not even 'schließen' (close), but always 'zubauen' or 'zumauern' (wall in). It is not so much a question of 'negligences of enthusiasm',[55] but rather a conscious policy of exaggeration and inflation. Words implode with a fierce dynamism, all are overlaid with a weighty value judgement which issues solely from that dynamism. Furthermore, many of the features which Siegfried Bork subsequently finds in his investigation of National Socialist language — for example, a predilection for superlatives and for the outsize — characterize Werfel's poetry. At a time when what Germany needed above all was clarity, concreteness and restraint, Expressionist poets like Werfel offered only hyperbole, mystification and strenuously vague and elusive yearnings. For many of their linguistic conceits — perhaps for all of them together — it is possible to find antecedents: the opening of Conrad Ferdinand Meyer's *Jürg Jenatsch* comes instantly to mind. But what is crucial is the historical context in which these abuses occur: they are worse in an age which is both much more sensitive (in its intellectuals) and much more brutal (in its politicians). In the 1920s and 1930s emotion spoke to emotion, a medium was shaped, and at least part of an audience was made ready for the 'right' strong, guiding voice. Werfel's moral obtuseness, which does not of itself make for bad poetry, should be seen against this historical background.

On the last day of 1933 Hitler wrote to Goebbels asserting that one of the first pre-conditions for the victory of National Socialism was 'the intellectual destruction of the inimical world of thought confronting us'.[56] Expressionism, with Werfel as its leading practitioner, was instrumental in that destruction. A warning had been sounded some ten years earlier by Hermann Hesse who, interestingly, does not demur to suggest a connection between what he predicts as the imminent downfall of the world and the linguistic iconoclasm of poets:

Others [of these contemporary poets] drive impatiently forward and seek consciously to hasten the disintegration of the German literary language — some with the sullen grief of the man who breaks up his own house, others with reckless humour and in the somewhat shallow mood of complete indifference to the ruin of the world.[57]

With that strange mixture of vainglory and contrition so typical of him, Werfel positively proclaims his part in lines written in 1920 and already full of *mea culpa*:

> I have caused yet greater catastrophe!
> Mankind's future is poisoned by me![58]

There is, though, even here more than a hint of the 'brazen self-deification of artists'.

NOTES

1 Thom Gunn, 'On the Move', in: *The New Poetry* (Harmondsworth, 1962), p. 135.
2 F. Werfel, 'Nur Flucht' (1915); *Das Lyrische Werk*, edited by A. D. Klarmann (Frankfurt a.M., 1967), p. 161 (hereafter referred to as WLW).

3 F. Werfel, *Barbara oder die Frömmigkeit* (1929; reprinted Frankfurt a.M., 1953), p. 571 (hereafter referred to as *Barbara*).

4 W. Paulsen, *Expressionismus und Aktivismus*, p. 97.

5 F. Werfel, 'Begegnungen mit Rilke', *Das Tagebuch*, 8, Heft 4 (1927), 140.

6 W. Hasenclever, 'Der politische Dichter', in: *Menschheitsdämmerung*, p. 215.

7 Mme de Staël, *De l'Allemagne* (1813; reprinted Paris, 1958), II, 277.

8 J. R. Becher, *Abschied*, p. 420.

9 H. Carossa, *Ungleiche Welten*, pp. 703–04.

10 S. Zweig, *Die Welt von gestern*, p. 250.

11 H. G. Kessler, *Tagebücher 1918–37* (Frankfurt a.M., 1961), p. 91.

12 F. Werfel, 'Brief an einen Staatsmann', *Das Ziel* (Munich and Berlin, 1916), p. 96.

13 F. Werfel, in the 'programmatische Ankündigung' (1913) of *Der Jüngste Tag*, and quoted in: P. Raabe, *Die Zeitschriften und Sammlungen des literarischen Expressionismus*, pp. 172–73.

14 F. Werfel, *Die Versuchung*, in: *Die Dramen*, 2 vols (Frankfurt a.M., 1959), I, 35.

15 A letter dated 28 November 1918 and sent by members of the Workers' and Soldiers' Council, Kreis Osterholz, to the 'Novembergruppe' in Berlin. Quoted in: *Germany in Ferment*, edited by D. Elliot (Durham, 1970), p. 8.

16 Alma Mahler-Werfel, *Mein Leben* (Frankfurt a.M. and Hamburg, 1960), pp. 221–24.

17 R. Musil, *Der Mann ohne Eigenschaften*, pp. 55–56.

18 F. Kafka, quoted in: P. Raabe, 'Franz Kafka und der Expressionismus', *ZfDP*, 86 (1967), 171.

19 A. Polgar, *An den Rand geschrieben* (Berlin, 1927), pp. 86f.

20 The phrase is Thom Gunn's in: 'On the Move', *The New Poetry*, p. 134.

21 For example in the second chapter of the third part of *Barbara*, pp 299–307.

22 F. Werfel, *Weißenstein, der Weltverbesserer* (1939), in: *Erzählungen aus zwei Welten*, 3 vols (Frankfurt a.M., 1954), III, 59 *(hereafter referred to as Erzählungen)*.

23 F. Werfel, *Stern der Ungeborenen* (Frankfurt a.M., 1946), p. 209.

24 Quoted in: Alma Mahler-Werfel, *Mein Leben*, p. 115.

25 A. Kurella, 'Brief an Franz Werfel', in: *Tätiger Geist. Zweites der Ziel-Jahrbücher* (Munich and Berlin, 1918), p. 222.

26 Annemarie Rheinländer-Möhl, 'Umbruch des Geistes in seiner Auswirkung auf die literarische Situation der Gegenwart. Nachgewiesen an der zeitbedingten und artfremden Romankunst Franz Werfels' (unpublished dissertation, University of Münster, 1936).

27 K. Kraus, 'Ich und das Ichbin', *Die Fackel*, 15 October 1918, Nos. 484–98, p. 101; and 'Dorten', *Die Fackel*, 18 January 1917, Nos. 445–53, pp. 133–47.

28 A. Siemsen, 'Zwei Dichter der jüdischen Emigration: Franz Werfel und Alfred Döblin', *Judaica*, 1, Heft 2 (1 July 1945), 157.

29 See the poem 'Junge Bettlerin an der Krücke'; WLW, 26.

30 The phrase is Robert Musil's. See *Der Mann ohne Eigenschaften*, p. 960.

31 The phrase is Rainer Maria Rilke's in: *RMR und Marie von Thurn und Taxis. Briefwechsel* (Zurich, 1951), p. 356.

32 H. Hesse, 'Recent German Poetry', *The Criterion*, I, October 1922 — July 1923 (London, 1967), p. 92.

33 Letter to Frau Dr Else Jaffé-Richthofen in: M. Weber, *Gesammelte Politische Schriften*, p. 481.

34 F. Nietzsche, *Werke*, Musarion edition, 23 vols (Munich, 1922–29), XIX, 231.

35 F. Nietzsche, 'Der europäische Nihilismus'; Musarion edition, XVIII, 54–55.

36 F. Werfel, introduction to: *Giuseppe Verdi, Briefe* (Berlin, Vienna and Leipzig, 1926), p. 38.

37 K. Kraus, 'Ich und das Ichbin', p. 110.

38 G. Büchner, *Dantons Tod*, I.I.

39 Quoted in: K. Langosch, *Hymnen und Vagantenlieder* (Basel und Stuttgart, 1954), pp. 54–55.

40 F. Werfel, *Die Geschwister von Neapel* (Frankfurt a.M. and Berlin, 1950), p. 208.

41 E. Pound, Draft and fragment of Canto CXV, *The Cantos of Ezra Pound* (London, 1975), p. 794.

42 W. Whitman, quoted in: *A Collection of Critical Essays*, edited by R. H. Pearce (Englewood Cliffs, 1962), p. 87.

43 T. S. Eliot, *On Poetry and Poets*, p. 94.

44 J. R. Becher, 'Der Tote Punkt', *Arbeiterstimme*, 3 November 1926, p. 127.

45 E. Mühsam, *Unpolitische Erinnerungen*, p. 147.
46 '. . . a debating-club for rootless writers or chaotic drawing-room Bolshevists'. Quoted in: H. Brenner, *Die Kunstpolitik des Nationalsozialismus* (Munich, 1963), p. 84.
47 Adolf Hitler, *Mein Kampf*, translated by R. Manheim (London, 1969), p. 345.
48 F. Werfel, *Der veruntreute Himmel* (Frankfurt a.M., 1951), p. 336
49 Bertolt Brecht, 'Dramatisches Papier und anderes', *Der Volkswille*, 14 December 1920.
50 J. C. Fest, *Das Gesicht des Dritten Reiches*, p. 339.
51 The phrase is Spengler's and is quoted in: R. d'O. Butler, *The Roots of National Socialism 1783–1933* (London, 1941), p. 250.
52 See Alex de Jonge, *The Weimar Chronicle — Prelude to Hitler*, p. 172.
53 'Cabrinowitsch', *Erzählungen*, I, 24.
54 And not 'merely' by mangling its grammar and syntax in the ways detailed during the first three months of 1952 in the usually sedate pages of *Neue Literarische Welt*, where there developed a fairly heated three-way feud about 'Language confusion in Franz Werfel's work' and his grammatical howlers.
55 Samuel Johnson, *Lives of the Poets*, 2 vols (Letchworth, 1968), II, 56.
56 Quoted in: J. Wulf, *Literatur und Dichtung im Dritten Reich* (Gütersloh, 1963), p. 145.
57 H. Hesse, 'Recent German Poetry', p. 90.
58 *Spiegelmensch* (Munich, 1920), p. 197.

VI KURT HEYNICKE

Das Heimweh ohne Heim, die leidigste,
schneidigste Herzensfrage, welche fragt:
'Wo darf *ich* — heimisch sein?'[1]
Darauf erglüht tiefeingeschrieben
das Wort: dem unbekannten Gotte.
Sein bin ich, ob ich in der Frevler Rotte
auch bis zur Stunde bin geblieben:
sein bin ich — und ich fühl' die Schlingen,
die mich im Kampf darniederziehn,
und, mag ich fliehen,
mich doch zu seinem Dienste zwingen.
Ich will dich kennen, Unbekannter,
du tief in meine Seele Greifender
mein Leben wie ein Sturm Durchschweifender,
du Unfaßbarer, mir Verwandter!
Ich will dich kennen, selbst dir dienen![2]

An image, Rilke says, will emerge from the carpet for the passer-by;[3] Stefan George calls one of his poetic cycles *Der Teppich des Lebens* (*The Carpet of Life*); and, in a notebook jotting in his wife's memoirs, Thomas Hardy writes:

As, in looking at a carpet, by following one colour a certain pattern is suggested, by following another colour, another; so in life the seer should watch that pattern among general things which his idiosyncrasy moves him to observe, and describe that alone.[4]

Hardy's analogy of the colour and the pattern in a carpet can be usefully applied to the poetry and life of Kurt Heynicke. The colour, the one thread which might suggest a pattern in his poetry is desolate loneliness and homelessness.

To say this is to say nothing very startling, for loneliness, homelessness, uprootedness, and alienation are the perennial themes of twentieth-century literature and the conditions from which much of the literature issued. Well before he wrote the famous lines in the 'Seventh Elegy' ('Each torpid turn of the world has such disinherited ones, | to whom no longer what's been, and not yet what's coming, belongs'). Rilke has described man's nomadic existence on earth, man's lack of a communal home: 'And we are a migratory people, all of us: not for the reason that none of us has a home to which he stays loyal and on which he builds, but because we do not share a home any more'.[5] The Expressionist poets, almost without exception, are prey to similar feelings of rootlessness. Iwan Goll, in his

H

autobiographical sketch in *Menschheitsdämmerung*, (p. 341), is dogmatic in his assertion that outsidership and homelessness are the central experiences of his life: 'I.G. has no homeland: a Jew by fate, born by chance in France, designated by rubber-stamp as a German'. Werfel stresses man's naked impotence and overwhelming sense of isolation in the face of the recalcitrance and discreteness of individual things:

We are all placed in an awesome situation to which we can see no end . . . we stand powerless before details which no externally imposed order can unite as a whole, the 'and' between things seems to have mutinied, everything lies for ever separated in a heap, and a dreadful loneliness reduces life to silence.[6]

The feeling of isolation and alienation need not be 'merely' a kind of existential angst: it can assume the sense of being estranged from all political parties so that the writer feels he has no control over his private or his public life. Döblin, having returned from a meeting held by the Social Democrats, relates how he was 'disgusted' by the Liberals, had 'no feel for' nationalism, was 'enraged' by the Conservatives and 'felt alienated from the Social Democrats'. 'It was clear to me', he adds, 'that I was swimming in the air, a hopeless stickler for principles'.[7] It is not surprising that, if homelessness of this order is the central experience of a whole generation of writers, some of them should place their art in the service of something bigger than themselves, in line with Becher's conviction that 'man craves for greatness. He demands something beyond himself' (*Abschied*, p. 407). Almost anything will do as long as it offers release from egotistic preoccupations and ultimate loneliness:

Spiritual uplift is necessary, and expansion! And both can be achieved only if we convert our feelings into actions, by working for some community or other and thus freeing ourselves from our selfish pleasures behind which painful loneliness always lurks. Whether it should be for a community, the whole of mankind or a single people, everyone must decide for himself![8]

The intensity of the will-to-self-surrender should be the only criterion, the commitment to a community should be unquestioning — 'just be determined to submit!'[9] Probably the most powerful of these paradigms of desolateness and homelessness is Gottfried Benn's strange autobiographical figure, Rönne, whose despairing 'Dear city, let yourself be occupied! Be my home! Accept me into the community!'[10] is answered by Tucholsky's joy at being admitted as a member of a club:

> In mein' Verein bin ich hineingetreten,
> Weil mich ein alter Freund darum gebeten,
>   Ich war allein.
> Jetzt bin ich Mitglied, Kamerad, Kollege —
> Das kleine Band, das ich ins Knopfloch lege,
>   Ist der Verein.[11]

I have joined my club | Because an old friend asked me to, | I was alone. | Now I am a member, comrade, colleague — | The little ribbon I put in my buttonhole | Is my club.

Kurt Heynicke's life and work provide a further representative example of the kind of isolation which Tucholsky has gleefully left behind. Goll's feeling of gross disorientation, Werfel's 'dreadful loneliness', Döblin's sense of isolation from all orthodox political parties, Dehmel's (and, more stridently, Rönne's) quest for a community — all these, in some degree, reappear in Heynicke's poetry. In an early poem Heynicke depicts Life and his life in the following terms:

> O dies Menschsein zwischen Himmel und Staub!
> Ich decke der Wälder Laub auf meine Stirne
> und kühle meinen Leib im Schatten der Bäume:
> ein ruhloser Gast auf den Straßen des Lebens.[12]

O this human life lived out between heaven and dust! I cover my brow with the forests' foliage | and cool my body in the shade of the trees: | a restless guest on the streets of life.

— 'a restless guest' in an intermediary kingdom, a kind of no-man's-land between the promise of Heaven and the certainty of dying, Heynicke has led a life which is typical of the Expressionist generation — footloose, uprooted, unstable. Werfel, for example, has titles like *Zwischen oben und unten* (*Between Above and Below*) and *Erzählungen aus zwei Welten* (*Stories from Two Worlds*) and a life characterized by sudden departures and lengthy peregrinations: his lines 'I a drifting cloud, | Without ties, a homeland, I a semi-dream, | I a refugee of spent cities | . . . |I with no home, no Hell, no Heaven, | Building my house on | Random and fleeting songs'[13] foreshadow the tone, the themes and many of the images of Heynicke's verse. Yet whereas one feels with Werfel that he is impelled, and his life shaped, by a series of feverish allegiances which might have taken him anywhere, there is a drifting, uncritically lazy quality about Heynicke's existence — the very ordinary beginnings in Dresden and Berlin, the frontline experience in France and Russia, a kind of 'will he, won't he?' relationship with Walden's *Sturm*, the five-year gap after the First World War when 'like lofty clouds | which do not know to whom they are drifting'[14] he wandered from job to job, the involvement with the theatre in Düsseldorf, the 1930s when he witnessed the advent of the Nazis in Berlin, wrote two plays in honour of the new régime and then vanished, resurfacing much later, a country-man, in the Black Forest. An early poem (1919) offers an accurate prediction of his life, pointing up its harried quality and his persistent yearning for peacefulness:

> O Welt, ich bin ein hingepeitschtes Leben!
> O Chor des Nacht, gieß Ruhe über mich!
>
> ('Der Jüngling', 1919; HLW, I, 129)

O world, I am a lashed along life! | O chorus of the night, pour calm over me!

Paradoxically, in view of the intellectual, spiritual, and physical rootlessness which he shares with his generation, he has always been reluctant to be assigned to a group: he resents being 'well entombed, not cared for in a museum called Expressionism',[15] and it is only very grudgingly and after much aimless procrastination that he concedes the obvious: 'With the volumes *Rings fallen Sterne*, *Gottes Geigen*, *Das namenlose Angesicht* I was borne along on the wave of young Expressionism as one of its fraternity'.[16] In theme, form, style, attitude, temperament, his cognates *are* the Expressionist poets in general and Stramm, Werfel, Stadler in particular. With hindsight we can see that his anthologizing contemporaries were right — with twelve poems, one fewer than Heym, he is well represented in Pinthus's *Menschheitsdämmerung*, and Soergel, in his early and influential account of Expressionism, *Dichtung und Dichter der Zeit*, devotes six pages to him. Since the Second World War he has felt caught between a past which he repudiates and a future where, he complains, young writers, re-enacting the hoary Expressionist inter-generational conflict, prevent older writers from having poems published and plays produced on the radio.[17] He is disillusioned, dissatisfied and yet determined to keep on . . . what?

> Zwischen Hold und Höllisch
> schwankt alles Gelebte einher,
> jeder Schatten ein Einst.
>
> ....
> Meine Pilgerschaft schläft nicht,
> die Lust,
> durch die Gewitterwand
> hinter die Blitze zu schauen,
> hochzeitet weiter mit mir.

('Die ewige Hochzeit'; HLW, III, 98)

Between graciousness and hellishness | everything lived reels along, | every shadow a once-upon-a-time. | My pilgrimage does not sleep, | the desire | to look through the storm-wall behind the flashes of lightning continues to make merry inside me.

'My pilgrimage does not sleep,' 'the desire . . . continues to make merry inside me' — these lines, written in 1969, appear in Heynicke's last volume of published verse. More than half a century earlier his first volume, *Rings fallen Sterne* (1917), is composed of such lines as 'And our path afflicts us with pointed stones . . . We all toil along our path' (HLW, I, 34) and 'I am a wanderer in the street | from my crown of thorns stars drip onto my breast' (HLW, I, 57): little has changed in the intervening fifty years. The restless fervour of the quest, the goal intentionally kept vague and overcast with pseudo-religious longing, the strenuousness and anxiety of the journey seen as values in themselves, the pervading sense of homelessness, the self-dramatizing religiose terminology — all this is common to both the 1917 and the 1969 volumes. By 1969 his poetry is full of a feeling of betrayal and disillusion-ment: everything has been a sham, and the voyager on his quest for the good place or the unknown god

> discovers nothing; he does not want to arrive.
> The journey is false; the false journey really an illness
> On the false island where the heart cannot act and
> will not suffer.[18]

The volumes between the first and the last are anchored in the same (wholly Expressionist) attitudes and assumptions: the voice, grown less frenzied in the course of time, the themes, the poetic forms and the prepossessions remain recognizably Heynicke's and manifestly Expressionist. For instance, the feeling of fierce, directionless longing which permeates the whole of Heynicke's œuvre is distilled in that mantological, talismanic Expressionist word 'Aufbruch'. If Stadler's

'Der Aufbruch' and Lotz's 'Aufbruch der Jugend' are the best known examples of the characteristically Expressionist call to set forth, Heynicke has his own, almost obligatory 'Aufbruch' which is composed of a series of frantic imperatives hurled at his heart 'to break out into the light, into love, into . . .' (written in 1919; HLW, 1, 122)

> A cloud has wept you,
> you raindrop, you do not know where you are
>   going,
> you have met other raindrops
> which, like you, are asking the direction.[19]
> We human beings are indeed homeless on
> earth, because we never come to rest anywhere
> . . . gradually we reach each other: the spirit of
> the resurrection, the release from the ego, the
> submission to a You, to a brother, to one's
> people is a bridge from this side to the other
> side.[20]

A peculiar danger lurked for poets like Heynicke, who, after the 1914–18 War, wrote out of an atmosphere of general economic, moral and spiritual collapse and out of a conviction of their own personal homelessness. There was an almost natural progression from the dawning realization that the self is not only inadequate but also devoid of all external support,[21] through the invocation of some vaguely defined and intensely sought 'Du' and a commitment to a community, to a more or less willing submission to the powers-that-be. Sometimes the commitment to something else, somebody else is a highly adventitious affair: Dehmel's 'some community or other' is matched precisely by Heynicke's 'das irgend-du' ('the any-you') in the 1917 poem 'Die Träume'. Becher, who in his autobiography continually parades the word 'Sozialismus' before us and intones 'Something will come. Something . . .'[22] with the ritualistic ardour of someone who is seeking to will the 'something', whatever it is, into existence by the very chanting of it, writes that his passionate allegiance to the ideals of Socialism could easily have been very different: 'I had the choice of becoming Becher or Benn, and Benn, too, was able to choose.• We decided to be what we became. This means that Benn had as much chance of becoming Becher as the other way round'.[23] Yet sometimes the commitment to an available -ism is not the result of a conscious choice amongst diverse possibilities, but amounts to an apparently irresistible and accelerating slither — as, for example, in the case of Arnolt Bronnen where the brutality of the Expressionist play *Vatermord* issues with ghastly predictability into all the nauseating compromises with National Socialism in the 1928/29 novel *O.S.* and the 1930 novel *Roßbach*. 'I had come to these men [the circle round Ernst Jünger], looking for something, looking for what was truly German . . .,' seeking for somewhere to console and accommodate 'this whole system, called I, . . . helpless, fluttering, fading, craving for integration'.[24] Heynicke, too, favours the image of the 'fluttering', homeless soul: in the 1918 poem 'Klage' he writes: 'My soul flutters high in the dark above things . . . risen from the earth, | upwards to | Him' (HLW, 1, 81). His poetry, no less than Becher's and Bronnen's work, is characterized by alternating moods of corrosive anxiety and irrationally high hopes, of hectic expectancy and profound disappointment:

> O daß einer käme mit jubelnder Fackel
> und schenkte uns wieder das Licht.
> Aber die Erde dreht sich höhnisch vorbei.
> Wir leben nicht.
> Wir sind schon lange tot.

> ('Lied der Armen', 1921; HLW, II, 38)

O if only someone would come with an exultant torch | and bestow the light on us again. | But the earth spins by in mockery. | We are not alive. | We have been dead for a long time.

And the feeling of rootlessness predominates, accompanied by an impulsion to move on to inevitably illusory goals:

> Regst du die Flügel, glühende Seele
> zu gläubig geahnten seligen Ufern?
> Wo aber sind sie, die seligen Inseln?

> ('Letzte Sehnsucht', 1925; HLW, II, 96)

Are you stirring your wings, glowing soul | to confidently anticipated blessed shores? | But where are they, the blessed islands?

Heynicke, Bronnen, Becher — these are three very different writers. Their particular careers and allegiances can best be explained by showing that they were writing at a time when there was in the air a universal craving for what another of their kind, Gottfried Benn, calls 'a new commitment', 'a new historical sense'.[25] Like Benn, like all 'genuine Expressionists' (Benn argues, I, 251), they followed the path 'out of their chaotic personality and past' to a new allegiance whose watchword is discipline. Again like Benn, they shared the German intellectuals' 'susceptibility to every conceivable infection — moral, spiritual and physical'[26] in an age when there was a pervasive uncertainty about values, opinions and truths. Their overriding feeling of homelessness and isolation — Bronnen's epithets 'fluttering, fading, helpless' could be applied to the whole generation of post-war writers — did nothing to stabilize values and moral standards. Moreover, there appeared on the scene in the shape of National Socialism (and, to a lesser extent, Communism) a highly pragmatic political party whose leader was quick to pour scorn on post facto literary sceptics and dilettanti among erstwhile supporters[27] and to capitalize on the historical angst of the bourgeoisie with its feeling of being déraciné:

Nothing is anchored any longer. Nothing is rooted within us any longer. Everything is superficial, flies away from us. The thinking of our people is becoming restless and hasty. All of life is being torn asunder . . .[28]

And the National Socialist movement was very willing and able to exploit feelings of discontent and personal failure, opening its arms to writers like Benn who have reached a dead-end in their work, to Bronnen who, corrupt anyway, is attracted by the cheap glamour of the National Socialists and their promise of gaining writers access to the elemental forces of the world, and to Heynicke who drifts along or Schumann who races to enlist, to 'come home to the Reich':

> Da bückte ich mich tief zur Erde nieder
> Und segnete die fruchtbare und sprach:
> Verloren, dir entwurzelt, lag ich brach.
> Ich komme heim, o Mutter, nimm mich wieder.[29]

So I stooped low to the earth | And blessed the fertile soil and spoke: | Lost, uprooted from you, I lay fallow. | I am coming home, o mother, take me back.

These lines are Schumann's, though Heynicke has poems in his early, unarguably Expressionist, volumes which voice identical sentiments. These writers (except Becher) sought in National Socialism the foothold, the recognition, the sense of their own importance, the 'reality', the stability, the substance which they missed in their lives. Yeats's comment in April 1933 can be applied directly to contemporary German writers: 'There is so little in our stocking that we are ready at any moment to turn it inside out, and how can we not feel emulous when we see Hitler juggling with his sausage of stocking'.[30] There came a point when Expressionist fervour was seen to be no longer adequate, to issue into chaos and confusion. Goebbels's Expressionist hero Michael, for example, notes in his diary:

I am so sated with the ecstasies of alien fervour that I long to return to reality. Is it then not possible to feel an unappeasable heavenward longing and, at the same time, to stand with firm, solid bones on the stable enduring earth? (*Michael*, p. 83)

Turning from the inchoateness of Expressionism, Benn, for example, seeks discipline and form. 'Sated with the ecstasies of alien fervour', Michael craves for 'reality' and for a reconciliation between his 'unappeasable heavenward longing' and a return to 'stable enduring earth'. And Heynicke? His poetry is founded in longings no less intense than Michael's — Michael's 'Something is in preparation . . . a man will come' reads like a direct response to Heynicke's early plea 'O if only someone would come with an exultant torch | and bestow . . .'. For a short time in the 1930s, he 'came back to earth' by declaring himself for the new régime. The two plays which he wrote at the time represent an overt welcome of that regime, and all the poetry which he had written from 1917 onwards provides the heady pseudo-religious rhetoric which the National Socialists were quick to exploit. Such rhetoric is a characteristic Expressionist mode, and thus Heynicke's two 'Thing'-plays, borne along on urgent emotional imperatives and metaphysical vapouring, can be seen as a continuation of the kind of rhapsodic Expressionism practised particularly by Werfel, Rubiner, Hiller, and Heynicke himself. It is interesting to note that once the rhetorical effluvium has been enlisted in the service of National Socialism and indeed becomes public property, the common currency of the day, Heynicke does *not* emerge into a sense of community. Nor does he ever repudiate the two 'Thing'-plays. After his 1936 volume *Das Leben sagt Ja* he withdraws from the public/political arena and falls mute (except for some slight novels and plays). The feeling of isolation is reaffirmed. But by then, if only for a time, he has settled for the safety of a 'blessed prison' and has found what Nietzsche calls 'a narrow belief' to accommodate his homeless spirit:

In the end even a prison seems blessed to unsettled people like you. Have you ever seen imprisoned criminals sleeping? They sleep peacefully, they enjoy their new security. Take care that ultimately you are not imprisoned by a narrow belief, a hard, rigorous chimera! After all, you are now seduced and tempted by anything that is narrow and stable.[31]

It can perhaps be shown that, as with Bronnen, there is something inexorable about Heynicke's 'progress' from early Expressionist beginnings to his affirmation of 'a hard, rigorous chimera' and about the way the blurred goal of the Expressionist 'Aufbruch' stabilized, in his case, into 'a narrow belief'.

> The restless spirit sows longing into the heavens. ('Das Unerfüllte', 1925; HLW, II, 97)
> I wear the white silk of great longing around my aching body and my hands fumble gently at the doors. ('Das erste Weib', 1917; HLW, I, 14)
> I am floating in a sea of indefinable wishes and longings. (Goebbels, Michael, p. 16)

The central experience of Heynicke's life, as it is articulated in his poetry, and the source of his insecurity and overwhelming sense of isolation is that God is, at best, distant and, at worst, dead. Yet Heynicke, in common with other Expressionist poets, has no very coherent idea of what he means by God:

God was the undefined, the great mystery towards which feelings floated. God was something awe-inspiring . . . something dreadful which dissolved all courage. But God was also the cave where we could sneak away from father, the spectacle of Headmaster Förtsch reprimanding us. God would come as a gentle, mysterious voice and stand on the easel in the drawing-room at home, in a light green voluminous cloth. God was the friend [das Du] when we did not know whom to turn to and who should be addressed as a friend. (J. R. Becher, Abschied, p. 167)

Becher's description of God and his explanation of the way in which the Expressionist generation used the word are echoed in the work of Heynicke, who fills his volumes of verse with musty invocations of some being who, raised above the merely mortal and invested (by the poet) with superhuman powers and a mystical aura, is summoned simply because he intimates a kind of redemption and assuagement. The result is that what may begin as sincere religious belief in God degenerates into an overheated religiosity. Becher writes of 'the great mystery towards which feelings floated'. 'Swimming, floating feelings' aimed at some divine, distant figure — much of Heynicke's poetry, much Expressionist poetry, is full of such feelings and thus, ultimately, empty. Feeling becomes the ultimate sanction for belief, experience, action, work:

The more profoundly the poet experiences people and the universe, and the wider his spiritual horizon is, and the more he is emotion and the less he is rationality — then the more profound, the more compelling and urgent the effect of his work will be.[32]

God does not even have to exist: the ability to *feel* Him is enough:

For a long time I was of the opinion that it is not at all necessary for God to exist — it's only necessary for me to believe in Him. Today I think differently . . . if we want to be what we have to be, we must feel the God who does not exist.[33]

Sometimes, in Expressionist poetry, such feelings are distilled into sanguine predictions and anticipatory visions. Sometimes, as in the case of Heynicke's poetry, the feelings are allowed to scatter in all directions so that already fuzzy, intrinsically self-regarding invocations of God topple into portentous statements about some, any, distant benevolent being:

> The any-you
> is great and has such distant lips.
>
> (HLW, I, 49)

Of course, the search, however undirected and vague, for (a) God as succour and assuagement of loneliness is not the monopoly of Expressionism, but once again the historical context is crucial here, for the point hardly needs making that the National Socialists soon saw the profit in exploiting such free-floating religiousness. Their poetry relies heavily on the vocabulary and images of the Christian faith: Michael, for example, is writing a drama entitled *Jesus Christus, eine dramatische Phantasie* (*Michael*, p. 70), and Hitler's admiration for the ritual and the organizational strength of Roman Catholicism was such that he sought to model National Socialism upon it. Max Weber in 1918, fifteen years before the National Socialists seized power, detects a strong religiosity amongst certain Germans and, perhaps with particular representatives of the Expressionist movement in mind, writes of the links between a 'religiosity of redemption' on the one hand and 'political disappointments and detachment'[34] on the other. What *is* certain is that Heynicke's poetry affords an incontrovertible example of the religiousness/religiosity which Expressionism purveyed. Brinkmann in his recent survey of literature about Expressionism throws down a challenge which should, at least in part, be met by consideration of Heynicke's work: 'The whole problem of "Expressionism and National Socialism" has hitherto been inadequately worked up and documented'.[35]

Loneliness, homelessness, rootlessness — the motive forces behind the quest for 'the any-you', like the self-validating urgency and heavy religious undertones of the quest, do not change from one poem to the next, from one volume to the next, in Heynicke's œuvre. The first volume *Rings fallen Sterne* (1917) is full of such lines as 'I am the hour which rises in loneliness' (HLW, I, 52), 'I am the cloud and have no shore as my goal', 'And I blossom . . . above suns into isolation' (HLW, I, 54) so that the poems in the volume become a series of strategies for finding some kind of asylum and resting-place in a universe where God chooses to remain inaccessible and incomprehensible. 'Mädchen' is a characteristic example. Like the poems of Werfel, it is gross with the rhetoric of effort and expectation, as a feeling of desperate alienation distends into an ecstatic, tremulous invocation of an unnamed DU:

> Ich gehe alle spitzen Wege
> und friere nackt vor fremdem Blick
> Ich trage meine Fragen in den Wald
> und bebe unfassbar
> blutumquollen
> sinnverlassen
> fern in das DU.
>
> (HLW, I, 25)

I walk all the jagged paths | and freeze naked before an alien gaze. | I carry my questions into the forest | and tremble incomprehensibly | surrounded by gushing blood | abandoned by my senses | distantly into the You.

A miasma of intense longings hangs over the lines which amount to little more than an illustration of Michael's confessional 'there is an impelling force in me, a longing for new goals and achievements. Within me sufficient strength for other gifts is concentrated . . .' (*Michael*, p. 45). The intense longing is sustained by an implicit assurance that a reservoir of fervent untapped emotion is available, waiting for the right cause to exploit it:

> We are very young. And are still feverishly hungering for world.
> We shine gently. — But we could burn.
> We are always looking for wind to swell us into flames. [36]

The 'burn'/'ignite' image recurs frequently in Expressionist poetry and National Socialist writing: it is a particular favourite with Werfel and is echoed in Michael's indignant 'if you are not burning inside, how can you catch fire?' (*Michael*, p. 12), whilst the same idea inheres in Heynicke's injunction 'Resolve to blaze fiercely' ('Sieger des Lebens', 1925; HLW, II, 100). With Heynicke the reason for 'catching fire', the object of the quest, is occasionally allowed to assume definite contours and *does* change within a small range of variations. The nebulous DU of 'Mädchen' is in *Rings fallen Sterne* often some kind of deus absconditus whom the poet, by the ardour of his song, reveals and chants back into the world. Because God stays remote, the poet resorts to various ploys. He wrenches aside the curtains which conceal God, he raises himself to God's side to be God's equal, he re-creates God by giving Him a name, he renders God human and, therefore, accessible or makes man divine. When all these ploys fail, the DU becomes a woman or womankind, but women too remain estranged and fail to provide consolation or stability for the poet. They are summoned with the same sort of desperate fervour as in a typical Stramm poem — the lines quoted from 'Mädchen' contain many *Sturm* school linguistic conceits — or depicted as exciting sex-objects. In the same way as the object of Heynicke's search for a divine being remains a hovering, arcane presence, nothing substantial or permanent attaches to his relationships with the opposite sex. Passionateness, excitement, lust are worked up and do not appear to emanate from a deeply involved heart. Empirical reality is hardly registered. Relationships, personal and religious commitments are proclaimed, undefined anxieties hover in the air, nostalgic cravings modulate into passionate outbursts, and the poet's predisposition for the cosmic ousts all concern for the details of everyday living, the minutiae of a particular landscape or the attributes of a carefully drawn individual. *Rings fallen Sterne* is awash with otiose abstractions or with beings merely summoned into existence. A war-poem such as 'Ferne Granate' is the nearest Heynicke comes to taking issue with a concrete, 'realistic' event, but such poems are rare and so derivative that they read like a more or less efficient parody of Stramm. Invariably Heynicke's verse is sustained by a hectic and mystical narcissism: as with all Expressionist poetry, the 'Ich', invested with an incantatory, heady quality and vast authority, must be taken as the artist. Heynicke favours a kind of vatic poetry where the poet is the point on which we focus, not himself focal on to a significant, common, recognizable world. There is also a trailing edge of Romanticism and 'Jugendstil', a loose hem of melodramatic sentimentality and whimsy of the sort to be found in some of Werfel's more rhapsodic verse, but *not* in Stramm. And, all the time, the urgent, usually aimless, quest goes on: a cycle which begins with a despairing appeal to 'you stars in the nights' closes with the poet's resolve 'to go with pure step into the infinite'.

The key-word of *Gottes Geigen* (1918) is 'fern' (distant). Likely assistance (from God, from the loved one, from an undefined 'Du') eludes the poet's grasp and withdraws into the distance, where it beckons alluringly to him. Heynicke's poetry is heavy with the attraction of a distant, indistinct goal:

> unten wir Welle im blaudunklen Spiel,
> ewig ist Ziel,
> ewig die leuchtende Ferne!
>
> (HLW, I, 98)

Below we are waves in the blue-dark game, | eternal is the goal, | eternal the gleaming distance.

God collapses, dead. Even 'death is dead' (HLW, I, 103). The poet's soul flutters over everything, seeking a way to God, yet disillusionment is total. Returning from the war, he watches his dreams founder. Even though we issue from God, we are tiny, our lives amount to nothing, for a thousand years is 'but a moment in the circle of the world' (HLW, I, 113). And then, after all, there is death, warmly welcomed and welcoming. He seeks refuge in a mother figure, Mary Magdalene is invoked in one poem ('Nonne'), and, in another, after the fashion of Gottfried Benn, he calls upon mysterious, irrational, chthonic forces to bear him away:

> Strom, der dunkel im Tiefen rauscht,
> trage mich hin.
> Trage mich meerzu der Unendlichkeit,
> Flußentgegen der seligen Quelle.
>
> (HLW, I, 100)

River which rushes darkly in the depths, | bear me along. | Bear me to the sea of eternity, | Towards the river of the blessed spring.

In *Gottes Geigen*, as in all his other volumes, Heynicke has an instinct for memorable lines, but they tend to come singly or, at most, in pairs, driven like plugs into layers of uneven material and muzzy incantations. God passes through the accustomed gamut of being a serenely superior spirit with an interest in man, then becoming a distant, indifferent deity, and finally evolving into a wholly immanent brother to man. The cycle ends on a note of defiance. The poet claims kinship, even equality, with the cosmos, with God, and demonstrates the kind of anthropocentric arrogance to which Werfel refers when he writes of the 'consuming, impudent, disdainful, diabolical arrogance . . . of avant-garde artists and radical intellectuals bursting with the vain passion to be profound and obscure and difficult (quoted above on p. 15).

Das namenlose Angesicht (1919) offers much familiar material. The poet still leads a harassed life, is still looking for someone to assuage his restless soul, but he is condemned to wander endlessly. At the beginning of the volume the poet seeks to place his faith in Man and the community of men. The influence of Werfel's *Der Weltfreund*, *Wir sind* and *Einander* is starkly obvious in such lines as:

> Ich will fließen, ewiger Bruder im Licht,
> in Unendlichkeit, Sternennebel und Allmacht
>   der Dinge,
> zermilliont mich senken in die hungernden
>   Herzen der Geschöpfe der Welt,
> ich selber will sein du und das Licht,
> hinsterben in die unendlichen Arme der Liebe!

(HLW, I, 138)

I want to flow, eternal brother in the light, | into infinity, star-lit mist and the omnipotence of things, | plunge myself, a million fragments, into the hungry hearts of the creatures of the world, | I myself want to be you and the light, | want to die away into the infinite arms of love!

Enormous hope is invested in Man, a great master-plan for the whole of mankind is confidently projected, the poet for a time feels all-powerful. Then confidence lapses, and old favourites reappear: an earnestly summoned DU, an elusive God, the madonna, the Virgin Mary, a mother figure, death, women, nothingness. The poet momentarily swears by the power of autonomy of his own ego as a bastion against loneliness, and in 'Aufforderung' he recommends a retreat to inwardness. But reference is repeatedly made to altogether more sinister saviours:

> Mein Volk,
> blüh ewig, Volk
> Einst wird kein Tag mehr deinen Traum
> zerschlagen . . .
> Mein Volk,
> einst werden alle Dinge knien
> vor dir.

(HLW, I, 120–21)

My people, | Flourish for ever, people | There will come a time when your dream is no longer smashed . . . | My people, | one day all things will kneel | before you.

Whilst this kind of poem isolates Heynicke within the Expressionist movement, it serves to forge a link between his early poetry and the 'Thing'-plays of the 1930s. It also makes a connection which Goebbels's Michael is determined to establish and retain — the connection between 'the people' and 'religion':

A people without religion, that is just like a human being without breath . . . perhaps our age is not mature yet? One is almost inclined to believe it. One day, in religious matters too, we will experience a glorious awakening. Until then let everyone seek his God in his own way. But the broad masses should even be left with their idols until they can be given a new God. (*Michael*, p. 145)

It is not a vast logical step from growing dissatisfied with 'feeling a God who does not exist' to creating a new god for oneself and giving him to the masses — a German god, perhaps? In a lengthy discourse on 'German Religiosity' Paul Ernst, writing in 1915, ventures that step,[37] and on the way employs terms which were shortly to assume grisly connotations. Could it be possible, he wonders, for mankind to find a purely spiritual religion which has no need of a body, of form, and would consist only of feeling? Then, turning his attention to Germany in particular, he appears to reject this incorporeal religion which has no historical and dogmatic expression and toys with the idea of 'the revelation of the German god' (Volkmann, p. 154). This mixture of abstract historicizing, vague but intense prediction and pious mystification formed an essential part of the currency of debate amongst German intellectuals during and immediately after the First World War.

An abiding feature of Heynicke's verse has always been its dense religiousness, but it is not until *Das namenlose Angesicht* that the 'Volk' is invoked (though there have been one or two unobtrusive references to 'Heimat' in earlier volumes). Now in *Das namenlose Angesicht* Ernst's hypothesis of a wholly 'unphysical', 'incorporeal' religion materializes into a paean to the 'Volk', couched in ecstatic, reverential, pseudo-religious terms. In identical vein, the poem 'Aufbruch' contains the lines 'And o my flourishing motherland, | clasp all my soul's roots!'[38] which Heynicke omits when he comes to reprint the poem in 1973. Moreover, it is the poet who plays a crucial role as leader, seer, and paragon:

> Fanfarengleich im Sturz der Zeit
> die Völker rufend zu heroischem Alarm
> einstürmt der Dichter in der Kämpfer Schwarm
> des Schicksals Wandlung kündend zu bereiten.
> ('Der Dichter: Prolog zu einer Schiller-Feier', 1936; HLW, II, 174)

Like a fanfare in the collapsing times | summoning the peoples to heroic alert | the poet charges in amidst the host of warriors | to herald and prepare destiny's transformation.

Elsewhere in this volume there is frequent reference to 'a dark god', to blood and 'bloodstream' in terms which are strongly reminiscent of Gottfried Benn's early Expressionist volumes and of the kind of poetry which Benn wrote in the 1920s. Heynicke's continual invocation of the stars in *Das namenlose Angesicht*, especially when God is seen to fail, prefigures a similar invocation in Benn's 1927 poem 'Sieh die Sterne, die Fänge . . .', in the second stanza of which the poet writes of the vacuum caused by the desuetude of old 'myths and words' and by the irretrievable loss of the splendour and glory of the gods. By 1927 Benn too has reached a state of inner emptiness and rejects many of the potential sources of consolation, many of the resting-places, to which Heynicke has constantly resorted in his poetry: this underlines once again how comparisons between Heynicke and Benn — in terms of their relationship with Expressionism, their fundamental prepossessions and convictions, their characteristic themes and styles, their suggested solutions to feelings of deep personal inadequacy and isolation, and, in the 1930s, actual political allegiance — could be pursued a good deal further than the scope of this chapter allows.

Little of this changes by the time Heynicke writes *Die hohe Ebene* (1921, 1925) and *Traum im Diesseits* (1932). He is still 'a restless guest', a nomad sentenced to loneliness. Sometimes man is worse off than that, sometimes man is nothing at all, nothing, that is, except for his soul which Heynicke is almost always intent on keeping free from blemish. And to alleviate man's desperate plight? God, a girl, 'du', death, love, a return to childhood, and once again the 'Volk':

> We were scattered leaves in autumn,
> People!
> We are now spring and steaming soil,
> People!
> Even if the plough rips our heart,
> we sing a song called sun . . .
>
> ('Sturmgesang', 1920; HLW, II, 46–47)

and on like that for almost forty lines with 'Volk' intoned ten times. The reference to 'Scholle' ('soil', 'clod') and 'Pflug' ('plough') in these lines is not an isolated one: more than once the healthy countryman is contrasted favourably with the sinful city dweller. The presence of Gottfried Benn again looms large: references to sexual lust, to 'primal blood', to the 'song of the primordial deity', to the primitive, to strange dark Eastern gods, all are reminiscent of themes popular with Benn. The hallucinatory mysticism of the previous volumes is now accompanied by a powerful vitalist impulse. Unquestioning assent is given to feelings, as long as they issue from the soul and as long as they are intense. Homage is paid to passion, to passionate acts of whatever kind. Adventure, excitement, action, a grand finale are coveted:

> Ich wünsche,
> daß mein Leben wild endigte
> und nicht faul im Schlafbett,
> daß ich im Wirbel wirbelte mit . . .
>
> ('Spruch', 1925; HLW, II, 101)

I want | my life to end wildly | and not sluggishly as I sleep in bed, | I want to be swept along in the swirl.

The 'I' of these lines, as so often in Expressionist poetry, is to be taken as the 'I' of the poet, and the sentiments expressed are very familiar to us from, for example, Werfel's *Gerichtstag* volume. Such sentiments make of Heynicke a paradigmatic Expressionist poet and link him directly with many of the other Expressionist poets

— such as Heym and Stadler — *and* with those who saw National Socialism as a potential source of invigorating deeds after the inertia of the Wilhelminian era and the Weimar Republic. Response to that inertia is couched in characteristically Expressionist language. Dissatisfaction swells into gross over-reaction:

> Reiße die Tore aller Dinge entzwei!
> Peitsch dich empor,
> reiße dich los,
> O uferlos jauchze dem Unendlichen zu.
>
> ('Nein', 1921; HLW, II, 17)

Rip the gates of all things in two! | Lash yourself upwards, | Tear yourself away, | O boundlessly exult as you move towards the infinite.

There is no chance of immediate salvation though the possibility of redemption is not denied and 'the perfect one' certainly exists:

> Nur der Vollendete leuchtet den Weg in dir,
> immer mußt du ihn kreisend beschreiten,
> bis dich Nirwana erlöst.
>
> ('Tempel des Buddha in Osaka', 1921; HLW, II, 34)

Only the perfect one illuminates the path in you, | circling you must always tread that path, | until Nirvana redeems you.

Heynicke's 1936 volume *Das Leben sagt Ja* is more subdued and more rigorously formed. It is about love and the seasons and God and war and growing old, but it is also about loneliness, aimlessness, restlessness and chances missed. There is one poem, 'Hymnus des Schicksals', where Heynicke appears to be commenting upon his own allegiance to a chimera which ends by letting him down. In this poem, which perhaps refers directly to political events, Heynicke burdens fate with the responsibility for *his* succumbing to temptation. This 'flight to a shadow' ('. . . die Flucht, | einem Schatten zu . . .' HLW, II, 165) has proved futile, and so he tries other ways of escaping from loneliness — love, a yielding to a vitalist creed predictable from the title of the volume, an appeal to the brotherhood of Man, a joyful surrender to fate and to whatever fate brings, a nostalgic invocation of his 'Fronterlebnis' and of the 'heroism of that time', and also a welcoming of severity and grief for their own sakes as a possible means of finding salvation. Even though the tone of the cycle is more muted than Heynicke's other volumes, many familiar features survive into it — the air of foetid expectancy, the central experience of living in a godless universe, the vague and directionless longing:

> Immer schwingt sich die Sehnsucht empor,
> still im blauen Raum
> wartet ihr Flug
> und ahnt nicht
> wohin.
>
> ('Oben und unten', 1936; HLW, II, 149)

Longing always soars upwards, | silent in blue space | its flight waits | and does not suspect | where it is going to.

Indeed some poems are thoroughly Expressionist in theme, form, and inspiration —
the best example is 'Wilde Werbung', a kind of litany of outrage, instinct with
Expressionist hubris where the poet's 'I' is both self-obsessed and solitary, where
any thought has to break clear of the scrum of vertiginous incantation and boisterous
verbiage which comes milling into every line, with the result that we are left with
poetry of hysterical and random gesture, fused not very successfully by the poet's
gabbling voice. The range of such a poem, for all its grandiose claims and references,
is narrow because the voice seldom modulates out of a hectic staccato. *Das Leben sagt
Ja* continues the traditional pattern in Heynicke's verse: on some occasions the poet
settles for various makeshifts, on other occasions (as in 'Wilde Werbung') he merely
voices his indignation and grief at not having and not finding love, a home,
consolation. Nietzsche has described this kind of insubstantial homesickness which
feeds upon itself:

Homesickness, not for a home, not for a family-house and a fatherland, for I had none of
these things: but the sickness, the pain caused by not having a home.[39]

> We are waiting for someone who will interpret
> our fate anew for us.[40]
>
> Here I sat, waiting, waiting — yet for nothing,
> beyond Good and Evil,. . .
> When suddenly, friend, one became two —
> And Zarathustra walked past me.[41]

Yet, for a time in 1933 and 1934, between the publications of *Traum im Diesseits*
and *Das Leben sagt Ja*, Heynicke does seem to have found a home, a fatherland, and
Ernst's hypothesis of a German God is realized. Sokel relates that his comments (in
The Writer in Extremis) about Heynicke's 'Nazi past' drew an indignant reaction
from the poet:

The Nazi affiliation of Heynicke had been reported to me by Kurt Pinthus. When I
included this information in *The Writer in Extremis*, Herr Heynicke protested to my
publisher that he had never been affiliated with the Nazis and that they had actually
ignored his fiftieth birthday . . . On further research, I found that Heynicke was the
author of two so-called 'Thing'-plays[42] in 1933 and 1934. The plays seem to be close to
the then prevailing ideology, but cannot be classified as out-and-out Nazi products . . .[43]

They *are* 'close to the then prevailing ideology', they *can* be 'classified as out-and-out
Nazi products'. Heynicke's name is included in an inventory of party-hacks drawn
up by Rudolf Erckmann, a reviewer and supervisor in the ministry which Goebbels
instituted to deal with literary questions and writers, as proof that 'a young poetry'
was guaranteed for the new Nazi state.[44] An official Nazi theatre critic maintains
that in *Der Weg ins Reich* (1934) Heynicke has toed the party line with such
consummate skill that 'the new Reich is no longer the yearned-for goal, but a real
fact'.[45] The approval of at least part of the Nazi administration, praise from the Nazi
press, the evidence provided by the plays themselves — all this has convinced

literary commentators and historians[46] that Heynicke should be placed directly in the National Socialist camp. Heynicke's *Neurode* (1933) and *Der Weg ins Reich*, which the authors of a wide-ranging book on German literature in the Third Reich[47] equate with Lersch's paean to the party, *Volk im Werden*, and Zerkaulen's sycophantic *Der Arbeit die Ehr'*, provide a classic example of the usurpation of the political sphere by criteria of an intensely personal, metapolitical nature and also of the obliteration of the whole area of public discourse and moderate rational values — the gap which arises is filled with giddy chanting and incantations to some mythic power.

Neurode and *Der Weg ins Reich* are of interest to us here only because they provide convincing evidence of Heynicke's (temporary at least) commitment to the National Socialist party and because, as literary artefacts, they can be used as sources of helpful comparison with the themes, the style, and the voice of the poetry which preceded them. In which ways, by virtue of which qualities can the poetry be said to prefigure Heynicke's commitment to the party as demonstrated in the two 'Thing'-plays? Heynicke, like the National Socialists (and the Expressionists), begins from the premise that a vast part of inherited culture is bankrupt. Something new must be created, prepared for, willed into existence in this 'age of the fled gods and the coming god'.[48] He fills his poetry, and his plays, with a vibrant air of anxious expectancy and earnest questing which is sustained by the firm conviction that he, the poet, is invested with huge messianic powers — powers which the National Socialist leadership does not for a moment deny him and which it is concerned to retain for him in the knowledge that it will be able to capitalize upon them for its own ends: Goebbels, opening the 'Reichskulturkammer' on 15 November 1933, is at pains to describe all 'culture-creating people' as 'trail-blazers, formgivers and shapers of a new century'. As late as 1941 Johst, who began his literary career as an Expressionist dramatist, appeals directly to the German poets:

With his soldiers the Führer creates the Reich . . . with his master-builders he controls the space which has been won — and with you poets, with the power of your words, he is resolved to go into history.[49]

Johst, as a matter of course, not only engages literature in the service of the National Socialist régime, but charges it with the most important (yet vague) task. More than twenty years before, when Expressionism was still flourishing, Rathenau's address *An Deutschlands Jugend* demonstrates the way in which literature and politics tightly interlocked during the immediate aftermath of the First World War — the same values obtain, the same misty visions are conjured up, the same longings and hopes are expressed in the same theatrical and vertiginously expectant voice with the result that literature and politics become indissolubly scrambled, and the idea of an heroic leap into the unknown becomes a familiar thought in both the politics and the literature of the day:

There is always someone — Lohengrin, Walther, Siegfried, Wotan — who can do everything and knock everything down, who can release suffering virtue, punish vice and bring general salvation, striking an exaggerated pose, with the sound of trumpets, and lighting and scenic effects. A reflection of this operatic manner could be seen in politics . . . People wanted the word of salvation to be spoken on every occasion with a great gesture, people wanted to see historical turning points presented before them, they wanted to hear the clash of swords and the flapping of banners.[50]

Heynicke's two 'Thing'-plays can be seen as a direct response to the kind of intense craving which, according to Rathenau, was a general phenomenon in German politics of the day — a direct *literary* response which fed, and was intended to feed, into German political life. The heady afflatus of Radke's speeches as he strives to enthuse the mining population, the way in which his earnest prayers are answered by the superhuman intervention of the diaphanous figure 'der Fremde', the soulful harangues of the chorus-leader whipping up his acolytes (in *Neurode*), the densely religiose and mystical tones of 'der Heimkehrer's' conversations with 'die Opfernde' as he tries to persuade her to surrender her land to the community (in *Der Weg ins Reich*) — all this has been anticipated and partially rehearsed in Heynicke's poetry. Indeed the plays offer temporary solutions to the endless, and endlessly unsuccessful, quests of the poetry in which heroic deeds and ultimate redemption are anxiously awaited:

> Ich warte mit euch [people], daß die Taten sausen,
> die Taten,
> die uns herrlich aufwärts brausen
> in den Raum der Welt,
> daß wir aufgelöst erlöst uns
> in den Herrlichkeiten fänden!
>
> ('Gedicht', 1921; HLW, II, 44)

I am waiting with you people for the deeds to resound, | deeds | which will hurtle us gloriously | into the space of the world, | I am waiting for us to find ourselves, dispersed, redeemed in glories.

If the plays and the poetry have this general voice and atmosphere in common, they also share a multitude of more detailed similarities which link Heynicke with National Socialism: a stress on the instinctual and organic which in Heynicke's verse is encapsulated in the verb 'blühen';[51] an invocation of the power of the blood which the National Socialists were quick to 'use' for its racial connotations and as a symbol for life; an undiscriminating admiration for and praise of 'das Volk' expressed in such injunctions as, 'Take thought, people! | Blossom and be! | Redeem yourself! | Then it will be May' (1921; HLW, II, 47) — an admiration which Heynicke shared with another member of the *Sturm* school, Lothar Schreyer, and which made a nonsense of Benn's assertion that Expressionism did not assume 'an historically national mission' ('Expressionismus'; p. 252); an uncritical attachment to the countryside, with the result that 'Scholle' like 'blühen' and 'Volk' and 'Seele', comes to be invested with cabbalistic force in his poetry; a fondness for big words which, freighted with mysterious authority, become magic runes and foreclose all chance of rational restraint. And all this, in poetry and plays and prose, is embedded in a language of high-tension enthusiasm, in a kind of 'poetry of violence', which, recruited to serve some mystical power, cajoles the reader or spectator into accepting uncritically all its premises and into relying totally upon an emotional response. Expressionism, like National Socialism, was above all 'a revolution of attitude'.[52] There are poems by Heynicke and by many other Expressionist poets where the reader is swept along on eddies of delirious, uplifting fervour of the kind which pervades Radke's and 'der Heimkehrer's' words *and* the speeches of the National Socialist leaders. Individual details of Heynicke's kinship with National Socialism — 'Blut', 'Volk', the organic, love of the countryside — are not shared by other Expressionist writers (except Benn, Johst and Bronnen), but the general miasma of frenetic volatility and free-floating enthusiasm, the grandiose claims in *all* spheres of public and private life, the violent switchback of emotions, the scornful repudiation of all rationality, the arrogation of vast moral, spiritual, and practical powers, the authority recklessly vested in the poet's word — all this links Heynicke's poetry with Expressionism *and* National Socialism. Poetry, of its nature, demands participation and response, from the clandestine physical echo in muscle and nerve that identifies us with the medium, to the imaginative enactment that stirs the deepest recesses where life and values reside. Few movements have insisted as fiercely as Expressionism on the submission of the reader or spectator to the work: it is not fortuitous that Werfel's 'Wolle mir, bitte, nicht widerstehn!'[53] became one of the movement's slogans. The Expressionist poet feels emboldened and entitled to demand such submission and in return, priding himself on the purity of his motives, he offers to assume the burden of the world (no less!) in a spirit of strenuous self-sacrifice:

> Aus tiefster Reinheit brennen meine Ziele:
> Ich will die Welt auf meine Schultern nehmen
> Und sie mit Lobgesang zur Sonne tragen.[54]

With deepest purity burn my goals: | I shall take the world upon my shoulders | And carry it with songs of praise to the sun.

Similarities with the terminology and the moral or emotional imperatives of National Socialism, which capitalized on the expectations raised and on the enthusiasms fomented by Expressionism and which was itself not so much a political party rallying round a set of political principles as an association of zealots who made demands on the whole man, need no elaboration here. Understanding that the behaviour of human beings and their responses are not motivated exclusively by economic forces and factors, Hitler soon saw the profit in vaulting beyond political problems and social distress and in offering suprapersonal goals, grandiose principles, urgent imperatives and the promise of great adventure at high odds.

Heynicke's work mediates directly between a literary movement which sought to trespass upon political life and a political movement which depended for much of its support on extra-political sources. The 1919 poem 'Erhebe die Hände' not only illustrates many of the characteristic themes and linguistic ploys of Heynicke's work, but also expresses, and at the same time fosters, the kind of 'nameless longing', the 'dreams which sway between heaven and earth'[55] so often purveyed by Expressionist writers.

The true German remains throughout his life a
God-seeker. (*Michael*, p. 32)

1 Erhebe die Hände,
2 Angesicht,
3 urnamenlos
4 über mein Haupt,
5 das feucht ist von Wein und Lachen!
6 Ich stürze in blitzende Stunden,
7 reiße mein Blut hoch in blühende Frauen,
8 und wiege dahin in singende Geigen —
9 siehe —
10 es neigen sich alle Stunden,
11 ich könnte jung sein,
12 und mein Herz ein Sommer —
13 aber tief in mir schluchzt ein Gedanke —
14 fern
15 verhaltenes Weinen steigt dunkelher
16 und umarmt meine Jugend . . .
17 Dies ist ewig:
18 Das Nein.
19 Hätte ich alle Lust,
20 fremd höben sich meine Schultern,
21 meine Lippe wäre Verachtung:
22 Ich bin ein Wanderer
23 und darf nicht verweilen.[56]

Raise your hands, | Face, | nameless from all eternity | over my head | which is moist with wine and laughing! | I plunge into glittering hours, | send my blood soaring into voluptuous women, | and sway thither to singing violins — | look — | all hours incline, | I could be young, | and my heart a summer — | but deep inside me sobs a thought — | distant | suppressed weeping rises from the dark | and embraces my youth . . . | This is eternal: | The No. | If I had all I desired, | my shoulders would hunch with indifference, | my lip would be contempt: | I am a wanderer | and may not linger.

The poem begins with an injunction to God to raise His hands above the poet's head.[57] God is not named, because He has no name, He never has had a name, He is 'urnamenlos', has been without a name from all eternity — at the end of the poem, God's anonymity will be the cause of the poet's assumption of brash independence, the cause of his frustration at being unable to summon by name somebody who is nameless. The poet has experimented with various makeshifts: in line 5 he tells how he has enjoyed himself with wine. God, the nameless one, seems not to be necessary to him and to his enjoyment. Yet 'Wein und Lachen' can be construed as a typical *Sturm*-school conceit and read as 'Wein-en' (crying), thus casting doubt on the poet's bravado in seeking to dispense with God. Perhaps, after all, he has not been revelling, but mourning. The fact that the poem begins with an invocation, an urgent call, shows what is important to the poet, even if he cannot name or find the God invoked. The revelry, the wine and the laughter, have been inadequate compensation for an absent God.

In line 6 the bravado persists, the feigned distractions are enumerated. The poet plunges into various excitements: the oblique assonants of 'stürze' and 'blitzende' somehow underline the gaudy, meretricious quality of the thrills which he pursues. Once again a kind of magic aura surrounds 'Blut' and 'blühen' (7). In line 8 the poet surrenders to the sensuous pleasure of music as a possible escape from the awful truth which is just about to press itself once more upon him. The verbs 'stürzen' and 'reißen' are wholly characteristic of Expressionist language and resound with the poet's sense of his own importance, his restless arrogance, his masterfulness and braggadocio. The dynamism and enthusiasm with which he has sought out his distractions are demonstrated in the emphatic use of the accusative case with the preposition 'in' (lines 6 and 7). In line 8 he lapses into grammatical incongruity and vagueness. What part does 'dahin' play in that sentence apart from serving to underline the feverish pursuit of sensuous pleasures? What does it mean? That the poet 'got to' his flashy pastimes (6), to his women (7), got 'thither', that is to that pitch of physical delight, to the luscious music of 'singing violins'?

'Siehe', picking up the sound in 'wiege', brings the rhapsody, which is threatening to take over the poem, to a sudden stop. A cooler appraisal starts. With 'siehe' the poet addresses God, himself and anyone else willing to listen. Things appear to be going well, time is on his side, optimism speaks out of line 10, there is sympathy and affection for the poet there, obedience and tractability are implied in the verb 'sich neigen'. He 'could be young', his heart full of joy, and yet . . . the word 'aber' brusquely interrupts his reverie, his playing with possibilities, and indicates that the masquerade is over. All the distractions, all the pleasures and joys which his youth might bring him are nothing against one thought which 'sobs' inside him. The verb 'schluchzt' (which, like 'verhaltenes Weinen', has a strong Rilkean resonance), poised in the middle of a line and in the middle of the poem, sounds and looks weighty: it *is* a dead weight after the enumeration of the superficial pleasures to which he has been abandoning himself. 'Fern', marooned as it is, attracts all our attention — God's distance from the poet is the theme of this poem and, indeed, of much of Heynicke's poetry. 'Verhalten' is an actional verb: his weeping, suppressed, wells up from deep within his consciousness. Heynicke's use of assonance here, once again in line with the *Sturm*-school canon, is noteworthy: in 'W*ei*nen st*ei*gt' and in the way the '-her' of 'dunkel*her*' parallels '*fern* v*er*haltenes'. The weeping 'embraces the poet's youth' — in a deadly gesture — for that weeping, provoked by the awful awareness of God's distance, is, *unlike* his youth and unlike the pleasures of youth, eternal. It is eternal because God's 'No!' is eternal — God will never reveal Himself to man, never respond to man's appeals. Sometimes in the course of *Das namenlose Angesicht*, the volume from which the poem 'Erhebe die Hände' comes, the poet approaches God and seeks asylum for his restless soul ('I want to kneel my restlessness before you'; HLW, I, 146): fleetingly he is assured of a sympathetic welcome ('Perhaps God will soon smile a sunrise | and, full of compassion, fold His infinite hands'; HLW, I, 161), but invariably he is met with a cavernous silence or a reverberating No! Questions about the meaning of life, the existence of God persist in obsessing him, but God is dead: He is lying out there on a First World War battlefield 'stabbed to death in the roaring No! of the cannons' (HLW, I, 189). And the poet senses that his belief in God is crumbling:

Meiner Jugend Traum:
Weib.
Meiner Sehnsucht Erfüllung:
Nichts!
Der Glaube fällt.

(HLW, I, 180)

My youth's dream: | Woman. | My longing's fulfilment: | Nothing! | Belief falls.

It is a feature of Heynicke's poetry that the longings expressed in it stubbornly come to nothing and that his questions go unanswered. In 'Erhebe die Hände' God's eternal No!, stranded like 'fern' before it, implodes with a sense of that isolation and vulnerability which are the central experiences of so many of the Expressionist generation, beginning with Benn's Rönne and continuing even into Heynicke's 1969 volume *Alle Finsternisse sind schlafendes Licht*. 'This is eternal: | The No' somehow encapsulates all the shattered dreams, the bankruptcy of the high hopes, the feelings of annihilating loneliness and despair of those who came back from the slaughter of the First World War, for, while there is no explicit reference to the events of that war in 'Erhebe die Hände', other poems in *Das namenlose Angesicht* establish clearly a connection between the poet's present state of mind and his experiences at the front. Moreover, a powerful strain of pessimism, almost of nihilism, runs through Heynicke's work: the 1921 poem 'Nein' begins with the blank, ineluctable assertion: 'Always there remains the eternal: | No' (HLW, II, 17).

In the last five lines, the poet attempts to achieve a kind of self-sufficiency and independence. Echoing I Corinthians 13 ('And though I have . . . all knowledge; and though I have all faith . . .'), he declares that, if he had all the pleasures in the world, he would shrug his shoulders indifferently, would curl his lip because, without God's presence, those pleasures would be nothing. In any case, he has no time for such indulgences. Picking up his constant theme of life seen as perpetual nomadism, he ends on a self-dramatizing, curiously vacuous note. He cannot linger. The belief that life is in a constant state of flux, the horror of anything fixed or finished, once again links Heynicke's work with Goebbels's *Michael* and, via that, with National Socialism and one of its mottoes rehearsed by Hitler in *Mein Kampf*: 'He who rests rusts'.[58] The quotation at the head of this section continues 'Pathetic the man who is complete', for a characteristic feature of Goebbels's diary-cum-novel is the hero's urge always to press on, to probe further, to experiment, to make a virtue of instability and incompleteness. The last couplet of 'Erhebe die Hände' is more than an expression of Romantic restlessness or superior unconcern and self-sufficiency. Nor is it just an example of the favourite Expressionist device of ending a poem in a state of unresolved tension. For Heynicke (as for Goebbels's Michael[59]) the compulsion *not* to come to rest is irresistible, the aimlessness of the 'pilgrimage' is its validation.

Contrast this with the devout poetry of an indisputably great religious writer like John Donne where an altogether different feeling and quality come through, for his work, reflecting the collision in a sensitive mind of the old traditions and the new learning, reads like the dialectical expression of a personal drama, devoid of anything rarefied or abstract, and yet rendering justice to the perfection and omnipotence of God. Or one thinks of the religious poems of John Whittier: for him, the search for God is no less anguished, protracted and arduous than in Heynicke's work:

> Have I not voyaged, friend beloved, with thee
> On the great waters of the unsounded sea,
> . . . ?
> Thou knowest how vain our quest; how, soon or late,
> The baffling tides and circles of debate
> Swept back our bark unto its starting-place,
> Where, looking forth upon the blank, grey space,
> And round about us seeing, with sad eyes,
> The same old difficult hills and cloud-cold skies,
> We said: 'This outward search availeth not
> To find Him.'[60]

But where Heynicke and Werfel and other Expressionist poets offer passionateness and religiosity, Donne and Whittier give the clear-sighted passion of the true believer; where Heynicke and the others, uncertain of themselves and their beliefs, fill 'the blank, grey space' left by an absent or undiscovered God with clamorous voices in the air, Donne and Whittier, drawing on powerful inner resources, vault the abyss 'in full assurance of the good' (Whittier, p. 466) which, they know, emanates not from a god created by human agency, but from God revealed in man, from the Redeemer whose magnanimity and love and grandeur are incontestable:

> We have set
> A strange god up, but Thou remainest yet.
> All that I feel of pity Thou has known
>
> Before I was; my best is all Thy own.
> From Thy great heart of goodness mine but drew
> Wishes and prayers . . .   (Whittier, p. 440)

Certain of God and of their faith in Him, Donne and Whittier allow that there is much beyond their comprehension and their reach and ultimately are happy to let it be so. Heynicke and other Expressionist poets pester and harangue God and will not be deterred:

> Seine Rätsel hausen in mir
> und ich jage sein Dunkel
> mit meinem Warum.
> . . .
> Ich bin sein Bumerang,
> er wirft mich
> und ich kehre zurück in seine Hand.
>   (HLW, III, 88)

His mysteries dwell within me | and I harry his darkness | with my why . . . I am his boomerang, | he throws me | and I return to his hand.

Implicit in their work is the feeling that, persistently confronted by miscarried beliefs, by the shortcomings of their own believing, they might in their despair settle for something else, anything else.

We come away from 'Erhebe die Hände' with the conviction that very little actually gets said. Heynicke all the time seems to be circling his material, he displays intricate footwork (in rhythm and the stresses and the manifold acoustic devices), but does not draw blood. God has no real presence in the poem: he inhabits it like some remote menacing ogre, rather as the family name inhabits the stately home, vapid and awesome behind the furniture. The interest shifts from the real (that is, poet invoking God, God remaining distant), to the apparent subject (that is, the poet's lonely lot on earth), from the clarification of a complex experience to the rehearsal of a simplified and very familiar one: the real subject has been lost in the general retreat to a perennial theme, and the poem expires on a note of Romantic kitsch. The being addressed remains wholly indeterminate, Heynicke's beliefs are only marginally involved, and what claims to be a sincere religious belief in God evaporates in amorphous conjurations. The poem is not, therefore, a religious poem in any respectable sense of the phrase, but it *is* a poem about a religious, or rather religiose, 'Stimmung'. The void left by God's silence or, indeed, by His eternal No! is filled with overheated longings and self-regarding rodomontade, so that the whole exercise is ultimately insubstantial, 'ein Beben nach Gott und Ruhe hin' ('a tremulous longing for God and calm'; HLW, II, 142), where the word 'God' means as much, and as little, as Becher's definition of it indicated. The slightness of the poem is further accentuated by the form in which it is cast. The monologue is an artificial, rhetorical mode. In his essay on Milton, Eliot remarks that 'a disadvantage of the rhetorical style appears to be that a dislocation takes place, through the hypertrophy of the auditory imagination at the expense of the visual and tactile, so that the inner meaning is separated from the surface, and tends to become something occult'.[61] In Heynicke's poetry and in Expressionist poetry generally very little is supplied to 'the visual and tactile imagination', and the poet, though perhaps not so much in 'Erhebe die Hände' as in other poems, is overly interested in melliflous sounds at the expense of meaning. The trouble is that, even when one has got past 'the surface', there is little 'inner meaning' to be garnered, and that, too, is true of a vast amount of Expressionist poetry.

It is certainly possible to argue (as Samuel Johnson does in connection with the poetry of Edmund Waller) that 'poetical creation cannot often please',[62] that because 'Omnipotence cannot be exalted, Infinity cannot be amplified . . . Perfection cannot be improved', poetry 'loses its lustre and its power when it is applied to the decoration of something more excellent than itself'.[63] The danger confronting the religious poet is clear: in his endeavour to describe God, to express his faith, his thanksgiving, his supplication, he may well allow his poetry to erupt and evaporate into emotions about emotions, into intense protestations of love and allegiance, profound feelings of adoration with nowhere to go, and in the process neither the object of the love *nor* the divine, magical qualities which inspire and justify such love and allegiance emerge from the welter of perfervid emotions. Donne and Whittier are examples of poets who circumvent that danger, demonstrating how, *pace*

Johnson, pious verse can do more than 'help the memory and delight the ear'. The Expressionist poets on the other hand, writing at a time when there was a felt need for new goals and new gods, set themselves up as oracles and priests and mediators between God and man:

The poet is the tool of the cosmic spirit. That is his pride and his humility. Poetic creation is a human symbol of divine creative power. In essence, art is: the performing of miracles. The poet's work is the miracle . . . in this, and in no other way, is the poet's priesthood to be understood — as pontifex, as the builder of bridges.[64]

They sought to satisfy their readers' and their own longings in poetry and ostensibly discursive prose where God remains shrouded in the ardent exhalations of the poet's own dominating ego.[65] Moreover, the words of oracles and priests and soothsayers are notoriously accessible to manifold interpretations, but rarely, if ever, did the Expressionist writers concern themselves with any secondary infection of doubtful, indeterminate meanings which their words might be carrying.

Compared with some of Heynicke's many other poems on the same theme and compared with the religious poetry of, say, Werfel, Lichtenstein and Becher, where anger at God's silence is not harnessed as a creative force and the poet's animus remains inarticulate, Heynicke's 'Erhebe die Hände' is impressive for its reticence. In Becher's poetry, in particular, the poet loses his temper, his anger becomes a pre-packaged attitude, whereas in Heynicke's case there is greater sobriety and control: the crying is, after all, restrained. Reticence involves a reluctance to devalue either the experience or the words by gushing out whatever first comes to mind with a confessional completeness of detail, rather after the manner of Rilke's picture of the Expressionist poet. Reticence means at the same time possessing yet withholding the features of extremity. One *can* sense in the poem a temptation to yield to fierce imprecations and accusations. There are certainly bitterness and disappointment, bravado and bluster, but, apart from one or two lines (8 and 19), no occasion where the poet's frustration clouds his meaning. On the page, and at a casual reading, the poem appears to limp and sprawl at will. In fact, it is carefully ordered *not* by stanzaic structure, but by the use of stress. There is a natural hiatus at line 12, that is at precisely the mid-point of the poem, where the truculent confidence which had prevailed until then gives way to a more sober acknowledgement of facts. There are five verse groups — lines 1–5 containing eleven stressed syllables, lines 6–8 twelve, lines 9–13 twelve, lines 14–18 eleven, and lines 19–23 eleven. This sequence of rhythmic periods of almost exactly equal length demonstrates how Heynicke uses stress as a substitute for stanzas and, incidentally, how much he owes *Sturm* school theories on stress and rhythm. Newton (pp. 216–18) shows in great detail that, in 'Erhebe die Hände', Heynicke relies on acoustic devices and line length variation for the shaping of his rhythm and that the whole poem rests upon a carefully structured pattern of alliteration, assonance and echoing vowels. Heynicke almost always retains a framework of logical, correct syntax. It can be argued that he takes issue with strict form on some occasions, but only rarely (and 'Erhebe die Hände' is no exception) does he produce poems where individual words implode with intensity, or poems where words become projectiles constructed out of fragmentary emotions and clamour and bawl against the indifference of the world and of God. Heynicke *is* 'capable' of that sort of poem, but it is not his customary voice. With him, traditional form persists.

Conclusions:

> The song is over —
> longing's sweet scream died in the mouth:
> a magician did it, the friend at the right time,
> the noonday friend —
> no! do not ask who it was —
> at noon it was that one became two. [66]

> Sail forth — steer for the deep waters only,
> Reckless O soul, exploring,
> I with thee, and thou with me,
> For we are bound where mariner
> has not yet dared to go,
> And we will risk the ship, ourselves and all. [67]

The argument of the preceding pages has sought to establish certain things about Heynicke and his work: that he began as an Expressionist poet and, in various ways, remained one; that his poetry can be regarded as a paradigm of Expressionist volatility and feverishness and is characterized by a studiously fostered instability; that the course of his life parallels, in many important respects, that of Benn and Bronnen; that, whatever he did or did not do in the 1930s, he wrote two plays which indicate more than lukewarm sympathy for the National Socialist régime; that there are features in his poetry which prefigure that sympathy, features which are in some cases peculiar to him and, in other cases, true of the Expressionist movement as a whole, and which serve to substantiate Sokel's claim that 'the confluence of late Expressionism and Nazism was neither a chance happening nor a reversal of the Expressionist current' (see above p. 7), that the theme of homelessness and loneliness runs throughout his work, mirroring his (and his generation's) 'Anfälligkeit', a susceptibility to the right offer of a home; that his poetry is fundamentally about a search for God, where God means all the things and all the people Becher says it does for his contemporaries; that his life and work demonstrate convincingly how the typically indeterminate Expressionist longing and searching can precipitate into an uncritical willingness to settle for 'a narrow belief . . . a hard, rigorous chimera' and that, finally, his poetry, as exemplified in one poem, represents something of a rejoinder to Rilke's criticism of Expressionism by offering a reticent passionateness as well as many characteristically Expressionist qualities.

Gottfried Benn is the obvious poet to discuss in this context, but his œuvre seems less consistently typical of the Expressionist writers and there is certainly a sense in which he is more self-aware (both in his links with Nazism and subsequent disaffection for it) than the writers under consideration here. In investigating the nature of a possible connection between Expressionism and National Socialism, one should bear in mind that, while there is never a one-to-one homology between poetic statement and political praxis, yet there are a number of factors peculiar to the political and cultural scene in Germany in the 1920s and 1930s. It is, for example, worth remembering that at least part of the Expressionist movement claims to be seriously involved in politics, that the National Socialists are anything but indifferent to poetry and are looking for ammunition wherever they can find it, that 'the Dichter occupied an exalted position in Germany', that 'before the Weimar Republic and during it poetry exercised a peculiar power over the German imagination' (as Peter Gay argues in Chapter 3 of his *Weimar Culture*), and that, furthermore, the Weimar Republic was an intensely fragile institution ('like a candle burning at both ends'[68]) in need of all the positive support it could muster. Here it might be useful to make a distinction between 'sins of commission' (that is, the party-hacks and those poets who made an open avowal of allegiance to National Socialism) and 'sins of omission' (that is, those poets who made no such avowal, but who in some way undermined potential resistance to National Socialism and did nothing to shore up the faltering Republic). Werfel, acknowledging his responsibility as one of 'the inconsiderable men who were the first to bring fuel to the hell-fire in which mankind is now roasting', could perhaps be said to belong in the second category, whilst such poets as Anacker, Menzel, Schirach and, for a time, Benn can be placed in the first category. Heynicke appears to occupy the middle-ground between these two groups. If he was not a party-hack like Menzel and Anacker, he certainly joined the ranks of the party-hacks for a time in 1933. And his poetry before 1933 not only made such an allegiance predictable, even likely, it also helped in a small way to create the kind of atmosphere in which the party-hacks could flourish. Edgar Jung, speaking in 1932 for the National Conservatives, underlines the complicity of German intellectuals in the rise of Nazism:

In countless little ways, especially among the cultured classes, we created the preconditions for the day when the German people gave its vote to the National Socialist candidates.[69]

Such complicity was not unique to Germany or to German intellectuals in their relationship with a totalitarian régime: writing of her country at an identical time in its history, Nadezhda Mandelstam (in a chapter called 'The Irrational') laments the alacrity with which the intellectuals 'succumbed to the plague that infected all our minds' and refers to the part they had played in earlier years in failing to halt the disease of Stalinism:

Can you explain the susceptibility of our intellectuals to this sickness only by reference to conditions after the Revolution? Weren't the first microbes already lurking in the prerevolutionary malaise with all its frantic searching and false prophecies?[70]

As a poet in Germany between the wars Heynicke was already assured of an audience. As an Expressionist poet, grudgingly or not, he had access to a much bigger audience than he might otherwise have expected, thanks to the enthusiasm with which the movement advertised itself and disseminated its magazines, periodicals and volumes of verse. It thus contributed positively to what Joachim Fest calls 'the enormous, chaotic potential of aggressiveness, anxiety, devotion and egotism [that] lay ready to Hitler's hand'.[71] Heynicke's contribution, like his influence, may not have counted for much, but it counted for something under a political régime which looked to the nation's poets for positive support. For a time Heynicke gave that support. He was one of a large group of writers who leapt at Goebbels's offer to relieve them of 'the feeling of inconsolable emptiness'.[72] It was a feeling which Heynicke knew well — in 1919 he is writing 'In mir ist unermeßlich lichtlos Leere' ('In me is unbounded lightless emptiness'; HLW, I, 158); in 1925 he describes his soul as 'ein leerer Kelch, | ausgetrunken ganz Leid und Freude vom Munde des Tags' ('an empty goblet, | grief and joy completely emptied by the mouth of day'; HLW, II, 95); and in a later poem (undated) he calls youth 'ein ungefüllt Gefäß | und offen jedem Tranke, | der ihr Ruhm verspricht' ('an unfilled vessel | open to every potion | which promises it fame'; HLW, II, 185). Hannah Arendt has shown how that feeling of emptiness and isolation is 'the most fertile ground' for any totalitarian government, how totalitarian government 'bases itself on loneliness, on the experience of not belonging to the world at all' and how loss of self and of a sense of reality make 'the ideal subject for totalitarian rule'.[73] The National Socialists' invitation to create 'a relationship of mutual interdependence between the state and intellectuals', to turn poetry from a personal to a public affair and to rescue the poet from the 'solipsistic loneliness of his feelings',[74] thus alleviating the sense of deadening failure distilled in 'the eternal No' of 'Erhebe die Hände', proved irresistible to Heynicke and writers like him. His œuvre lacks the vehement stridencies of, say, Becher's work, though it has its angry moments. Indeed there is a tentativeness and vacillation about it — 'Wir suchen den Standort | von Spätervielleicht'[75] in his retrospective comment upon himself. And yet, as Nietzsche observes at the end of a piece called 'Wir Heimatlosen' ('We Homeless Ones'), when a choice has to be made, 'the hidden Yes in you homeless ones is stronger than all the Noes, all the perhaps with which you and your age are sick: and if you emigrants have to take to the sea, you too are driven by — a belief!'[76] Heynicke's poetry has enabled us to watch him fumble towards an ardent belief, the object of which typically remains unstated and unimportant,[77] and to see 'the No!' of 'Erhebe die Hände' gradually swell into an ecstatic Yes, the Yes of his 1936 volume *Das Leben sagt Ja*:

> Sturm des Daseins!
> Sang voll Klage!
> O die unbegriffne Reise: Ja und Ja!
>
> (HLW, II, 143)

Storm of existence! | Song full of lamentation! | O the uncomprehended journey: Yes and Yes!

And the result of that joyous affirmation when Heynicke's voice is joined by the voice of so many others? Hitler is indeed welcomed as 'the friend at the right time, the noonday friend':

Now he stands before us, he whom the voices of our poets and sages have summoned, the liberator of the German genius. He has removed the blindfold from our eyes, and through all political, economic, social and confessional covers has enabled us to see and love again the one essential thing — our unity of blood, our German self, the homo germanus.[78]

The 'German God' had truly, and at last, arrived. Faith, undirected and shapeless in the beginning, ends by creating the god to which it then blindly adheres.

NOTES

1 'Homesickness without a home, the most painful, the deepest cutting question of all: "Where can *I* — be at home?"'; F. Nietzsche, *Aus der Zeit des Zarathustra* (1882–88), Musarion edition, XIV, 19.
2 'On them [altars] glows deeply inscribed | the word: to the unknown God. | I am his even if I in the blasphemers' band | have remained until this hour: | I am his — and I feel the snares | pulling me down as I struggle, | and, even if I want to flee, | forcing me to serve him. | I want to know you, you unknown God, | reaching deep into my soul | passing through my life like a storm, | you incomprehensible one, yet related to me! | I want to know you, even serve you!'; F. Nietzsche, 'Dem unbekannten Gott', Musarion edition, XX, 63.
3 R. M. Rilke, *Die Weiße Fürstin. Eine Szene am Meer* (1898); *Sämtliche Werke*, 6 vols (Frankfurt a.M. and Wiesbaden, 1955–56), I, 225.
4 Florence E. Hardy, *The Early Life of Thomas Hardy* (London, 1928), p. 198.
5 R. M. Rilke, 'Auguste Rodin' (1907); *Sämtliche Werke*, V, 241.
6 F. Werfel, 'Aphorismus zu diesem Jahr', *Die Aktion*, 5 December 1914, cols 902–05.
7 See 'Die Vertreibung der Gespenster' (January 1919), in: A. Döblin, *Schriften zur Politik und Gesellschaft* (Olten and Freiburg im Breisgau, 1972), pp. 71–72.
8 Letter to Frau Grete Buchholz of 15 August 1915 in: R. Dehmel, *Ausgewählte Briefe aus den Jahren 1902–20*, pp. 382–83.
9 Arnold Zweig, 'Der Einsame' ('The Lonely One'), *Die Weißen Blätter*, 10 October 1919, p. 456.
10 G. Benn, 'Die Eroberung' (1915); *Gesammelte Werke*, II, 20.
11 K. Tucholsky, 'Das Mitglied' (1926); *Gesammelte Werke*, 10 vols (Reinbek bei Hamburg, 1975), IV, 455–56.
12 From the poem 'Gedicht' (1921); *Das lyrische Werk*, 3 vols (Worms 1969–74), II, 19 (hereafter referred to as HLW).
13 See Werfel's 1915–17 poem 'Benennung'; WLW, 243–44.
14 K. Heynicke, 'Zwei Liebesgedichte' (1917); HLW, I, 19.
15 HLW, III (1969), preface. Heynicke's wordplay — 'wohlversargt' against 'nicht versorgt' — cannot be reproduced in English.
16 K. Heynicke, '"Ich unterscheide mich von der Gegenwartslyrik und ihrer Artistik"', *Die Horen*, 94 (1974), 34.
17 For an account of Heynicke's 'odyssey' to 'half a dozen publishers' see: R. Hochhuth, *Die Hebamme. Komödie. Erzählungen. Gedichte. Essays* (Hamburg, 1971), pp. 335–46.
18 W. H. Auden, 'The Voyage'; *Collected Shorter Poems 1930–1944* (London, 1950), p. 176.
19 K. Heynicke, 'Unterwegs', printed in: *Jahresring* (1971–72), p. 115.
20 J. Goebbels, *Michael*, p. 33 and p. 7.
21 Compare Benn's picture of 'the modern I' as 'over-ripe, decaying, giraffe-like, uncircumcizable, devoid of belief and doctrine, of science and of myth . . . assailed by afflictions, meaningless' in: 'Das moderne Ich' (1920); *Gesammelte Werke*, I, 20.
22 J. R. Becher, *Abschied*, p. 348. Compare the promise-cum-prophecy of Michael's 'Something is in preparation . . . A man will come' (Goebbels, p. 41).
23 Quoted in: H. Daiber, *Vor Deutschland wird gewarnt* (Gütersloh, 1967), p. 14.
24 A. Bronnen, *Arnolt Bronnen gibt zu Protokoll* (Hamburg, 1954), p. 190 and p. 125.
25 G. Benn, 'Expressionismus'; *Gesammelte Werke*, I, 251.
26 F. Schoenberner, *Bekenntnisse eines europäischen Intellektuellen* (Icking and Munich, 1964), p. 299.

27 See Hitler's comment: 'Today the old women amongst the writers are screeching "betrayal of the mind" at me. And not so long ago they were sounding off about the mind's betrayal of life. As long as it was a literary delicacy they inflated their own importance. Now that we are in earnest, they react in wide-eyed innocence and amazement'; H. Rauschning, *Gespräche mit Hitler* (Zurich, Vienna and New York, 1940), p. 255.

28 Adolf Hitler, quoted in: H. Preiss, *Adolf Hitler in Franken: Reden aus der Kampfzeit* (Munich, n.d.), pp. 39 f.

29 Quoted in: K. C. Hayens, 'Gerhard Schumann: Poet of the Third Reich', *GLL* (Old Series), 2 (1937–38), 65.

30 W. B. Yeats, *Letters*, edited by A. Wade (London, 1954), p. 808.

31 F. Nietzsche, 'Der Schatten', *Also sprach Zarathustra; Nietzsche Werke*, VI/I, 337.

32 K. Heynicke, quoted in: Daiber, p. 59.

33 The First Officer in Paul Ernst's 1915 'Invented Conversations'. See E. Volkmann, *Deutsche Dichtung im Weltkrieg 1914–1918*, p. 208.

34 M. Weber, *Wirtschaft und Gesellschaft* (Cologne and Berlin, 1964), pp. 394–95.

35 *Expressionismus: Internationale Forschung zu einem internationalen Phänomen* (Stuttgart, 1980), p. 306.

36 E. W. Lotz, 'Hart stoßen sich die Wände in den Straßen . . .', *Wolkenüberflaggt* (Munich, 1916), p. 53,

37 Paul Ernst (1866–1933) was a versatile writer who, having associated with the Naturalist movement, adopted the neo-Romantic style and then neo-Classicism. He wrote plays, novels and many Novellen and was also a critic and essayist. He was nominated as one of the fourteen founder members of the National Socialist 'Dichter-Akademie', but he died before the first meeting. See Paul Ernst, 'Der deutsche Gott', *Zeit-Echo. Ein Kriegs-Tagebuch der Künstler*, Heft 6 (Munich, 1914–15), 82 ff.

38 For a full version of the poem see *Die Erhebung*, (Berlin, 1920), 21. The altered version is in HLW, I, 122.

39 F. Nietzsche, *Nachgelassene Fragmente 1884–85; Nietzsche Werke*, VII/ 3, 59.

40 The Third Critic in Sorge's play *Der Bettler*, in: R. Sorge, *Sämtliche Werke*, 3 vols (Nuremberg, 1962–67), II (1964), 23.

41 F. Nietzsche, 'Sils-Maria'; Musarion editions, XX, 120.

42 A 'Thing'-play, just about the Nazis' solitary contribution to a theatrical art form, was a mixture of a politico-religious service, Nazi agit-prop, death-cult, judicial assembly, military tattoo and inauguration into the 'Volksgemeinschaft'.

43 In a letter to me, dated 29 December 1976.

44 D. Strothmann, *Nationalsozialistische Literaturpolitik* (Bonn, 1960), p. 391.

45 W. Braumüller, *Deutsche Bühnenkorrespondenz* of 24 July 1935, quoted in: J. Wulf, *Theater und Film im Dritten Reich* (Gütersloh, 1964), p. 170.

46 e.g. U-K. Ketelsen, *Völkisch-nationale und national-sozialistische Literatur in Deutschland 1890–1945* (Stuttgart, 1976), p. 99.

47 H. Denkler and K. Prümm, *Die deutsche Literatur im Dritten Reich* (Stuttgart, 1976).

48 The phrase, 'die Zeit der entflohenen Götter und des kommenden Gottes', is Heidegger's and is quoted in: W. Stuyver, *Deutsche Expressionistische Dichtung im Lichte der Philosophie der Gegenwart* (Amsterdam, 1939), p. 195.

49 H. Johst, 'Der Dichter in der Zeit', in: *Die Dichtung im Kampf des Reiches* (Hamburg, 1941), p. 14.

50 W. Rathenau, *An Deutschlands Jugend* (Berlin, 1918), p. 83.

51 This verb also meant something to Bronnen. In *Vatermord*, the son, raping the mother, feels a kind of sexual ecstasy and exclaims in the last words of the play: 'Ich | Ich blühe —'. Quoted in: Bronnen, *Gibt zu Protokoll*, p. 39.

52 Ernst Deuerlein, quoted in: G. L. Mosse, *The Crisis of German Ideology* (London, 1966), p. 310.

53 'Do not, please, resist me!' from the 1911 poem 'An den Leser'; WLW, 62–63.

54 The poet speaking in *Der Bettler*. See R. Sorge, *Sämtliche Werke*, II, 80.

55 The phrases are Hans Blunck's and are quoted in: P. Viereck, *Metapolitics — The Roots of the Nazi Mind* (New York, 1961), p. 155.

56   This poem appears in the 1919 volume *Das namenlose Angesicht*. It is also the first of the dozen poems by which Heynicke is represented in *Menschheitsdämmerung* (pp. 71–72).

57   One might (pedantically) ask how 'face' can have 'hands'. Heynicke is prone to such odd juxtapositions: the poem 'Wiegenlied' in the 1918 collection *Gottes Geigen* contains the phrase 'from the countenance of your voice . . .', whilst 'Augenblick' in the same volume begins 'My heart raises its hand'.

58   Adolf Hitler, *Mein Kampf*, p. 362.

59   See Michael's urgent injunction 'We must thrust forward into eternity' (*Michael*, p. 72).

60   J. Whittier, 'In Quest' (1873); *Selected Poems of J. G. Whittier* (London, 1913), p. 439.

61   T. S. Eliot, *On Poetry and Poets*, p. 143.

62   Compare Cowper's 'Pity religion has so seldom found | A skilful guide into poetic ground!'; W. Cowper, 'Table Talk', *Cowper's Poems*, p. 218.

63   Samuel Johnson, *Lives of the English Poets*, I, 173–74.

64   K. Heynicke, quoted in: Daiber, pp. 59–60.

65   We think of Donne's 'To see God only, I goe out of sight'. See his poem 'A Hymne to Christ' in: *John Donne*, edited by J. Hayward (Harmondsworth, 1966), p. 176.

66   F. Nietzsche, 'Aus hohen Bergen'; Musarion edition, xx, 158.

67   W. Whitman, 'Passage to India', quoted in: W. Whitman, *A Collection of Critical Essays*, p. 87.

68   Quoted in: K. D. Bracher and others, *Die nationalsozialistische Machtergreifung*, p. 18.

69   Quoted in: K. Sontheimer, *Antidemokratisches Denken in der Weimarer Republik* (Munich, 1962), p. 363.

70   N. Mandelstam, *Hope against Hope* (London, 1971), pp. 47–48.

71   J. Fest, *Hitler* (London, 1974), p. 754.

72   On the occasion of the 'Rede zur Eröffnung der RKK' on 15 November 1933.

73   H. Arendt, *The Origins of Totalitarianism* (New York, 1966), pp. 474–79.

74   These phrases are Josef Nadler's and are taken from his *Deutscher Geist Deutscher Osten: Zehn Reden* (Munich, Berlin and Zurich, 1937), pp. 11–27.

75   'We seek the standpoint | of later perhaps'. K. Heynicke, from the poem 'Position', printed in: *Jahresring* (1971/72), p. 114.

76   F. Nietzsche, *Die fröhliche Wissenschaft*; *Nietzsche Werke*, V/ 2, 313.

77   See the 1936 poem 'Warum' which contains the line: 'Eternally the last tear shouts: Believe! Believe!'; HLW, II, 143.

78   K. Adam, 'Deutsches Volkstum und Katholisches Christentum', *Theologische Quartalschrift* (1933), p. 59.

VII WILHELM KLEMM

> Now Parmenides plunged into the cold bath of
> his dreadful abstractions[1]

In 'Untersuchungen zur Lyrik Wilhelm Klemms', Jan Brockmann suggests that
Lukács's criticism of Expressionism has a particular relevance to the poetry of
Wilhelm Klemm (see p. 8 above). Application of that criticism should serve to
illuminate both the validity of the critical categories employed by Lukács (at least
with regard to one Expressionist poet) *and* the characteristic voice, forms and
themes of Klemm's poetry. The burden of Lukács's polemic, it will be remembered,
is that Expressionism, in its flaccid 'abstracting away from reality', its self-regarding
and hysterical refusal to engage in contemporary social and political issues, amounts
to no more than an arbitrary shadow-play of fragmentary and insubstantial images
and hence to a wholly pinchbeck, ultimately inane movement. Although some of
Klemm's poems are difficult to date with any precision, his poetry can, for practical
purposes, be divided into three groups, of which the last two will be the principal
concern of this chapter: the early poetry (that is, the poems written between the
beginning of 1908 and the end of 1913 for the periodicals *Simplicissimus, Licht und
Schatten* and *Jugend*), the war-poetry (contained in Klemm's first volume, *Gloria,
Kriegsgedichte aus dem Felde*), and the rest (poems written between 1913 and 1922, but
not included in *Gloria*).

> A barrage of disruptive sound, a petal on a sleeping face,
> Both must be noted, both must have their place;
> It may be that our later selves or else our unborn sons
> Will search for meaning in the dust of long deserted guns,
> We only watch, and indicate and make our scribbled pencil notes,
> We do not wish to moralize, only to ease our dusty throats.[2]

Klemm's early poems are the poems of an 'angry young man', though perhaps at
twenty-seven (his age in 1908) he was not such a young man. The voice is truculent,
the attitude is non-conformist and oppositional, the form is fundamentally traditional. Sokel must have got the wrong poet when he writes that 'the mere look of the
printed page of poems by J. R. Becher and W. Klemm spells aggression against the
reader . . . exclamation marks, question marks and dashes follow the one-word
sentences in menacing crescendos'.[3] Klemm very rarely writes like Becher: with
him the belligerent tone is usually reined back by a timid conservatism straining ever
so slightly to be audacious, by an aestheticizing neo-Romanticism, an idyllic brand

of religiousness, a rather precious choice of vocabulary and, above all, by the worst elements of 'Jugendstil' poetry. The targets of Klemm's satire are the ossified conventions of the older generation, philistinism, the clergy and contemporary art. The satire is not very scathing, its point is blunt, the mind from which it issues not sure enough of its own poetic means of expression, with the result that it adds up to a rather invertebrate predecessor of Tucholsky's, Kästner's and Eugen Roth's verse. Yet the early poems do give us a foretaste of the kind of poetry which Klemm comes to write subsequently — unrhyming four-line stanzas, traditional in appearance, ruminative, marked by a log-jam of solid-looking substantives, fluid but not dynamic and impassioned. This is a huge generalization which does not do justice to *all* the thirty-one early poems. It does no justice at all to Klemm's *Gloria* (1915), but then (and here Klemm differs from Stramm) his war-poetry is not of a piece with all his other poetry.

Chosen for Klemm by Langen, the publisher of *Simplicissimus*, *Gloria* is a misnomer: there are just three instances of strident chauvinism of the 'Up and into the holy war!' sort. Perhaps the best way to introduce the poems which Klemm wrote from the battle-field is to say what they are *not* like: they are not like Stramm's intensely concentrated triangles, nor are they like Becher's hectoring outbursts (see his 'Mensch, stehe auf!') or Werfel's garrulous rhetoric (see his 'Der Krieg') — the 'Bleibe Mensch!' of Klemm's poem 'Spuk' is not some empty Werfelian injunction, but a heart-felt plea to 'remain human' in the holocaust of war. A strong subjective element juts into Becher's and Werfel's poems on war. In a memorable sentence in his introduction to *The Oxford Book of Modern Verse 1892–1935* (Oxford, 1936) Yeats writes that, 'when man has withdrawn into the quicksilver at the back of the mirror, no great event becomes luminous in his mind' (p. xxxiv). Klemm does not make such a withdrawal: instead of rhetoric and pathos, he provides the impression of things seen and events experienced. His war-poetry is marked by objectivity and restraint, selection and control, with the result that events on the battle-field are ordered and stabilized. Sorley disparagingly uses the phrase 'small-holdings type'[4] for some of his own poetry: this might serve as an initial characterization of Klemm's *Gloria*.

Klemm recaptures the utter futility and annihilating boredom of much of an individual soldier's life at the front, whilst all the time retaining the looming presence of Yeats's 'great event'. Occasionally, too, he succeeds in recording an incident from 'the scorching cautery of battle'.[5] There is no over-personalized response (of the kind which vitiates much English war-poetry), and yet, although Klemm insists on being scrupulously honest to the limitations of experience, he offers more than sympathetic photography and vivid reportage, more than the notations of a stenographic eye. The insistence on detail is remorseless — the haggard troops, the horses in heavy blankets, the grey-faced soldiers huddled round a camp-fire, the endless marching, the drooping eyelids, the burning villages, the cigar-smoke spiralling into the night-sky, the rain, the puddles, the seeping blood, the terrible wounds, the skeletal towns and, especially, battle-field noises. Klemm is determined to render a punctiliously full account, not to gloss and not to exaggerate, and at the same time to link the sufferings of the struggle to a philosophic concept.

The inchoate sensations, the data of a terrible experience can assume meaning and coherence only if they are registered and interpreted by a mind capable of relating them to a dominant conception of action and endeavour. In, for example, Stramm's 'Patrouille' the war has taken possession of everything, filling even inanimate objects with its urgent dynamism, whereas a feature of Klemm's war-poetry is that the author makes us aware of a time and a place beyond war where, perhaps, 'the earth no longer trembles'.[6]

The first verse of Klemm's famous 'Schlacht an der Marne' is cumbered with detail:

> Langsam beginnen die Steine sich zu bewegen und zu reden.
> Die Gräser erstarren zu grünem Metall. Die Wälder,
> Niedrige, dichte Verstecke, fressen ferne Kolonnen.
> Der Himmel, das kalkweiße Geheimnis, droht zu bersten.
> Zwei kolossale Stunden rollen sich auf zu Minuten.
> Der leere Horizont bläht sich empor.
>
> (*Gloria*, p. 27)

Slowly the stones begin to move and to speak. | The grass congeals to green metal. The forests, | Low, dense hide-outs eat up distant columns. | The sky, the chalk-white mystery, threatens to burst. | Two mighty hours unfold into minutes. | The empty horizon swells up.

The detail is supplied poetically, in images which know their place and do not deflect the attention — the shifting stones (contrast Klemm's deliberate circumlocution with Stramm's spare 'The stones are hostile' in 'Patrouille'), the grass congealing into a green metallic colour, the forests 'eating up' distant columns of men, the heavens (if not godless, then certainly inscrutable) about to pour down, time passing, an empty bloated horizon. Then the scenario widens and expands beyond the range of immediate perceptions and sensations, taking in the individual soldier's response on the way:

> Mein Herz ist so groß wie Deutschland und Frankreich zusammen,
> Durchbohrt von allen Geschossen der Welt.
> Die Batterie erhebt ihre Löwenstimme
> Sechsmal hinaus in das Land. Die Granaten heulen.
> Stille. In der Ferne brodelt das Feuer der Infanterie,
> Tagelang, wochenlang.

My heart is as big as Germany and France together, | Pierced by all the shells in the world. | The battery raises its lion's voice | Six times out into the country. The grenades howl. | Silence. In the distance infantry fire splutters, | For days on end, for weeks on end.

What looks like developing into an access of self-pity and self-dramatization signals, in fact, the opening stages of the onslaught. The 'sechsmal' underlines Klemm's almost pedantic determination to get things right, and the last line, the marooned 'tagelang, wochenlang', opens up the whole perspective and places this particular attack into a routine, into a wider setting and continuity, thus creating an impression of temporal depth whilst retaining a thorough notation of particularized reality.

Contrast this poem with five lines from Heynicke's war-poem 'Schrei in der Schlacht':

Und [Ich] überschreit die eisernen Vögel aus dem Nest der Kanonen,
und steigt über Gott hinaus hoch in das All!
Denn Ich ist ewiger als der Wein des Todes in der Schlacht.
Ich ist das Kreisen von Anfang zu Anfang,
Ich hat in den Händen den Tag und die Nacht.

(HLW, I, 154)

And [I] outscreams the iron birds from the nests of cannons, | and rises way beyond God into the cosmos! | For I is more eternal than the wine of death in battle. | I is the circling from beginning to beginning, | I has the day and the night in its hands.

Here, if anywhere, is an example of a poet's 'withdrawing into the quicksilver at the back of the mirror' — self-dramatization, abstractions (where Klemm had offered a ballast of concrete details), 'an impoverishment of content', unsuccessfully cryptic images and the intensely distracting *Sturm*school conceit 'I is', 'I has'. Heynicke's lines are held up by nothing more than the poet's own breathless enthusiasm — the same is true of Werfel's, Becher's and Ehrenstein's war-poetry, where anger, pity, indignation and sympathy are not only crude and visible, but are allowed to dominate and distort the character of the poetic vision. With Klemm the quality of a battle-field scene or incident may evoke an emotion, but the emotion is an effect and not a predisposing cause of the visualization. His war-poems are firmly anchored in quotidian particulars, thus fully earning their shifts beyond the personal and the immediately visible into the universal and mythopoeic. The weight of meticulously depicted detail which goes to make up Heym's poems underpins *Gloria*, and with Klemm the detail is recruited to a definite historical event and scrupulously observed landscapes. A poem like 'Rethel' with its gloomy army in grey ghostly helmets moving through a devastated town, or 'Nächtliche Aussicht' with its invocation of dark cannons and the night prodding 'brazen arms into the ribs of armies', or 'Tristissimus' with its picture of a cathedral of death looming menacingly on the hem of the world — such poems in *Gloria*, such images, echo the work of Georg Heym. In contrast, Heynicke's and much other Expressionist war-poetry establishes no real or direct relationship with its subject, it is characterized by an oratorical pathos which attenuates the horrors of battle, and any attempt to widen the perspective, to 'search for meaning in the fust', invariably slithers into vagueness and declamation. Klemm, unlike many other Expressionist poets, does not regard war as a substitute for revolution, as a kind of necessary and salutary 'Aufbruch'. With him there are no ulterior motives. War is 'the infernal activity' (*Gloria*, p. 19), is 'always the same delirium of destruction' (p. 61). And death? That may come at any time: 'Death is as indifferent as the rain which sets in' (p. 45). The bitter, slangy, Kästner-style 'God knows how it will end' (p. 58) rings altogether truer than Heynicke's hectoring invocations of the deity and somehow works towards a religious enlargement. The poems of *Gloria* are not visions: they are born in the field and sustained by closely documented detail. 'The shrapnel speckles the heavens

| Like a panther' (p. 16), 'The blood seeps diffidently through the tunic' (p. 19), 'The moon plunges its torch into the black canal. | The countryside clings fast to darkness' (p. 50) — such lines, demonstrating a dogged allegiance to the detail of empirical reality with no loss of strikingly vivid imagery, are the rule in *Gloria* which, with the work of the now rarely read Alfred Vagts (and, for very different reasons, August Stramm), is the most substantial volume of German poetry to emerge from the First World War.

The poems of *Gloria* can justifiably be adduced as a rejoinder to Marxist criticism of Expressionism, but a problem arises. Is Klemm's war-poetry Expressionistic in any respectable sense of the word? 'Schlacht an der Marne' appears in *Menschheits-dämmerung* and other anthologies of Expressionist verse: whether that makes it an Expressionist poem or not is far from certain. Pinthus, writing almost fifty years after the first publication of his anthology, is in no doubt about the correctness of his ascription of these 'war- poems which, in spite of the realistic depiction of experience, make more and more frequent use of simultaneity, one of Expression-ism's principal means of communication: the widely divergent images, metaphors and comparisons juxtaposed for no apparent reason and heedless of all logic, but all visualized at the same time'.[7] The shy caveat 'in spite of the realistic depiction of experience', hidden away amongst the technical paraphernalia, is the very nub of the matter. Expressionism, if it is to mean anything at all, amounts to a rejection of the mimetic approach to art and of all the assumptions upon which realistic art is based. To the extent that Klemm's war-poetry is sustained and stabilized by realistic depictions of a soldier's life at the front, to the extent, in other words, that his war-poetry is not Expressionistic, it is far superior to that of other *Aktion* war- poets. In connection with 'Schlacht an der Marne', Pinthus is certainly right to list simul-taneity, alogicality, acausality and enumeration as important features of the poem *and* of Expressionist poetry. Yet there is no denying that Klemm begins from things seen and gives us things seen. The images of stones 'beginning to move and to speak', of grass 'congealing to green metal', of forests 'eating up distant columns', of heavens 'threatening to burst' — all these contain a characteristic Expressionist dynamism and urgency, but the fact remains that these images are firmly anchored to the studiously rendered world of trench warfare with its fierce assaults and lengthy hiatuses, and for this reason alone it is difficult to justify devoting more time to *Gloria* in the context of Expressionism. Even at the time of writing *Gloria*, Klemm's view of empirical reality is fundamentally dialectical:

> Ein verirrtes Geschoß schlägt ein. Hart wie die Wirklichkeit
> Und traumhaft wie sie. Lern es begreifen, mein Herz.
>
> ('Der Abgrund'; *Gloria*, p. 73)

A stray shell strikes home. As hard as reality | And as dreamlike. Learn to understand it, my heart.

The stray shell, like 'reality', is both 'hard' and 'dreamlike': 'hard', because, apart from its obvious physical qualities, it carries with it the prospect of death and destruction: 'dreamlike', because man as soldier is a powerless, passive figure in the landscape of war, someone to whom things happen. The poet is committed to

138

registering the données of man's existence, the facts of this 'hard' and 'dreamlike' reality, for 'nothing is nobler than reality'.[8] But for Klemm, 'reality' comes to be invested with more and more of a chimerical, ethereal quality,[9] until its 'hardness' has all but dissolved and the poet surrenders himself to his own familiar, safe thickets of dreams and is content to 'beat vain hands in the rosy mists of poets' experiences':[10]

> Wenn alles sich als Täuschung erweist,
> Es gibt Träume, denen man unbedingt glaubt.
>
> (*Ergriffenheit*, p. 97)

When everything turns out to be deception | There are dreams which one believes unconditionally.

It is not fortuitous that post-*Gloria* poems bear such titles as 'Weltflucht' ('Flight of? from? the World') and 'Magische Flucht' ('Magic Flight'). It is as if the poet feels that he has paid adequate obeisance to hard facts and now, dissatisfied, shifts his attention elsewhere:

> Manchmal kommt ein Gast zu Besuch.
> Macht eine Verbeugung vor den Tatsachen
> Mit der kühlen Nachlässigkeit des Überlegenen.
> Wendet sich unbefriedigt anderen Dingen zu.[11]

Sometimes a guest drops in. | Gives a bow to the facts | With the cool nonchalance of a superior being. | Finding no gratification turns to other things.

This self-conscious change of focus is an ever-accelerating process through varying degrees of abstraction until, by 1919, the emptiness of the poet's own existence has become his sole consideration and, in one of those moments of self-awareness which recur in his later volumes, he writes: 'My incorporeal longing sobs wildly — | I am only a dream, a flitting silhouette' (*Ergriffenheit*, p. 41). And all the time his vision becomes more and more attenuated, his poems less and less substantial, until that expedient, too, leaves him profoundly disillusioned and he plunges back into the grossly carnal and sybaritic world of *Die Satanspuppe*:

> Es genügt mir zu wissen,
> Du hast die schönsten Beine Europas.
> (p. 45)

It is enough for me to know, | You have the most beautiful legs in Europe.

— 'the most beautiful legs in Europe' are ultimately 'the only truly plastic thing in this world of false appearances' (ibid.). It is, then, a process whereby 'essence', that favourite Expressionist catchword, is not won: on the contrary, substance is lost. Perhaps the best way of following this process is to examine in some detail Klemm's second volume of verse, *Verse und Bilder* (1916), as a means not only of highlighting the wide differences between *Gloria* and all Klemm's subsequent poetry, but also of indicating the characteristic themes and linguistic ploys common to the post-*Gloria* volumes.

> The place is
> not found but seeps
> from our touch in
> continuous creation.[12]

The shadow of the 'Jugendstil' epoch lies heavily across *Verse und Bilder* and the volumes which succeed it. Typical features of 'Jugendstil' art[13] are a refined elegance, a satyric sensuality, a love of ornamentation and floral motifs, preciousness, asymmetry, stylization and decorative luxuriousness. *Verse und Bilder* teems with the topoi, the figures, the stylistic devices of 'Jugendstil'. Such lines as:

> Sein Herz ist die Sonne, aus deren Burgen
> Feuerkaskaden die Augen des Raumes blenden.[14]

His heart is the sun from whose castles | Cascades of fire dazzle the eyes of space.

and, even more abstract,

> Alles Ersehnte verklärt sich
> Mit dem Liebesrausch des Unmöglichen —
> Aber nur das Nieerfüllte stillt sich
> Am Urgrund des Göttlichen.
>
> *(Verse und Bilder, p. 24)*

All that is yearned for becomes transfigured | In the ecstatic love of the impossible — | But only that which is never fulfilled is appeased | At the primordial source of the divine.

— such lines, saturated in 'Jugendstil' mystique and impalpability, are commonplace in *Verse und Bilder*. The 'sun's castles', the 'eyes of space', 'the primordial source of the divine' are the kind of loose, abstract, bloodless, decorative terms and images which fill Dominik Jost's study of 'Jugendstil' *and* Klemm's volume of poetry. In the latter we find phrases like 'enigmatic rapture', 'galleries of desires', 'radiant finery' and 'adorned columns and rose-arches'; there are swarms of colourful things, birds, fish, moths, tents, cathedral spires, magic palaces, bed-rugs with patterns, silent trees, congregations of white apostles, Aladdin's lamp, ranks of pagan gods, sensual long-limbed girls, half-child half-cat women, evening stars, 'caravans of colours', thrushes, moons, vineyards etc . . . *Verse und Bilder*, it can readily be seen, does *not* suffer from a shortage of carefully itemized detail of the kind which characterizes Georg Heym's poetry. But, and this is certainly *not* true of Heym's work, that detail always serves a rather winsome, surrealistic, superficially mannered imagination and is immersed in a hallucinatory aura. When Klemm writes in one poem: 'Wrestling on my knees for enchanted goals . . .' ('Auf den Knien ringend nach verzauberten Zielen . . .'; *Verse und Bilder*, p. 27), he not only previews the name of his 1921 volume, but also furnishes an adequate definition of his poetic aims as manifested in *Verse und Bilder* and, ever increasingly, in subsequent volumes. In another poem, called appropriately 'Das neue Paradies' and composed, to a large extent, of compound nouns and adjectives ('sunray-spears', 'morning-sun torches', 'mane-covered', 'star-miles', 'river-intertwined') typical of all Klemm's work *and* 'Jugendstil', he writes of the world, reality, in terms not all that different from the ones used by Jost and Hermand:

Denn dies, mein Kind, ist eine fremde,
Eine Welt voll Widerspruch, reicher als Wahrheit,
Wo des Lebens zarteste Prismen
Aufglühen in wunderbaren Nuancen.

(Verse und Bilder, p. 10)

For this, my child, is an alien world, | A world full of contradiction richer than truth | Where life's most delicate prisms | Begin to glow in miraculous nuances.

This is the 'reality' for which Klemm settles — one where he might find, and concentrate on, 'enchanted goals', on richness of colour, on 'delicate prisms' and 'miraculous nuances'. And in his description of Prague he again unconsciously provides a sketch of his own poetic practice:

Das gebärdet sich toll und gespreizt,
Unterdrückt, verzehrt, überreizt,
Voller Zauber und Exorzismen,
Ein verhundertfältigter Lug,
Ein prachtvoller Höllentrug
Für der Seele phantastische Prismen.

(Verse und Bilder, p. 16)

It puts on an extravagant pompous air, | Restrained, consumed, overexcited, | full of magic and exorcisms, | A centuplicated fraud, | A magnificent, consummate deception | For the soul's fantastic prisms.

In these lines, emphasis is placed on magic, exorcism, splendour, fantasy, prisms, excessive stimulation, illusion and surrealistic effects. By the same token Klemm comes to see art as some kind of conjuring trick, whereby the fragmentariness of existence can be filled out:

Wir wollen Taschenzauberkunststücke,
Wir suchen im Dasein eine fatale Lücke
Zu stopfen.

(Aufforderung, p. 102)

We want juggling tricks, | We are seeking to stop up a fatal hole in existence.

At the time of *Verse und Bilder* he sees poetry in terms of Gottfried Benn's 'Artistik' and the poet as a spinner of dreams, a sorcerer and, in true Expressionist fashion, creator of a surrogate reality. Later, poetry, and indeed all art, becomes *mere* conjuring, *mere* fashion, *mere* sensation.

Verse und Bilder for all its detail is insubstantial and thematically threadbare. It amounts to a shadowland of abstract symbols, neo-Romantic-cum-'Jugendstil' furniture and cloying imagery. There is a tendency towards the architectural and statuesque of the same kind that some critics note in Hofmannsthal's work, dreadful lumps of abstraction proliferate, and there are occasions when wispy abstractions disintegrate into embarrassing tweeness: 'Ein zartes Wiederfinden atmet beklommen' ('A tender reunion breathes anxiously'; *Aufforderung*, p. 40). The poem 'Aufforderung' provides important clues to Klemm's methods and attitudes. It is a twenty line chunk, non-rhyming, with haphazard line-lengths. In it the poet addresses his friend, 'scion of the earliest human race', and enjoins him:

> Stoße von dir, was du mitbrachtest an alten Fetzen.
> Sie sind vergänglich.

He recommends art:

> Denn die Kunst ist schön. Eine uralte Hydra,
> Bäumt sie viele Häupter, etliche tragen
> Kronen, andre eiserne Masken, Federschmuck . . .

Thrust from you all the old rags you brought with you. | They are ephemeral . . . For art is beautiful. An ancient Hydra, | She raises many heads, several wear | Crowns, others iron masks, feather head-dress . . .

The expectations raised by the title 'Aufforderung' ('Summons') are not fulfilled — the summons is to a literary revolt, and even that dissolves into an enumeration of various sorts of headgear and heads. The poem 'Aufforderung', like the volume in which it appears, like all Klemm's poetry (with the exception of *Gloria* and one or two poems, such as 'Der Bettler' and 'Abendgesellschaft', in *Aufforderung*), demonstrates no concern for, or interest in, contemporary social problems or political events. The injunction to shake off all tradition (a common enough Expressionist rallying-call) and to begin again occurs with some frequency in Klemm's poetry, but, as in 'Aufforderung', the summons never shifts beyond the purely literary. The glee in that other Expressionist mantra 'Aufbruch' and in the achieved tabula rasa state of mind is followed by a determination to fill the void (left by the discarding of tradition) with clutters of nouns which conjure up images of exotic worlds and with the invocation of dream worlds and magical lands. A kind of applied surrealism takes over, blurring the edges of things. It is, however, wrong to give the impression that *Verse und Bilder* is composed of nothing but 'Jugendstil' fossils and anaemic abstractions. There *are* powerful lines and two or three wholly successful, substantial poems where Klemm speaks in an individual voice. But the powerful lines tend to come in isolation, wedged between long abstract nouns ending in '-ung' or an equally tedious neuter '-te'. A moth fluttering through the night is memorably pictured in the following lines:

> Geister wehen ihm nach und stille Wälder.
> Dann wie ein weißer Zauberpriester
> Hängt er zitternd am schwarzen Herzen der Nacht.
>
> (*Verse und Bilder*, p. 53)

Spirits glide after him and silent forests. | Then like a white magician-priest | He hangs trembling on the black heart of night.

Though even these lines bear 'Jugendstil' marks, Klemm has hit upon a striking image with the 'white magician-priest' which seems exactly right for a moth against a gloom-laden background, and, for once, 'trembling on the black heart of night' is not mere whimsy.

As a premise for this examination of Klemm's poetry we referred to Lukács's criticism of Expressionism, but can *Verse und Bilder*, which we have argued is almost submerged beneath the weight of 'Jugendstil' detritus, be called Expressionist? Only once in *Verse und Bilder* (and very rarely in subsequent volumes) does Klemm write in an *immediately* recognizable Expressionist vein. Exclamation marks, belligerent derring-do, overweening bluster à la Becher, calls to destruction and anarchy, cosmic sabre-rattling, all are there:

> Trichterstürme will ich zusammenraffen,
> In Scherben schlagen, was noch steht und hält,
> Das Meer zertreten und die Erde zerklaffen,
> Leviathan des Untergangs wälz'ich mich über die Welt.
> Vernichte! Zerschmettre! Verderbe!
> Bäume auf! Schlag die blaue Zunge heraus!
> Verpaffe! Werde klein wie eine Laus.
> Kurz muß das Feuerwerk sein! Sterbe!

> (*Verse und Bilder*, p. 42)

I want to gather up storms in funnels, | Smash to pieces anything that is still standing and holding, | Trample down the sea and split open the earth, | A Leviathan of destruction I roll through the world.
Annihilate! Crush! Ruin! | Rise up in revolt! Thrust out your blue tongue! | Evaporate! Become as small as a louse. | The firework-display must be brief! Die!

This cacophony obtrudes into a volume, the characteristic voice of which is one of solemn rumination. Moreover, and this again distances him from Expressionism, there is no evidence in *Verse und Bilder*, or indeed in any of Klemm's poetry, that he believes in the power of poetry to solve all mankind's problems. Far from regarding his verse as some kind of panacea, he knows it is consigned to swift oblivion:

> Ich brüte über meinen 1500 Gedichten,
> Die ich zusammengestoppelt habe in schweißigen Nächten,
> Und ich wundere mich nicht mehr, daß ich verrückt geworden bin dabei.
> Es ist alles Mode, es ist alles nur Mode.[15]

I brood over my 1500 poems, | Which I have pieced together on sweaty nights, | And it no longer surprises me that in the process I have become crazy. | It is all fashion, all nothing but fashion.

Yet, if he does not repeat Expressionist claims to omniscience and omnipotence (indeed, in the poem 'Philosophie', he lists all the things which we do not and cannot know), or share certain Expressionist prepossessions, his cognates are, in some significant respects, the Expressionist poets. He has, it is true, nothing in common with the dynamic and hectic bluster of Becher, with the overheated religiousness of Werfel, with Heym's invocation of bleak threatened cities, with Stramm's meticulously chiselled verbal precipitates, or with the activists' call to revolution and moral and political renewal. Nor is there much evidence of urgent social concern or of interest in the world of the worker. Nevertheless he begins from the premise that everything must be demolished and then rebuilt from within the poet's self:

Wenn einst alles niedergerissen ist,
Alle Irrtümer zerstört, alle Gefühle gelöscht,
Wenn die Welten leer sind für so vieles Neue:
Welch eine Freiheit wird sein!

(Ergriffenheit, p. 20)

Once everything has been ripped down, | All errors expunged, all feelings obliterated, | When the worlds have been evacuated to make way for so many new things: | What freedom there will be!

In true Expressionist fashion, he seizes upon that 'freedom' to build a fictitious world, a world more fanciful than even the inveterately Utopian dreamworlds of Expressionism — a fairy-tale alternative to a world which, to the end of his life, he saw as fragmented, illusory and devoid of a higher purpose. Moreover, *Verse und Bilder* contains echoes of many Expressionist poets. His conviction that man is no longer in control of his destiny, that sinister forces lurk nearby and that life is an ineluctable cause for despair, together with his occasional retreat to the comfort of traditional verse forms, establishes his kinship with Georg Heym — indeed, the *Aufforderung* volume has a poem called 'Umbra vitae', the title of one of Heym's best known poems. The moth with its connotation of stubborn suicide, the 'horned graves' and 'the dogs which bark so loud' (in the poem 'Herbst'), the old men dying and then scurrying across 'grotto landscapes and volcanic craters' (in the poem 'Halbschlaf'), a pervasive atmosphere of armageddon though Klemm's demons operate within the realm of allegorical innocuousness and do not usually menace the modern industrial city — all this is again strongly reminiscent of Heym. Klemm, unlike Heym, hardly ever expresses a longing for some great final catastrophe, for some, any, kind of adventure:[16] on the contrary, an aura of gentle pessimism and melancholy, a kind of introspective taedium vitae, hangs over his depictions of the decay of a mummified world, calling to mind the poetry of Georg Trakl. The very title and shape of the poem 'Herbst' which contains lines like 'Rauch duftet fern und traurig' ('Smoke smells distant and sad') and 'Wir trinken einen toten Wein' ('We drink a dead wine'), the image of 'des Wahnsinns Abgrund' ('the abyss of madness') in the sonnet 'Meine Zeit', the spectacular intrusion of ghastly effects, the subdued soliloquizing voice, all reinforce the comparison with Trakl — and the volume *Ergriffenheit* has such titles as 'Abendruhe', 'Nachsinnen', 'Schwermut', 'Trüber Abend' and 'Winterabend'.

Yet the Expressionist poet who most readily comes to mind in any discussion of Klemm's work is Gottfried Benn. Both share a yearning for exotic climes, for sensual pleasures, for self-created dreamworlds, for irrational diversions. Emotion and oblivion and a Benn-like primitive sensuality are explicitly recommended and sought:

Die Sonne sinnt rot
Durch die geschlossenen Lider.
Alle Buchstaben stäuben
In den goldenen Trichter des Lichts.
Warmes Vergessen
Strömt ihnen nach. Wachstum atmet still.   (Verse und Bilder, p. 26)

The sun muses red | Through the closed eye-lids. | All letters dissolve | Into the golden funnel of light. | Warm oblivion | flows after them. Growth breathes silently.

This poem, 'Mittagsstunde', with its sunbathing bodies and general sultry atmosphere of hedonistic drift and lines like 'Frauen ziehen vorüber . . . um die Schläfen Mohn' ('Women move past . . . poppy around their brows'), is directly reminiscent of Benn's 1915 poem 'Ikarus' with its opening quatrain:

> O Mittag, der mit heißem Heu mein Hirn
> zu Wiese, flachem Land und Hirten schwächt,
> daß ich hinrinne und, den Arm im Bach,
> den Mohn an meine Schläfe ziehe.

O noon that with hot hay reduces my brain | To meadow, flat land and shepherds, | So that I flow away and, my arm in the stream, | Draw the poppy to my brow.

Indeed, the very titles of two of Klemm's volumes, *Verzauberte Ziele* anud *Traumschutt*, are heavy with resonances of Gottfried Benn's work. Klemm, like Benn, suffering from the curse of possessing a brain, seeks comfort and possible salvation in the example of animals which live by instinct:

> Und Tiere stehen da mit Heiligenscheinen,
> Indes wir Zauberer, Ketzer und Sophisten,
> Uns bäumen in Erkenntnisqual und schreien.
>
> (*Aufforderung*, p. 35)

And animals stand there with haloes, | Whilst we magicians, heretics and sophists | Writhe in the agony of knowledge and scream.

Klemm, a slave to thinking, longs for the instinctual, irrational world of the animal:

> Wir denken und erreichen das Ziel nie,
> Wir quälen uns und kommen nicht weiter.
>
> (Quoted in: Brockmann, 'Untersuchungen', p. 98)

We think and never reach the goal, | We torment ourselves and get no further.

The hallucinatory quality of the poetry in *Verse und Bilder*, the preoccupation with dreams and imagination and sensuality, the implicit repudiation of rationality, recall much of Benn's post-*Morgue* work.

Of approximately forty-five poems in *Verse und Bilder* less than a quarter rhyme either in full or in part. That is the usual proportion of rhyming to non-rhyming in Klemm's poetry. Lengths of lines vary bewilderingly within the same poem, within the same stanza even. Klemm occasionally writes perfectly shaped and regular sonnets, but his typical form is the shortish poem (that is, not more than four four-lined stanzas) consisting of free-rhythmic, non-rhyming quatrains with verse ends linked assonantly either with other verse ends or with some accentuated interior word. He regards poetic form, in theory and apparently in practice, as a kind of natural development or as the organic outgrowth of an active vital principle:

> Ich wuchs unaufhaltsam in meine Form.
> Nun stehe ich so, wie du mich gewollt hast.
>
> (*Ergriffenheit*, p. 69)

I grew irresistibly into my form. | Now I stand the way you wanted me.

Accordingly, he does not often use self-contained poetic forms. He offers bundles of lines rather than stanzas tightly organized into units by rhythmic means or by content. He favours unmediated transition, without apparent nexus, from one stanza to the next, from one image to the next. Metre and rhyme are generally discarded. A clear contrast exists here between the thumping, dynamic stresses and rhythmic tension of Heym's work and the prosaic, soliloquizing, laissez-aller rhythms and voice of Klemm's poetry. Instead of Stramm's taut triangles of energy and intensity, Klemm gives us short-lived torrents of self-generating images or sheaves of free-wheeling, reflective or metaphorical associations in stanzaic form. This chain-reaction, which makes the end of each stanza, indeed of each poem, something of a matter of chance (recalling Rilke's general criticism of Expressionism), is invariably not sustained by a thematic ductus, but is urged ever onwards by the imperious thought or idea or emotion which is tied only loosely to its object and, drifting further and further from it, gradually and irresistibly dissolves. In this respect at least, Klemm belongs to that group of Expressionist poets which includes Werfel and Becher, for they, too, make a virtue of not reining back the flow of images and nouns. Literary critics have tended to be generous in their praise for Klemm's facility with free-floating images and associations. Yet what these critics, in their efforts to establish his kinship with Expressionism, have called 'richness of imagination', 'wide-ranging kaleidoscopic effects' and 'brilliantly evoked phantasmagoria'[17] can be shapeless and repetitive. The general effect of his fondness for compound words, for neologisms, and tongue-twisting queues (like 'begeisterungsbrausend', 'Silberkaskadengelächter' and 'Jugendunschuldsschlaf') is to add to an already over-populated, sclerotic[18] verbal tableau and, once again, to bring him into line with such Expressionist poets as Ehrenstein and Stadler. Unlike their poetry, however, Klemm's — and this is the point at which the influence of 'Jugendstil' makes itself most clearly felt — is hardly ever anchored to the worldly world in which there is some kind of an awareness of, and some attempt to take issue with, contemporary political, moral and social problems. His interest is in 'parallel worlds which silently crumble'.[19] An aura of timelessness which, it is true, hangs over a great deal of Expressionist poetry is diluted ever thinner and spread ever wider in Klemm's work. The almost invariable movement of the best Expressionist poetry (for example, Heym's and Trakl's) — from observed to observer, from an outer to an inner reality and back again on a return journey — is not reflected in his work. Only briefly and rarely does the outside world impinge upon the poet's world of self-generating images and abstractions where 'the chimera gives birth to the chimera' ('Die Chimäre gebiert die Chimäre'; *Entfaltung*, p. 52):

> In mir träumen die Träume ihre Träume.
>
> (Entfaltung, p. 69)
>
> In me the dreams dream their dreams.

After *Gloria*, and beginning with *Verse und Bilder*, the imponderable nature of his verse becomes more and more evident. He knows it:

Das Gestaltete geht über in Traum,
Der heraustritt aus blinzelnder Versunkenheit.

(*Ergriffenheit*, p. 79)

That which has been shaped issues into dream, | Which emerges from eye-blinking absorption.

In the same way, he knows about the elusive, ever mobile nature of things. Yet the hope abides that at least some shapes will take on substance and clarity:

Gestalten heben sich ab,
Verschwommen und körperlos.
Ich weiß nur, daß sie vorhanden —
Einiges von ihnen wird deutlich.

(*Ergriffenheit*, p. 109)

Figures come into focus, | Indistinct and bodiless. | All I know is that they are there — | Some of them become clear.

Analysis of the poem 'Phantasie' from *Verse und Bilder* will demonstrate how swiftly after *Gloria* the debilitating process of anaemia sets in and how Klemm's poetry is composed of the kind of abstractions which critics customarily find in Expressionism — decked out, in his case, with 'Jugendstil' paraphernalia.

Ich muß suchen nach unbesetzten Bühnen,
Ausweichend ins Phantastische . . .[20]

Es gibt Tiefen, wo Kitsch und Kunst eins werden.[21]

Ich sehe die Geister in dunklen Lauben zechen
Und schimmernde Weiber sich dehnen auf nackten Thronen.
Ich höre, wie Riesen ihre Fesseln zerbrechen.
Fahl schimmern die Schlösser, in denen die Greifen wohnen.

Kolosse schwanken heran. Cherubgestalten,
Nacht im wilden Auge, schwarz rauscht ihr Gefieder
Empor. Lodernde Fahnen entfalten
Sich. Chöre verhallen und wilde Sturmlieder.

Wohlan! Wohlauf! altes Herz! Mit unzähligen Maschen
Ziehen die schimmernden Träume über die Welt.
Wer hat sie gewebt? Wer will ihre Enden erhaschen?
Strahlender Schmuck, der ins Unendliche fällt.

I see the spirits carousing in dark bowers | And shimmering women stretching out on naked thrones. | I hear giants smashing their chains. | Pallidly shimmer the castles in which the gryphons live.

Colossi totter up. Cherub figures, | Night in their wild eyes, their wings rustling black | As they soar up. Blazing flags unfurl. | Choruses and wild revolutionary songs fade away.

Come on! Cheer up! old heart! With countless stitches | The shimmering dreams drift across the world. | Who has woven them? Who will catch hold of their ends? | Radiant finery which falls into infinity.

'Phantasie' consists of three free rhythmic quatrains — the typical form of a Klemm poem. It rhymes and, in line 9, it apostrophizes — two factors a good deal less typical of Klemm's work, as is the heavy enjambment in the second stanza. It is impossible to date the poem. 'Phantasie' appears in both *Verse und Bilder* and *Entfaltung*, which probably means that it is an early post-*Gloria* poem. It is typical of that whole band of Klemm's poetry which mixes Expressionist features with 'Jugendstil' influences, surrealistic effects and many of the components which Frye enumerates as integral parts of 'the ironic mode'. It is not glutted by abstract nouns. On the contrary, for the first two stanzas at least, it describes a series of incidents which the poet sees in his mind's eye. It does not 'say' much, but then precisely that has been the cardinal feature of Klemm's poetry.

From the beginning, the poet makes it clear that *he* is responsible for seeing and hearing the events of the first two stanzas. In spite of the generalizing nature of the title, it is his imagination which is at work here. '*I see . . . I hear . . .*', though metrically they are not stressed, direct our attention to the poet's own creative powers. Here we have an Expressionist poet fulfilling what he sees as his principal role — recreating reality:

Wilhelm Klemm abandons the landscape of the earth and all that our consciousness has gleaned from sense impressions and experiences of reality; his mind creates a new universe in which there are no dimensions, no natural laws, no causal nexus.[22]

Pinthus's words help to explain what Klemm is seeking to achieve in 'Phantasie': to invoke an alternative world to the one which is being torn asunder by war and in which man has so little control over his destiny. The poet sees spirits carousing and women lying prostrate on thrones — presumably it is the women, not the thrones, which are 'naked'. The word 'schimmernd' ('shimmering') underlines the insubstantiality and ephemerality of the whole imaginative venture. Reference to reclining women reminds us that Klemm's last volume, *Die Satanspuppe*, is a paean to sexual and erotic delights:

> Aus allen Gelenken schlagen zuckersüße Flammen,
> Ein eisiger Bogen der Lust krümmt sich tief.
> O ihr ewigen Gefühlswege,
> Eure Bahn ist himmlischer als alles andere!
>
> (p. 43)

From all the joints of the body shoot sugar-sweet flames, | An icy curve of desire squirms low. | O you never-ending ways of feeling, | Your course is more heavenly than everything else.

In 'Phantasie' the poet yearns wistfully for some kind of medieval, fairy-tale, amoral world in which physical needs are unconditionally satisfied. It is a world peopled by giants. These the poet does not see, but he hears them breaking free from their chains — perhaps as a symbol of his own desire to liberate himself from the bonds of conventional morality and launch himself upon the kind of hedonistic life depicted in *Die Satanspuppe*. Line 4, with its shimmering castles in which the gryphons live, is undiluted 'Jugendstil'. 'Fahl' ('pallidly') is the right adverb to invoke the evanescent nature of the world which the poet's imagination has constructed: it suggests the gauzy character of much 'Jugendstil' writing. The first stanza provides then the picture of a medieval-cum-mythical region: that picture is composed of four constituents with no necessarily logical and causal nexus, though the image of the giants' breaking their chains leads tentatively to the 'shimmering castles' where the giants may be being held captive. For the moment at least, there is nothing arbitrary or adventitious about the way in which the four elements are strung together. They are part of an unreal, illogical dream-world, a world which is a good deal less intimidating and eerie than the nightmare engendered by Georg Heym's imagination in, say, 'Die Dämonen der Stadt'.

In the second stanza more figures appear from Roman and Greek antiquity — colossi, who are so tall that they totter up unsteadily. The rest of the stanza, which is all bits and pieces of staccato verse, has to do with 'cherub figures'. They are wild-eyed, the reference to night and blackness in line 6 suggests menacing belligerence, as does the way their plumage (that is, their wings) rustle. They are waving flags — 'lodernde Fahnen' is an accepted image, yet not perhaps a cliché. Presumably these flags are meant to conjure the idea of rebellion, though no hint is given about the possible target of the 'cherub figures'' revolt. 'Phantasie' is the one poem of Klemm's work which Pinthus places in the 'Aufruf und Empörung' ('Appeal and Rebellion') section of *Menschheitsdämmerung*, and so it is obvious how Pinthus interprets it. Just as in the first stanza the giants break free (to go where? to do what?), in the second the preliminaries of a rebellion (against what?) are described. Klemm fills these first two stanzas with verbs denoting a considerable amount of movement and activity ('stretch out', 'smash', 'totter', 'rustle' and 'unfurl') apparently for their own sake. A great deal seems to begin to happen, and then, like the choruses and revolutionary songs in line 8, just subsides and fades away. This is another example of the continual itch to be on the move, to set off anew, which informs, as we have seen, the poetry of Heynicke and indeed much Expressionist poetry. Another symptom of the same intense restlessness[23] is an abiding suspicion of anything finished or integral, and here too Klemm's poetry interlocks with a fundamental Expressionist tenet — *and* with that part of National Socialist philosophy which decrees that 'the true German remains throughout his life a God-seeker: pathetic the man who is completed' (*Michael*, p. 52). Klemm's version of the same basic belief reads:

> Gib Sprünge, gib Risse, Mängel und Widerspruch,
> Bögen, die klaffen, Krakelüren, Spaltensysteme, o gib
> Verschiebungen, Rätsel und Dissonanzen. Nur nicht den Fluch
> Des unermeßlich Vollendeten, das tolle Prinzip
> Deiner unerhörten, aalglatten Richtigkeit,
> Diese Ewigkeit aus einem einzigen Guß!
>
> (*Aufforderung*, p. 13)

Give cracks, give lacerations, flaws and contradiction,/ Arches which yawn open, craquelures, methods of fission, o give/ Displacements, puzzles and dissonances. Anything but the curse/ Of the immensely perfect, the crazy principle/ Of your absurd, slippery rightness,/ This eternity of time from one single mould!

The poem 'Phantasie' provides an illustration of just such a fragmentary, aimlessly active, jarring world. Its first two stanzas depict a scene filled with movement and are composed of shards of information, as if the poet were concerned to recapture the ever-changing and unstable tableau which his imagination has conceived and which is on the retreat from the harness of concept and logical categorizing. The problem confronting Klemm is how to 'express' this movement which he sees as the essence of life:

> Bewegung schwingt, hört niemals auf.
> Das Leben pflanzt sich fort mit tausend süßen Wurzeln . . .
> Die Seele drängt immer zu Gott.

(Verse und Bilder, p. 60)

Movement swings, never ceases. | Life propagates itself in a thousand sweet roots . . . the soul is always straining to reach God.

Usually he has recourse to the periphrastic accumulation of abstract nouns, which amount to no more than empty husks and mere structures, as if the constant flux of life has swamped them and evacuated them of all content. Or, as in 'Phantasie', he adopts the method of enumerating a series of apparently haphazard activities. In fact, in this instance, they cohere into a reasonably ordered scene.

The first line of the last stanza goes a little way towards supporting Pinthus's ascription of this poem to the 'Aufruf und Empörung' section of his anthology. The poet calls upon his aged heart to cheer up, wearied as it is by what Klemm elsewhere calls 'our trashy existence, the sullen funeral procession of slavery' (*Die Satanspuppe*, p. 13). The shimmering (again!) dreams, which he sees as woven by unknown hands, drift across the world. Optimism, as well as encouragement, is evident in the first couplet of this stanza, in the epithets 'unzählig' and 'schimmernd'. And then, in the final two lines, comes the only slight hint of portentousness when the poet inquires after the source of the dreams, and asks, returning to the image of the 'countless stitches', who there will be to 'catch hold of their ends'. There is no bitterness, no anger, let alone 'Empörung', in the penultimate line, as there is on other occasions when the poet wonders aloud about the creator of the world. The last line, again pure 'Jugendstil', assembles all dreams and all figments of imagination into 'radiant finery', which he then proceeds to consign to the safety of infinity. His dream of carousing spirits and shimmering women and unfettered giants will never end: he can, as he maintains in the poem 'Phantasie' (another one), 'rely on his imagination'.[24] He has built a dream-world: Brockmann writes in terms of Klemm's 'dream architecture' ('Untersuchungen', p. 141), and Klemm himself in *Verzauberte Ziele* invents such words as 'dream pagodas', 'dream apocalypse' and 'dream fissures'. This dream-world is as secure as anything 'shimmering' and 'pallid' can be. The magic flight[25] which 'Phantasie' recounts appears to end, or rather not end, happily.

'Phantasie' is rhythmically is messy hotchpotch. Newton's claim in *Form in the 'Menschheitsdämmerung'* that it is 'ruined by inexcusable rhythmic laxness' and that it is an unhappy blend of dactylic and anapaestic metre is well justified (Newton, pp. 135 & 147). He also sees it as a paradigm of 'disformation' — that is, 'the establishment of certain formal expectations, either categorically (by starting with a known verse form) or inductively, and the subsequent noticeable abandonment of this form to gain some expressive effect' (p. 228). Newton does not tell us what this 'expressive effect' might be, though the general bittiness and confusion of the rhythm probably has something to do with Klemm's associative technique of stringing image on image and with the way he views the world, even his dream-world, as something essentially fragmentary. The six pairs of rhymes are weak ('Gefieder' | 'Sturmlieder' and 'Maschen' | 'haschen' are especially feeble), the lengths of the lines vary considerably and apparently, in lines 7 and 8, at random, and the metre hops about waywardly. Frequently in his poetry Klemm displays a nonchalant contempt for prosody: in comparison with the poems of *Verzauberte Ziele* and *Die Satanspuppe*, 'Phantasie' is a mild example of that contempt. It is manifestly controlled and consciously shaped. Nevertheless it illustrates the validity of Loerke's strictures with regard to Klemm's poetic form:

Klemm's imagination is too full of densely coloured life and light, gentle movement. The consequence is that it had no time to perfect a considerable number of images which are loose and flimsy in construction, he becomes careless and over-hasty . . .[26]

Carelessness, haste, lack of tight control — we are once again put in mind of Rilke's criticism of Expressionism.

Conclusions

> Blow your soap-bubbles, mystical magician,
> Each one mirrors a sublime symbol.
> (*Verzauberte Ziele*, p. 32)

Klemm's later volumes pick up and develop many of the themes which are to be found in *Verse und Bilder*. God, immanence, oblivion, loneliness, purposelessness, movement, time passing, inadequacy of words, invocations of the soul, vitalism, lust, profound hostility to learning and rationality, existential despair, mythical regions, hybrid creatures, strange deities, dream-worlds — these are the figures, themes and landscapes which recur in the six volumes following upon *Verse und Bilder*. The influence of 'Jugendstil' remains strong: Brockmann is wrong to intimate that 'Jugendstil' was a fashion which Klemm simply outgrew. Klemm does nothing in these volumes to fill his poems with the kind of substance and social-political-historical awareness and insight which Lukács misses in Expressionism. On the contrary, by *Traumschutt* and *Verzauberte Ziele* — the very titles are a pointer — Klemm's language and style have become ever more abstract and gossamer. In *Verzauberte Ziele*, for example, he develops the habit of concocting abstract nouns in 'Ge-' — 'Geträum', 'Gerank', 'Getürm', 'Geklüfte', 'Säulengeschiebe', 'Trüm-mergeschiebe', 'Getuschel' etc . . . Such substantives, in which, usually, physical or mental activity is precipitated and ossified, have the effect of some kind of verbal rennet and illustrate the progressively glaireous nature of his verse. And the abstract world which he constructs is rendered so remote, so pure that its surface is never clouded by anything as substantial as a thought or idea.

L

Examination of one volume of verse and one poem in detail, supported by quotations and references from other volumes, suffices to indicate the character of Klemm's poetic development and achievement. The pattern which emerges can be seen as a series of stages: non-conformism, war, taedium vitae, an interest in the grotesque and the erotic, recourse to the landscape of the imagination, then to aestheticism and the hectic confusion of abstract and phantasmagoric images, and finally, in *Die Satanspuppe*, a heedless plunge into sensuality. These stages overlap, but they represent an accurate sketch of the particular emphases and concerns in Klemm's poetry at a given time in its evolution. Invariably it is not a dynamic or passionate poetry: its tone is contemplative and subdued, its form is nonchalantly conservative, it looks as if it is (and often turns out to be) a conglomeration of heterogeneous fragments. His conviction of the fragmentariness and flux of existence is balanced by a belief in the power of the moment to transcend time and the passing of time. In the moment, lifted out of causal necessity and the spatial dimension, Klemm finds the mystic experience of the unity of the human soul and God: the moment for him represents the blissful encounter between thought and object, between thing and image in a metaphor or line of verse. In this respect, Klemm is fulfilling Picard's view of the Expressionist poet (quoted derisively by Lukács)[27] as someone who 'plucks things out of the eddying chaos' and fixes them with no regard to causality or historical context. In offering enthusiastic assent to the moment, Klemm follows the example of Benn and Nietzsche. The plaintive 'O meine Zeit! So namenlos zerrissen' ('O my age! So dreadfully rent asunder . . .'; *Aufforderung*, p. 124) with all its separate bits and pieces ('Gesang und Riesenstädte, Traumlawinen, | Verblaßte Länder, Pole ohne Ruhm, | Die sündigen Weiber, Not und Heldentum . . .'; 'Song and giant towns, dream avalanches, | Faded countries, poles without fame, | The sinful women, need and heroism . . .') is offset by an urgent demand for fragmentation and discontinuity in such a poem as 'Heraklit'. This is the opposite end of the spectrum to the Marxist view of reality. Klemm attempts to illustrate thought processes by abstracting away from their content, to win metaphors from conceptual compositions, to depict ideas lyrically; he chooses allegories not to convey abstract things in a sensual image, but to offer a kind of morphology of thought by grasping abstract processes physically. The result is that his poems become a sort of relaystation, hanks of metaphorical fragments and lumps of abstraction which have no reference to empirical reality and bear titles like 'Form', 'Verses', 'Series', 'Scene', 'Phenomena' and 'Summons'. It is impossible to find substance in such wholly characteristic lines as:

> Aus edler, freier Luft, wo sich zarter als Glück
> Die wunderbaren Einheiten des Göttlichen verflüchtigen,
> Denen nachahmend die Meilen des Augenblicks
> Zerspringen in schwelgenden Offenbarungen.
>
> (*Verse und Bilder*, p. 37)

From noble, free air where, more tender than happiness, | The wonderful units of the divine evaporate, | Imitating them, the miles of the moment | Explode in luxuriating revelations.

Here, above all, Lukács's criteria are relevant, though his polemic against Expressionism is directed towards what he sees as the movement's *political* 'abstracting away from reality'. Uninterested in political issues (at least on the evidence of his poetry), Klemm raises no expectations in that field and hence disappoints none. Only if Lukács's criticism of Expressionism can be regarded as 'purely literary', divorced from all politics and economics — which, of course, it cannot — can that criticism be directly applied to Klemm's poetry. Nevertheless, his categories and criteria have been helpful in assessing Klemm's work.

It is certainly possible to overestimate Klemm's achievement and to exaggerate its Expressionist aspect. Pinthus consistently does both ('. . . creating a thousand new lyrical means, Klemm multiplies a thousandfold the lyrical effect'[28]). In retrospect, Pinthus's inclusion of nineteen of Klemm's poems in *Menschheitsdämmerung* (when Heym is represented by thirteen, Trakl by ten, van Hoddis by five) seems wrong-headed — wrong-headed, moreover, by Pinthus's own standards as propounded in the introduction of his anthology. There he declares that he has not sought to present either 'a comprehensive picture of the lyric poetry of our age' or 'a selection of the best contemporary poetry compiled on the basis of (spurious) absolute standards of qualitative judgement', but 'the characteristic poetry of . . . the young generation of the last decade'.[29] Klemm's poetry is *not* typical of the Expressionist generation: the abstractions which fill his poems and, Lukács argues, all Expressionist art are not summoned in the name of some Socialist Utopia (as with Becher), some master-plan for the redemption of all mankind (as with Werfel), or even a fervent religiosity (as with Heynicke), but come and go at the arbitrary behest of the poet's imagination. By what Pinthus calls 'absolute standards of qualitative judgement', too, the sample of Klemm's poetry in *Menschheitsdämmerung* now appears too generous. When thought has its own impotence for subject matter, when a poet ignores the content of reflection (convinced as he is that the world is not to be explained by rational thinking) and seeks to illustrate in images thought's empty processes, reflection and thought become vacuous brooding and obsessive introspection, the heart is left out of account, and the state of abstractedness which results expresses itself in verbal husks. Klemm's 'we seek the glittering something. | Everything else is but the world's refuse' (*Verzauberte Ziele*, p. 22) is not just a cynical aside aimed at his generation, but a neat comment on his own poetic practice. He is on occasions capable of providing detailed graphic and concrete evocations of natural phenomena. On such occasions he matches the power of much of Heym's verse:

> Das Gewitter erhob seine Ebenholzstirn,
> Die ungeheure Quadriga rollte langsam herauf,
> Das Land versinkt gelb, Täler gehen unter,
> Wälder stieren, Gespenster kreischen vorüber.
>
> (*Aufforderung*, p. 60)

The storm raised its ebony brow, | The huge quadriga rolled slowly up, | The countryside is immersed in yellow, valleys disappear from view, | Forests stare, spectres screech past.

The presence of something menacing and huge and real informs such lines as these, and the menace, instead of being allowed to coagulate in clumsy substantives, issues from a genuine picturing of a storm-scene. Sometimes, too, Klemm achieves a combination of Heym's power and Trakl's elusive mystery without diluting that elusiveness to wan shadow-boxing:

> Die Wälder bluten schwarz hinab ins Tal.
> Die Nacht schließt sich darüber wie eine Falle.
> Der Himmel ist matter Tuff. Alles schweigt.
> Im Hintergrund wird einer vom Teufel geholt.
>
> (*Aufforderung*, p. 66)

The forests seep black blood down into the valley. | The night closes in like a trap. | The sky is dull tufa. Everything falls silent. | In the background someone is fetched by the devil.

Klemm is good at natural descriptions like these, he is good at individual lines, but *Gloria* is the only volume in which this kind of concreteness and careful precision, combined with vivid imagining, is sustained over long stretches of verse. His war-poetry lacks the profound humanity of Owen's, the controlled anger of Sorley's or the interesting linguistic experimentation of Rosenberg's or Stramm's, but its unsensational allegiance to detail and to fact and its determination not to be self-indulgent or over-awed by the size of events make it a considerable achievement. Examination of a poet who is allegedly an important practitioner of German Expressionism has thus led to the following paradoxical position: the strengths of his first volume of verse reside in precisely those qualities which cannot be called Expressionist, and the style and themes of subsequent volumes have more to do with 'Jugendstil' than with Expressionism.

This does not, however, mean that the Expressionist aspect of his work must be *under*-estimated. In many important ways his poetry is apodeictically Expressionist. For example, the abstractions which go to make up his poems are all part of a fictive redemption of the world. The influence of Lichtenstein's self-deprecating irony and collage technique, of van Hoddis's method of free association whereby a poem consists of a dead-pan concatenation of apparently dislocated images, can be discerned throughout Klemm's work. Yet, again and again, it is of the poetry of Gottfried Benn that we think when we read Klemm's verse. Like Benn, Klemm experiences the fragmentariness of a destroyed world *and* of his own ego and, incidentally fulfilling the second of the three pre-conditions which Nietzsche stipulates for the onset of nihilism as a psychological state,[30] comes to an intrinsi-cally nihilistic view of life. Perhaps it is not over-stretching the comparison to see Klemm's life and work in something like the same terms in which Benn's are customarily interpreted, to regard Klemm's poetry as a symptom of what Thomas Mann calls 'the impotence of the mind and reason in comparison with the powers latent in the depths of the soul, with the dynamics of passion, the irrational, the unconscious'.[31] There are obvious overt parallels between Benn and Klemm — both were medical doctors, Benn's 1924 volume *Schutt* is matched by Klemm's *Traum-schutt* (1920), and both poets became more or less silent in the early 1920s. There is in their verse the same almost total lack of interest in politics and the state, a rejection of the ideas of religion and progress, an embracing of nihilism and irrationality, a retreat to dreams and dream-worlds and self-induced hallucinatory states and exotic climes and past ages, a sense of aimlessness and profound personal and artistic failure, and a similar degree of self-loathing and historic fatalism. Benn's *Ithaka* (1914), in which a biology professor is brutally murdered, is paralleled in sentiment and tone by the vicious amorality of *Die Satanspuppe*; the 'destruction of reality' which Benn welcomes in Expressionism[32] corresponds to Klemm's call for a tabula rasa; Benn's fascination for formal patterns within associative connections,[33] his cult of formalism and abstraction in art, all have much in common with Klemm's view of art as a kind of magic, with his recourse to abstractions and his habit of associative images; Benn's theory of 'Artistik' and 'Form' is intended to be a means of hallucinating the intellect, and where he speaks of 'value of intoxication' and 'value of high emotion',[34] Klemm writes of 'hashish of the soul' as a possible way of dulling potential rational protest; Benn's 'Ardour passes itself on. | Sap prepares to trickle. Earth calls . . .'[35] is echoed generally throughout *Die Satanspuppe* and more particularly in the lines 'O du großartiges Wort; primitiv! primitiv! | Ich könnte dich lallen bis zur Benommenheit!' ('O you magnificent word; primitive! primitive! | I could stammer you out until my mind goes numb'; *Die Satanspuppe*, p. 53 and p. 56) repeated twice in the poems 'Magdalene' and 'Umgang'; neither poet evinces any interest in writing about the way other people are living at that time, singly or communally, in that historical situation; and both poets, by 1922, come to regard their artistic careers as failures. These are the obvious and important similarities between a major European poet and a comparatively minor German poet. The differences between them in terms of range, ability and poetic achievement are considerable.

The purpose of venturing a comparison between Klemm and Benn is twofold: to demonstrate that Klemm has much in common with a poet who, at least in the early part of his career, was irrefutably an Expressionist writer, and, following Sokel's example in linking Klemm's name with the National Socialist party (Sokel, p. 96 and p. 103), to seek to establish a connection between Expressionism and National Socialism. It is certainly possible to *imagine* Klemm reaching, eagerly if temporarily, like Benn,[36] for the 'poisonous goblets'[37] proffered by the Nazis. But that would be pure speculation. Unlike Bronnen, who was pleased to place himself at the disposal of the Nazi leadership, unlike Benn, who in the 1930s briefly declared himself for the National Socialists, unlike Heynicke, who wrote two plays in their honour, Klemm (as far as is known) fell silent and stayed silent after 1922 and was hounded out of the 'Schrifttumskammer' in 1937. Again unlike Bronnen, Benn and Heynicke, Klemm after 1922 enjoyed the security of being a very successful publisher, perhaps finding in that security and success consolation for whatever sense of poetic failure he may have felt, and was consequently less likely to share the potential and, as it turned out, actual vulnerability of the other three. Examination of Klemm's poetry in the light of Lukács's criticism of Expressionism has served to demonstrate above all that Klemm cannot be placed unequivocally amongst Expressionist poets, that the Expressionist aspect of his work is balanced and diluted by other influences, and that, therefore, in any attempt to verify (or refute) the Marxist claim that Expressionism somehow issued into National Socialism, his work can be of only limited value. Moreover, it seems inappropriate to think in terms of the possible political implications of an oeuvre which remains so resolutely unpolitical and consists principally of individual items as insubstantial as 'soap-bubbles'.

NOTES

1   F. Nietzsche, *Die Philosophie im tragischen Zeitalter der Griechen*; *Nietzsche Werke*, III/ 2, 336.
2   D. Bain, 'War Poet', quoted in: *The Terrible Rain: The War Poets 1939—1945*, edited by B. Gardner (London, 1966), p. 159.
3   Sokel, *The Writer in Extremis*, p. 20.
4   In: *The Letters of Charles Sorley*, p. 273.
5   See Wilfred Owen's poem 'Insensibility'.
6   W. Klemm, 'Gedanken', *Gloria* (Munich, 1915), p. 61.
7   K. Pinthus, 'Wilhelm Klemm', *Jahresring* (1968), p. 317.
8   W. Klemm, 'Neigung' (1919), *Ergriffenheit* (Nendeln and Liechtenstein, 1973), p. 25.
9   By his last volume, *Die Satanspuppe* (1922), he is proclaiming 'Friends, reality is not at all reality'. See 'Zweifel', *Die Satanspuppe* (Nendeln and Liechtenstein, 1973), p. 42.
10 The sentence is Rupert Brooke's and is quoted in: F. R. Leavis, *New Bearings in English Poetry* (Harmondsworth, 1972), p. 52.
11 W. Klemm, 'Dinge' (1917), *Aufforderung* (Wiesbaden, 1961), p. 51.
12 Thom Gunn, 'Touch', *Touch* (London, 1967), p. 27.
13 For information on 'Jugendstil' see D. Jost, *Literarischer Jugendstil* (Stuttgart, 1969) and J. Hermand, *Lyrik des Jugendstils. Eine Anthologie* (Stuttgart, 1964). Hermand uses such headings as 'Spring feelings', 'The great god Pan', 'Artificial paradises', 'The wonder of the body', 'Dream through twilight' and 'Pool and boat'.
14 W. Klemm, 'Das Licht', *Verse und Bilder* (Berlin, 1916), p. 7.
15 W. Klemm, 'Gegen Mitternacht' (undated), quoted in: Brockmann, 'Untersuchungen zur Lyrik Wilhelm Klemms', p. 88.
16 Exceptions are 'Wintermorgen' (in *Ergriffenheit*), 'Verzweiflung' (in *Aufforderung*) and 'Qualen' (in the same volume).
17 See, for example, H. Benzmann in: *Zeitschrift für Bücherfreunde*, 10 (1918–19), col. 266, and K. Pinthus in: *Zeitschrift für Bücherfreunde*, 9 (1917), col. 557.
18 In the *Aufforderung* poem 'Qualen', referring to lightning flashes, Klemm appropriately (he was, after all, a doctor!) speaks of 'Arteriosklerosengeäder' — arterosclerotic veins.
19 W. Klemm, 'Ablehnung', *Entfaltung* (Nendeln and Liechtenstein, 1973), p. 53.
20 'I must look for unoccupied stages, | Slipping away into the fantastic . . .'; 'Die Satanspuppe', *Die Satanspuppe*, p. 11.
21 'There are depths at which kitsch and art become one'; 'Duett', *Die Satanspuppe*, p. 15.
22 K. Pinthus, *Jahresring* (1968), p. 317.
23 To reinforce this point, see Klemm's 1916 poem 'Die Stunden' which begins, after the fashion of Kurt Heynicke, with the rhetorical question: 'Where to, o my restless heart, where to?'; *Verse und Bilder*, p. 5.
24 In: *Verzauberte Ziele* (Nendeln and Liechtenstein, 1973), p. 15.
25 'Magische Flucht' is the title of a poem in *Aufforderung*.
26 O. Loerke, *Literarische Aufsätze* (Heidelberg and Darmstadt, 1967), p. 95.
27 G. Lukács, *Werke*, 17 vols (Neuwied and Berlin, 1962–75), IV, 137.
28 K. Pinthus, *Die Aktion*, 25 August 1917, col. 461.
29 *Menschheitsdämmerung*, p. 23. The quoted words were written in the Autumn of 1919.
30 The second pre-condition is that a totality is postulated and subsequently *not* found in the world. In: 'Hinfall der kosmologischen Werte'; Musarion edition, XVIII, 14–16. Interestingly, Werfel, performing a complete volte-face, echoes Nietzsche by linking free association with nihilism in a late (1937–45) aphorism in: F. Werfel, *Zwischen oben und unten*, p. 361.

31 T. Mann, 'Die Stellung Freuds in der modernen Geistesgeschichte' (1929); *Gesammelte Werke*, X, 261.

32 G. Benn, 'Expressionismus'; *Gesammelte Werke*, I, 243.

33 G. Benn, 'Schöpferische Konfession' (1919); *Gesammelte Werke*, IV, 189.

34 G. Benn, 'Probleme der Lyrik' (1951); *Gesammelte Werke*, I, 512.

35 G. Benn, 'Mann und Frau gehn durch die Krebsbaracke'; *Gesammelte Werke*, III, 14–15.

36 Or Bronnen: for example, a comparison could be developed between the perverted depravity and sensationalism of Klemm's *Die Satanspuppe* and Bronnen's *Vatermord* and *Roßbach*.

37 The phrase ('nach giftigen Kelchen greifend') is Klemm's and appears in his poem 'Menschliches', *Entfaltung*, p. 58.

VIII CONCLUSIONS

> Poet: A thing slipp'd idly from me.
> Our poesy is as a gum, which oozes
> From whence 'tis nourish'd . . . my free drift
> halts not particularly, but moves itself
> In a wide sea of wax.[1]

> The idealism of the young is no more than a
> jelly of sentiment. Infuse this jelly with the
> germ of an idea and it sets into a Communist
> or Fascist.[2]

> How much of this mobilized feeling could have
> been expended on a different future! . . . The
> Expressionists split up. The feeling dispersed
> in all directions. Fascism seized upon
> some of it.[3]

Many of the critical categories with which this study of Expressionist poetry began emerged naturally in the course of discussions and analyses of individual poems. This does not mean that any generalized critical onslaught on Expressionism should be accepted without reservation. On the contrary, application of Rilke's, Mann's, Lukács's, George's and Musil's criticism has served to highlight what is lastingly valuable in Expressionism — in particular Stramm's miniaturist distillations of battle-field events and sexual conflict, Heym's nightmarish visions and powerful invocations of the destructive forces lurking in that eerie limbo immediately before the First World War, and Klemm's (as it turned out, largely *un*-Expressionistic) war-poetry. No doubt, examination of other Expressionist poets, for example Trakl or Benn or Ehrenstein, would have led to a similar need to qualify the critical obloquy to which much of literary Expressionism has been subjected. Werfel's and Heynicke's poetry, on the other hand, issues directly from the spirit of the age: poetry like theirs modifies and shapes the sensibility of the age in the very act of responding so uncritically to it, and, as verse written for and in the moment, risks a swift demise. If Stramm and Heym emerge comparatively unscathed from the examination to which their work has been subjected, Werfel's poetry (but *not* his prose) now seems a pot-pourri of haphazard thinking and reckless heart-baring, Heynicke's verse remains stubbornly and justifiably the work of a minor writer, and Klemm's poetry can be termed Expressionist only with the severest qualifications.

Yet examination of five Expressionist poets in the light of particular criticisms has enabled us to do more than confirm received critical opinion. It has served to flesh out the practical meaning of the term 'Expressionism'. What has become clear is that Expressionism was, above all, a movement. For a time at least it answered a need, especially amongst young people in Germany. Egon Larsen who lived in Munich during the 'Soviet Republic' of 1919 and the Hitler Putsch of 1923 gives an eyewitness account of the way Expressionism found a special resonance — 'We youngsters were, of course, fascinated by everything that seemed to contradict the life-style of our parents, of the dead Wilhelminian establishment. We sided with the innovators. For a while, Expressionism was for us the emotional manifestation of the welcome upheaval.'[4] Again and again, Expressionist writers gave notice of their ambition to unsettle and disconcert, and their all-or-nothing mentality drove imperiously ever onwards to some stridently trumpeted Promised Land. The predictable consequence was moral anarchy and a repudiation of all 'intermediary consolations',[5] of all dispassionate public debate and controlled private imperatives. The sentiments voiced in Charles Tomlinson's plea for moderation would have been anathema to any self-respecting Expressionist writer:

> Let there be treaties, bridges
> Chords under the hands, to be spanned
> Sustained: extremity hates a given good
> Or a good gained . . .
> Against extremity, let there be
> Such treaties as only time itself
> Can ratify, a bond and test
> Of sequential days, and like the full
> Moon slowly given to the night
> A possession that is not to be possessed.[6]

To any recommendation of the virtues of patience and gradualness, to the call for slow maturation and the injunction *not* to possess fully, the Expressionist poet opposes not only a fiercely uncompromising attitude towards poetic form and utterance, but also an unconditional confidence in immediate man-made panaceas and the earnest intention to embrace the whole world in an ecstasy of love. Once again the poetry of Whitman is recalled: 'With the twirl of my tongue I encompass worlds and volumes of worlds'.[7] Expressionist writers, moving effortlessly from the national to the international and the global, proclaimed the belief that their art would bring them 'to that almost forgotten community which means not only the spiritual and moral unification of the Germans, but — perhaps — of all men dwelling on earth'[8]: the interpolation 'perhaps' carries no hint of irony. They thus displayed the traditional aloofness of German 'poets and thinkers' from practical affairs and, at the same time, felt an apparently contradictory yearning for community that was often the corollary of their sublime self-confidence.

When the promises went unredeemed and the hopes unfulfilled, the result was a numbing inner collapse: the Expressionist poet suddenly feels helpless before the forces of history, unequal to what he takes to be his especial calling, and he slumps into aimless inertia. Benn's famous confession of fatalism in 1929 'Wer Geld hat, wird gesund . . ., wer Gewalt hat, schafft das Recht. Die Geschichte ist ohne Sinn . . .'[9] is paralleled by Werfel's 'Wir sind erwählt oder verworfen durch unsre

Geburt. | So grauenvoll, grausam, hoffnungslos ist diese Welt'.[10] Yet whether he is promising to save the world or writing from the nadir of despair, the Expressionist poet invariably resorts to a grossly overheated, emotional language and to a kind of frenetic vagueness: Trakl's gently elegiac tones provide a stark and rare contrast. 'Greedy after vicious provocatives',[11] activist writers such as Hiller and Rubiner as well as essentially unpolitical *Sturm* poets purveyed the same declamatory, high-tension rant. The poetry which, for example, Walden promoted in the pages of *Der Sturm* was sustained by emotional intensity as its only criterion for objective truth, by a perfervid irrationalism, and by a deep-seated conviction of the value of dynamism and dynamically new words.

This faith in words, words, words, and in the efficacy of words is demonstrated, as Musil points out, in the continual resort to words-for-all-seasons like 'Seele' and 'Geist'. The habit spread to politicians, to intellectuals, to those whom Hermann Rauschning calls 'the men of tradition, continuity and balance' who should have been the first to defend 'the bastions and dykes by means of which people seek to protect themselves from one another'.[12] Walther Rathenau, when he was not being an extremely shrewd business-man and efficient minister of munitions, wrote precisely like an Expressionist poet. For example, in 1906 (when he was not yet a politician and Expressionism was still unheard of in Germany) he produced *Breviarium Mysticum* which consists of ten vertiginously metaphysical statements about the 'Seele'. The lifelessness of his early philosophical speculations re-emerges in the misty visions of the future which he spins in his 1918 appeal to the youth of Germany — *An Deutschlands Jugend*. At a time when what was important for Germany was to make present political arrangements work in a spirit of realistic and practical conciliation, his Romantic appeals to the younger generation and his reliance on intense emotionality sound very like Expressionist blather and like the ideals which his murderers believed they were serving.[13] Contrast his words and sentiments with the views of a traditional Liberal English political thinker: 'All government', Edmund Burke writes, 'indeed every human benefit and enjoyment, every virtue, and every prudent act, is founded on compromise and barter. We balance inconveniences; we give and take; we remit some rights that we may enjoy others; and we choose rather to be happy citizens than subtle disputants.'[14] Few German writers or politicians at the end of the First World War were advocating the qualities of prudence, moderation, compromise and pragmatism. Instead, the call went out for a mystical order of things governed by an enlightened elite in the name of some inspiring idea:

We must try to find an order in which man can hold faith with man. For that, it is necessary that we have men who can claim to possess loyalty unto death, and we also need an idea which can inspire such outstanding men so that they place themselves at the head of the people instead of the pathetic charlatans who stand there at the moment; [an idea] which produces the kind of men who can lay claim to loyalty unto death from others.[15]

This is a syntax not of discursive argument and thought, but of feeling and fervent directionless longing, a syntax rendered familiar by many a pre-war Expressionist anthology and magazine, and in the 1920s and 1930s it was common to Expressionist and non-Expressionist writers alike.

Karl Kraus for one does not doubt the damage inflicted by Expressionist poets on the health of the German language: 'Ten third-rate scribblers — each one a harbinger of devastation — cannot approach a good Expressionist when it comes to wreaking havoc' ('Dorten'. p. 146; see p. 80 above). The political and social anarchy for which Werfel and other Expressionist poets call in their work is mirrored in the anarchic form of their verse. There are several occasions in Werfel's long, nostalgic *Barbara oder die Frömmigkeit* when, in the account of the 1918 revolution, his political characters declaim like true Expressionist poets, erupting into lengthy harangues which depend for their effect upon unbridled emotion and instant inspiration. For example, Weiß, having whipped up the mob into an almost uncontrollable hysteria of directionless passion, seeks to explain his astounding popular success to the protagonist, Ferdinand: 'I just suddenly did it. I swear to you, I didn't give it a second's thought. That's the way history is made! God knows what will come of it. Anyway it had a really strong effect?! Didn't it?' (*Barbara* . . ., pp. 409–10). It is at this point that radical artist and radical politician, sharing a community of language and voice, tone and slogan, are seen to merge in indissoluble identity, in the same way as the three great theatre-directors of the day — Reinhardt, Jessner and Piscator — admitted of no dividing line between the revolution in the theatre and that in the streets. It is not fortuitous that Hannah Arendt, in the course of seeking to explain how the totalitarian movements' preference for terrorism attracted the intellectual elite and the mob alike, should maintain that 'terrorism had become a kind of philosophy . . . a kind of political Expressionism which used bombs to express itself'.[16]

By the 1920s Expressionist language had become the common currency of many politicians. Moreover, Siegfried Bork has demonstrated[17] how many of the characteristic features of that language survived into the 1930s and were echoed and exploited by National Socialist orators and writers, who reduced the diverse uses of speech — as communication, debate, monologue, prayer and incantation — to a single incantatory, hectoring one. Once language is corrupted in this way, 'the plain humanities of nature are thrust out of sight'.[18] Probably the only duty a writer has as a citizen is to protect his language, and this is a duty of which, traditionally, German poets have been exceedingly jealous. Günter Grass, for example, in a recent novel, summons to a meeting at Telgte at the end of The Thirty Years' War the great poets of the day 'to rescue their cruelly maltreated language', for the poets 'had knitted the German language as the last bond, they were the other, the true Germany . . . they alone had the power to preserve for all time whatever truly deserved the name of German'.[19] But is should be added that Grass's poets, unlike Expressionist writers, are painfully aware that they are without power ('except to write true if useless words'; p. 69) in the realm of political decision-making, although, as they well know and plan, Telgte is conveniently placed between Münster and Osnabrück, the sites of the peace negotiations.

> And 'tis this fever that keeps Troy on foot,
> Not her own sinews. To end a tale of length,
> Troy in our weakness stands, not in her strength.[20]

Poetry is not simply a conglomeration of words: it is also an expression of temper and mood, of spiritual and moral disposition. And if poets are invariably without power to shape political decisions, they are not without influence in creating the intellectual background against which these decisions are made and received — especially in Germany and especially in the particular circumstances which obtained between 1910 and 1930, when cultural trends proved to be such powerful subversive forces for unreason in the public, political sphere, and when one of those trends, Expressionism, shared a common language and diverse other prepossessions with contemporary politics and political thinking. Thus it is not surprising that of all the critical categories with which we began, the one to which we find ourselves constantly returning is that of Expressionism's political (ir)responsibility and defective response to political and social issues. Responsibility was, after all, something which Expressionist writers were delighted to assume and to bear — responsibility for mankind's future, no less:

The spiritual ones — what does that mean? It means those who feel responsible . . . And responsible means: liable to be called to account — not for the past, but for the future. To feel responsible: to bear the experience of one's missions; to suffer fruitfully the world's suffering; to be possessed by the idea of improving the world.[21]

To attempt to assess Expressionism in its historical context — and we have focused throughout this book only on literary Expressionism and, in this résumé, are continuing to do that — and to judge it in the light of what it saw as its responsibility for future events and its mission to improve the world is to examine it in its own frequently invoked terms. In referring to Expressionism's historical context, we mean, of course, the rise of National Socialism and the part which, according to many critics and the Marxists in particular, literary Expressionism played in that rise. All events are an intermeshing of causes from which neither spiritual nor material, neither cultural nor emotional environment can be excluded. Art in its widest sense is the outward and visible sign of a civilization and if, at its highest level, it remains a minority interest, it can also, as the record sleeves, posters and street fashions of the last fifteen years have shown, involve more or less everybody — involve *and* somehow change, a writer like T. S. Eliot would maintain with regard to poetry:

In the long run, poetry makes a difference to the speech, to the sensibility, to the lives of all the members of a society, to all the members of the community, to the whole people, whether they read and enjoy poetry or not: even, in fact, whether they know the names of their greatest poets or not. The influence of poetry, at the furthest periphery, is of course very diffused, very indirect, and very difficult to prove . . . (but) you will find it present everywhere.[22]

Hitler did not fall upon Germany in the way that Pizarro fell upon Peru, he did not come like a thief in the night or like a bolt from the sky, Germany did not decide, like a Richard III, to become evil, National Socialism does not stand like 'an erratic block in the landscape of German history and culture'.[23] Hitler's path was paved:

Hitler did not come from outside, he was not a demonic beast snatching power for himself, though that is the way many people see him today [1967]. He was the man whom the German people wanted and whom we ourselves, by our excessive adulation, made the master of our fate.[24]

In the space of twelve years National Socialism changed the face of the world and modified the thinking of succeeding generations. Such tremendous processes cannot be adequately explained by reference to political, economic and material problems which Germany shared with many other countries or to the whims and ambitions of one individual in power (however tyrannical he may be) or to the political success of National Socialism: after all, Italy, Turkey, Spain, Poland and Austria also had Fascist or Fascist-orientated movements. The fact that National Socialism proved to be the most radical form of Fascism and that it took such a hold in Germany must be seen in the light of Germany's particular psychological, emotional, intellectual and spiritual roots and of that multitude of ideas produced by German thinkers and writers down the years. Ideas have consequences, and poets as creators and propagators of ideas and as heirs to traditions shape consequences, or they influence responses to ideas, or they help to create an atmosphere in which certain responses to certain ideas can be predicted or engineered. The relationship between the poet and the 'world of action' is delicate, fragile and intangible, but none the less real for that. The effect of works of art is not measurable. Their influence is so much dissolved in memory and experience and so interwoven with them that it does not allow of individual representation. Expressionist poets gave little, if any, thought to the way in which their words might be (mis)interpreted: they did not object to being taken to mean more than they actually said, they set themselves up as oracles, inevitably indeterminate in meaning, and revelled in their wide readership and subsequent notoriety.

Moreover, Expressionism was prescriptive and not descriptive, far from neutral in the stances which it ostentatiously adopted. It was wilfully provocative and subversive of anything stable, orthodox and reasonable. It flourished in a country which has always attributed to its writers profound insights and wide-ranging powers. Two articles in *The Daily Telegraph* from the early 1980s demonstrate how in Germany literature is *still*[25] respected (and feared) for its potential influence on its readers. The work in question is Goebbels's *Michael*. In the first article (22 April 1981) notice is given that a novel by Joseph Goebbels will be dramatized and staged by the Municipal Theatre of Heidelberg: this work 'tells the story of a youth who does not know how to cope with life until he meets Hitler' and the theatre management says that 'the aim of the production is to give a picture of the age that led to the triumph of the Nazis'. Three weeks later, in the second article (15 May 1981), it is announced that the dramatization will not be staged 'in case it is misunderstood'.

Expressionist poets exploited a public taste for a poetry, for any form of art, where the boundaries between religion and literature became blurred and a vague religiosity of the heart was perpetuated (as in *Michael*). Once again following a familiar German tradition, they implicitly belittled the routine aspects of politics and placed poets above thinkers and politicians in the belief that poets could easily do the work of politicians anyway:

Anyone who has created, for example, some great work of art can achieve in politics in ten minutes what the bureaucratic animal, drowning in his own sweat and getting through countless pairs of trousers, would take thousands of years to do.[26]

The breathtaking presumptuousness of Heym's comment is nothing new in German literature. It is succinctly prefigured by Richard Wagner who received more veneration from the high priests of National Socialist culture than any other artist and who chose the following quatrain for the motto to his treatise 'Art and Revolution':

> Wo einst die Kunst schwieg, begann
> die Staatsweisheit und Philosophie:
> wo jetzt der Staatsweise und Philosoph
> zu Ende ist, da fängt der Künstler an.

Where once art fell silent, statecraft | and philosophy took over: | now that the age of the statesman and philosopher | is at an end, the artist begins.

In their self-appointed roles as 'legislators of mankind' and 'army-commanders',[27] Expressionist poets claimed that their poetry was an instrument of salvation. The heady mixture of religiosity, poetry and metaphysics, in league with an exhilarating bellicosity, has proved, over the years, well nigh irresistible to the mystical part of the German character and its yearning for the far-flung and infinite. By April 1932, when the air was buzzing with declarations of allegiance and commitment, Kessler writes in his diaries that he has come to recognize precisely this basic feature in his fellow-countrymen, an 'absolute and immutable' feature: 'the flight to metaphysics, to any "belief" (Marxism, Communism, Hitlerism, philosophy or whatever)' (*Tagebücher 1918–37*, pp. 600–01). Indeed, as one such 'belief', Expressionism in the 1920s served to discredit reasonability, Weimar and Weimar reasonability. It raised hopes, disappointed and then offered the disappointed up into the arms of the KPD or the NSDAP. Among the disappointed must be counted some of the Expressionist poets themselves, who, according to Hermann Hesse in his survey of the literary scene in the early 1920s, had already then shown worrying symptoms of what he calls 'abandonment to the doctor . . . a blindly enthusiastic submission to the one who first appeared to the patient as a liberator, whether it be Freud or Sternheim',[28] or indeed someone much more sinister, one might add. Hitler's party offered sanctuary to such disillusioned writers. In an important speech, delivered during the course of the seizure of power, Hitler draws attention to the political impotence and confused state of mind of the average German, to the compensatory dream-worlds which the latter has devised and to the role which art has played in offering the only possible means of redemption:

The German, at odds with himself, with deep divisions in his mind, likewise in his will and therefore impotent in action, becomes powerless to direct his own life. He dreams of justice in the stars and loses his footing on earth. . . In the end, then, only the inward path remained open for the Germans. As a nation of singers, poets and thinkers they dreamed of a world in which the others lived, and only when misery and wretchedness dealt them inhuman blows did there perhaps grow up out of art the longing for a new rising, for a new Reich, and therefore for new life. [29]

A debt is clearly being acknowledged here.

For some time it looked as though Expressionism might have the same kind of accommodating relationship with the National Socialists as Futurism enjoyed with the Fascists in Italy. The Third Reich, after all, gave special prominence to the role of art in general and poetry in particular. There was a remarkably high proportion of frustrated aesthetes in the top echelons of the Nazi party — Hitler, Goebbels, Rosenberg, Speer, von Schirach, all had burning ambitions in the sphere of art, which they regarded not as a hobby, but as an integral part of their lives, in constant need of nourishment. Hitler was a painter, considered himself an architect, and, as a young man, stayed up late night after night in the Stumpergasse in Vienna working on plays and operas. Goebbels wrote poems, prose pieces and essays: his manuscripts are entitled *Gypsy Blood, Those Who Are Loved by the Sun, I'm a Wandering Scholar*, and for his poems he devises such titles as 'Deep in Dreams I Wandered the Dark Wood', 'Prayer', 'Sleep, Baby Sleep', 'At Night'. In 1927 his drama *The Wanderer* was produced. Ribbentrop wrote a play, Streicher nursed ambitions as a water-colour artist and Hess took his own Romantic poetry very seriously. It is not surprising, therefore, that in 1934 Goebbels asserts that 'National Socialism is not only the political and social, but also the cultural conscience of the nation', [30] or that in the 1938 anthology *Germany Speaks*, in which many prominent Nazi officials seek to present the Nazi world-view, Hans Blunck, a poet and writer of fairy-tales, and *not* one of the party's strictly political leaders, should be selected to write the official article on Nazi 'Kultur' policy. The party, Blunck maintains, is fortunate in having leaders with 'religious convictions' about 'the importance of artists' as the Volk's 'mediators'. The terminology, the attitudes, the assumptions of Blunck's article have all been made very familiar to his readers by such movements as Expressionism: he perpetuates the same vague idealism, the same misty yearnings for suprapersonal goals or for 'The One', and the same urge to put overwhelming mythical surrogates in place of pragmatic solutions. But, it should be added, the Nazis themselves were pragmatic enough (after 1933) to ensure that literature, with its wide-ranging influence, was strictly supervised. Within four and a half months of coming to power they began the purge with the notorious Book Burning episode, and before long Goebbels had set up his Chamber of Literature with its immense apparatus for controlling and shaping public taste. Many Expressionist writers, called upon now to make a firm political commitment and to enter into the beckoning community of Nazi culture, found themselves unable to do so and fell foul of the new system.

Thus the result of Expressionist writers' endeavours to discharge their 'responsibility to reality' had been to enfeeble, even to corrupt, the few forces for moderation and for good in ramshackle, fragile Weimar, which was hamstrung already by a conviction of its own provisional, makeshift nature. Expressionism helped to undermine those institutions which customarily sustain and stabilize a democratic state — tradition, the family, morality, and authority — and to confuse and distort its readers' emotions and thoughts, thus smoothing the National Socialist seizure of power, especially amongst the young where the NSDAP made its most remarkable inroads. 'Our emotional life is warped, sick and vulgar' is the comment of one fictional observer surveying the scene in Germany in the 1920s (Werfel, *Barbara* . . ., p. 424), whilst Albert Speer, in his reminiscences, refers to a collapse of values and moral standards, to which, we have argued, Expressionism made a small, but significant, contribution:

> I think of my own father, and of his father. For them there were still wholly unassailable values. They had no doubts whatsoever about right and wrong, good and evil. It is unimaginable to think of my father or grandfather with Hitler and his cronies at Obersalzberg on one of those dreary movie nights. How brittle all aesthetic and moral standards must have grown before Hitler became possible.[31]

It will be seen how Speer links 'aesthetic and moral': he assumes that the two interlock. The Expressionist poet, a frivolous and amoral exploiter of intoxicating feeling, foreshadowed, and thus rendered familiar and in part acceptable, the kind of hysterical emotionalism upon which Hitler founded his appeal. According to a contemporary reviewer in the *Times Literary Supplement*, Expressionism 'attempted to achieve an intellectual end by emotional means, and this involved a fundamental fallacy which is now [1933] being repeated in the whole sphere of German politics and culture'.[32] One party hack, writing gleefully in 1934, observes:

> Das Morsche stürzt und das Faule fällt,
> Vom göttlichen Licht durchdrungen —
> O starker Geist, der nun Einzug hält:
> Es spricht das neue Deutschland zur Welt
> Mit hundert feurigen Zungen.[33]

That which has decayed tumbles down and the rotten falls, | Pierced by the divine light — | O powerful spirit which now comes upon the scene: | The new Germany speaks to the world | With a hundred fiery tongues.

The first three lines of this, at least, steeped in Expressionist bravado and religiose euphoria, could have been taken at random from almost anywhere in *Menschheitsdämmerung*. And as for the last two lines, we have seen how one Expressionist poet, Kurt Heynicke, with very little adjustment of the characteristic Expressionist features of his work, did more than 'merely' stifle the voice of rationality and decency beneath a welter of intensely emotional longings. In establishing 'the new Germany', National Socialism grew strong on its opponents' internal confusions and inherent weaknesses. Expressionist writers, in many cases with the best of intentions, regarded dissension and confusion, indiscipline and immoderation as fertile manifestations of the restless spirit by which they swore, and thus compounded the weakness of National Socialism's potential antagonists. For ever aspiring to 'their mystic goal of Chaos',[34] they set themselves up as saboteurs and iconoclasts, with no thought of the morrow: at the height of his Expressionist phase, Becher exclaims: '. . . We are explosive forces. To serve what purpose? That

is not the question. We hate all meaning! And what a lovely little fire we shall light!'
(*Abschied*, p. 384)

> It is now or never, the hour of the knife,
> The break with the past, the major operation.[35]

Expressionist writers also liked to see themselves as great innovators, breaking with a stale and discredited past, serving present society in a spirit of self-sacrificial zeal and breathing new life into a moribund culture. In fact, in many important ways, they do not shake off the past: they can be regarded as neurotic and terminally violent heirs to Romanticism, to what Speer (p. 391) calls 'all the perils of the Romantic relationship toward the world, all the blindness, the obscurantism, the reckless enthusiasm, and potential inhumanity of it'. In their spurious relationship with political reality, and in the elevation of their overweening egos into oracles and divine mediators, they do *not* appear incongruous — or even unannounced — in the tradition of German literature and thinking. Schiller's Idealist-Poet, prone to restless speculation, exclusively interested in absolutes and in the maximum, expert in oversight but not insight, is already more than a preliminary sketch of the kind of writer who was to emerge one hundred and twenty years later with qualities which Schiller denigrates. His anticipation of such qualities appears at the end of *Über naive und sentimentalische Dichtung* in his depiction of 'the false idealist', a remarkable prefiguring of an Expressionist poet. In an earlier paragraph Schiller had written of a special poetic elite, 'a class of people' who do not work, who are not at the mercy of everyday events, who can 'preserve the beautiful totality of human nature' and who, through the purity of their feelings, can lay down general aesthetic guidelines.[36] In positing such an elite group of writers (like the artistic hierarchy in Goethe's Weimar and Klopstock's ideal of a republic of letters) and according them a certain degree of leadership in society, Schiller indulges in the common enough practice (in Germany) of granting writers the status of priests, exegetes and missionaries. No wonder that at times in its history Germany has looked to outside observers more like 'a poetic and demonic conspiracy' than 'a social and human enterprise'.[37]

It is particularly difficult for a reader who is not German to grasp that literature can wield a profound influence over public life or that the slogan 'nation of singers, poets and thinkers' is anything more than a tedious cliché. The role that, for example, Grass and Böll play in contemporary public life in Germany is inconceivable, for example, in England: their actual influence cannot be measured, the changes they may have effected in public attitudes cannot be pinpointed, but their intervention is far from unique and surprises no one. An illuminating parallel can be drawn with Russia, though vast differences between the two countries (in terms of the régime in power and of writers' relationship with that régime, especially in the 1920s) must be granted: Nadezhda Mandelstam's memoir *Hope against Hope* brings to the fore many of the factors and features which were prominent in the 1920s and 1930s in Germany — the desecration of words and poetry when speech is used heedlessly 'by high priests, soothsayers, heads of state and other charlatans', a vague longing for 'the appearance of the Wise Leaders', the way that under a dictatorship people 'are killed for poetry', the fact that one poem (Mandelstam's verses about

M

Stalin written in November 1933) could put an author's life at great risk, the conviction that 'ideas shape the minds of whole generations' and impose themselves with radical effects on human consciousness, the progressive loss of a sense of reality and the craving for an all-embracing idea, the way that the twenties 'prepared the ground for the future' and 'the thirty-year-old iconoclasts led their hosts of followers into the coming era' and, finally, Mandelstam's abiding belief that, judging by the reactions of politicians, 'poetry is power'.[38] Whereas — and at this point the difference between the countries comes sharply into focus — Mandelstam's poem about Stalin was, and was meant to be, an overtly subversive act, Expressionist writers in the 1920s, often unconsciously, often in subterranean ways, helped to subvert a democratically organized government and, then later, some of these number found it easily possible to adjust to, and swing their support behind, the Nazi régime. Yet much of what Nadezhda Mandelstam depicts as being true of Russia under Stalin was also happening in Germany even *before* Hitler came to power. Many of the same assumptions, convictions and responses are instantly recognizable. It seems, therefore, that 'poetry is power' either in countries where writers have no freedom (as in Russia and, subsequently, in Germany) or in countries like Germany where there exists a long-standing, deeply ingrained tradition of writers' enjoying special status. What is ultimately 'irresponsible' about Expressionist writers is that, knowing of this tradition, they exploited it, and exploiting it, they paid no heed to possible consequences.

One consequence of their poetry and of the extra-literary expectations which it raised soon became very clear: given their literary tradition, their contemporary historical situation and the innate qualities of their writing, Expressionist poets were always likely to be susceptible to political (mis)interpretation — of the kind to which Hellmuth Langenbucher, an important figure in cultural affairs in the National Socialist hierarchy, subjects Stefan George's poetry in seeking to claim that poet for the National Socialist party.[39] Expressionist poetry is open to the same kind of exegesis and representation as George's, and not just by National Socialist hacks. In the ways indicated in this study, Expressionist poetry, pitting its radical demands and desperate dreams against the inevitable compromises of political reality, helped to create an atmosphere in which National Socialism could take hold. By 1933 Ernst Toller, himself a writer of Expressionist drama, comments despairingly:

Everywhere the same lunatic belief that a man, a leader, a Caesar, a Messiah will suddenly appear and work a miracle; will arise and take upon his shoulders all responsibility for the future; will master life, banish fear, abolish misery, create a new people, a new kingdom of splendour; will emerge with supernatural powers to transform the old Adam into a new man.[40]

Toller's German readers would not have been at all startled by the thought of the advent of such a leader. Becher, amongst many other Expressionist writers, had anticipated that thought *and* the destruction necessary to its realization. But by 1933 the 'little fire' which he had promised was already moving out of control, and an earlier prophecy that the weakness of the twentieth-century mind would be 'in locating the ideal of perfection, not in equilibrium and the middle path, but in the extreme and exaggeration'[41] had been borne out. Excess, unreason and indiscipline had become, if not accepted, then familiar and integral parts of private and public life, of personal and cultural life in Germany. 'The great and golden rule of art, as well as of life' had been broken — the rule which states 'that the more distinct, sharp, and wiry the bounding line, the more perfect the work of art . . . leave out this line, and you leave out life itself; all is chaos again . . .'[42] 'Grenzenlos' (boundless) had always been one of the most popular epithets with Expressionist poets and polemicists, just as chaos, in part willed, in part craved, and rarely repudiated, was the inevitable consequence of their writing:

'What is it you're hoping to see happen?' asked Augustine. 'Chaos', said Franz . . . 'Germany must be re-born and it is only from the darkness of the hot womb of chaos that such re-birth is possible.' (Hughes, p. 164)

NOTES

1 Shakespeare, *Timon of Athens*, I.1.
2 J. Symons, *The Thirties* (London, 1975), p. 18.
3 Written in 1934. See K. Mann, *Prüfungen* pp. 205–06.
4 E. Larsen, *Weimar Eyewitness* (London, 1976), p. 26.
5 The sentence 'Ein Zwischentrost gilt nicht' ('An intermediary consolation is not valid') is Kurt Heynicke's and appears in the poem 'Einsicht in Aussicht' (1969); HLW, III, 30.
6 C. Tomlinson, 'Against Extremity', *The Way of a World* (London, New York and Toronto, 1969), p. 11.
7 W. Whitman, *Leaves of Grass*, edited by M. Cowley (London, 1960), line 567.
8 K. Pinthus, 'Zur jüngsten Dichtung', p. 1510.
9 'Anyone who has money becomes healthy . . . anyone who has physical force creates the law. History is devoid of sense . . .'; G. Benn, *Gesammelte Werke*, IV, 210.
10 'We are chosen or rejected by our birth,/ This world is so full of horror, so cruel, hopeless'; F. Werfel, 'Gebet gegen Worte' (1919), WLW, 289.
11 W. Wordsworth, 'Essay, supplementary to the Preface to the Lyrical Ballads', *Poetical Works*, edited by E. de Selincourt (London, New York and Toronto, 1965), p. 744.
12 H. Rauschning, *Men of Chaos* (New York, 1943), pp. 4, 9–10.
13 See, for example, the words written in 1933 by Ernst-Werner Techow, one of his murderers, and quoted in: E-W. Techow, *Gemeiner Mörder?! Das Rathenau-Attentat* (Leipzig, 1933), p. 20.
14 E. Burke, 'On Conciliation', quoted in: G. W. Chapman, *Edmund Burke, The Practical Imagination* (Cambridge, Massachusetts, 1967), p. 56.
15 Paul Ernst, writing in 1919, quoted in: Volkmann, *Deutsche Dichtung im Weltkrieg 1914–1918*, p. 283.
16 H. Arendt, *The Origins of Totalitarianism*, pp. 331–32.
17 See his *Mißbrauch der Sprache* (Berne and Munich, 1970).
18 The sentence is Wordsworth's: interestingly, he is condemning the way in which language is being distorted by contemporary writers aspiring to be poets and employing rhetorical, excessively powerful lines. See his essay on 'Poetic Diction' in: Wordsworth, *Poetical Works*, p. 741.
19 G. Grass, *The Meeting at Telgte*, translated by R. Manheim (London, 1981), pp. 13, 67 and 129.
20 Shakespeare, *Troilus and Cressida*, I.3.
21 K. Hiller, 'Philosophie des Ziels', in: *Tätiger Geist. Zweites der Ziel-Jahrbücher* (Munich and Berlin, 1918), pp. 206–07.
22 T. S. Eliot, 'The Social Function of Poetry' (1945), in: *On Poetry and Poets*, p. 22.
23 R. Taylor, *Literature and Society in Germany 1918–1945* (Sussex, 1980), p. 250.

24 B. von Schirach, *Ich glaubte an Hitler* (Hamburg, 1967), p. 160. Von Schirach, as Youth Leader of the German Reich, was a leading member of the National Socialist party.

25 *Pace* Lord Macaulay, according to whom, by 1825 in Germany, the influence of literature is on the wane: '. . . the power which the ancient bards of Wales and Germany exercised over their auditors seems to modern readers almost miraculous'. Lord Macaulay, *Critical and Historical Essays* (London, 1877), p. 4.

26 G. Heym, 'Über Genie und Staat'; PD II, 175.

27 The phrases are Richard Dehmel's. See his letter dated 24 March 1899 to Harry Graf Kessler in: R. Dehmel, *Ausgewählte Briefe 1883–1902*, (Berlin, 1923), p. 291.

28 H. Hesse, 'Recent German Poetry', *The Criterion*, I, 91.

29 On the Day of Potsdam, 21 March 1933, quoted in: K. D. Bracher and others, *Die national-sozialistische Machtergreifung*, p. 269.

30 *Berliner Lokal-Anzeiger* of 7 December 1934.

31 A. Speer, *Spandau: The Secret Diaries* (London, 1976), p. 370.

32 Review of A. Eloesser's *Modern German Literature* in: *TLS*, 13 July 1933, p. 476.

33 H. Anacker, quoted in: A. Schöne, *Über politische Lyrik im 20. Jahrhundert* (Göttingen, 1969), p. 17.

34 R. Hughes, *The Fox in the Attic* (Harmondsworth, 1964), p. 279.

35 C. D. Lewis, 'Consider these, for we have condemned them', *The Magnetic Mountain* (1933), quoted in: Symons, *The Thirties*, p. 24.

36 F. Schiller, *Über naive und sentimentalische Dichtung*, edited by W. F. Mainland (Oxford, 1957), pp. 70–71.

37 See Act I, Scene 2 of Giraudoux's 1928 play *Siegfried*.

38 N. Mandelstam, *Hope against Hope*, pp. 74, 96, 159, 161–63, 168 and 170.

39 For a further development of this argument, see R. Taylor, *Literature and Society . . .*, pp. 237–38.

40 E. Toller, *Eine Jugend in Deutschland* (1933), in: *Prosa, Briefe, Dramen, Gedichte* (Reinbek, 1961), p. 28.

41 Made in 1910 by A. Gide, *Journals I*, edited by J. O'Brien (New York, 1947), p. 136.

42 W. Blake, 'Outline in Art and Life', in: *The Poems of William Blake* (London, 1969), p. 254.

BIBLIOGRAPHY

The bibliography extends to those social, historical and ideological fields that impinge on literature. For reasons of size it excludes works of literature used in my argument merely to provide incidental examples or to illustrate points that are not central to the book. Such material is given in the footnotes only.

The following major bibliographical aids have been used:

C. G. *Kaysers vollständiges Bücherlexikon* (Leipzig, 1834 ff., from 1911 entitled *Deutsches Bücherverzeichnis*)

Kosch, W., *Deutsches Literatur-Lexikon*, revised edition, 4 vols (Berne, 1949)

Merker, P., and Stammler, W., *Reallexikon der deutschen Literaturgeschichte*, 4 vols (Berlin, 1925–41), revised by W. Kohlschmidt and W. Mohr (in progress)

The bibliography is divided into the following sections:
1. Literary and Cultural Periodicals
2. General Literary, Philosophical and Historical Background
3. General Accounts of Expressionism
4. August Stramm
5. Georg Heym
6. Franz Werfel
7. Kurt Heynicke
8. Wilhelm Klemm

Entries in the bibliography which are preceded by an asterisk denote recent secondary literature which has appeared since this book was written or which was not available to the author at the time of writing.

1. LITERARY AND CULTURAL PERIODICALS

The following two books are particularly recommended:

Raabe, P., *Die Zeitschriften und Sammlungen des literarischen Expressionismus 1910–21* (Stuttgart, 1964)

Schlawe, F., *Literarische Zeitschriften 1910–1933* (Stuttgart, 1962)

Lillian Schacherl's dissertation 'Die Zeitschriften des Expressionismus' (unpublished dissertation, University of Munich, 1957) is also useful.

As Raabe's and Schlawe's books give a very full account of magazines and periodicals, the following list is brief and selective:

Aktion, ed. F. Pfemfert (Berlin, 1911–32; reprint of years 1911–18, ed. Raabe, 1961–67)

Argonauten, Die, ed. E. Blass (Heidelberg, 1914–21; Kraus reprint, 1969)
Blätter für die Kunst, ed. C. A. Klein (Berlin, 1892–1919)
Blätter, Die Weißen, ed. R. Schickele (Leipzig, 1913–16, Zurich and Berne, 1916–18, Berlin, 1919–20; Kraus reprint, 1969)
Brenner, Der, ed. L.v. Ficker (Innsbruck, 1910–15, then irregular; Kraus reprint, 1969)
Fackel, Die, ed. K. Kraus (Vienna, 1899–1936)
Hochland, ed. K. Muth (Munich, 1903–41, 1946–)
März, ed. L. Thoma, H. Hesse and others (Munich, 1907–17; Kraus reprint, 1970)
Pan, ed. P. Cassirer, A. Kerr and others (Berlin, 1910–14)
Rundschau, Die Neue, ed. O. Bie (Berlin, 1904–)
Schaubühne, Die, ed. S. Jacobsohn (Berlin, 1905–18)
Simplicissimus, ed. A. Langen and others (Munich, 1896–1944)
Sturm, Der, ed. H. Walden (Berlin, 1910–32; Kraus reprint, 1970)
Tat, Die ed. E. Horneffer (Jena, 1909–38)
Ziel, Das, ed. K. Hiller (Munich, 1915–23; 5 'Jahrbücher' in all)
Zukunft, Die, ed. M. Harden (Berlin, 1892–1922)

2. GENERAL LITERARY, PHILOSOPHICAL AND HISTORICAL BACK GROUND

Abel, T., *Why Hitler Came into Power* (New York, 1938)
Adorno, T. W., *Gesammelte Schriften*, 22 vols (Frankfurt a.M., 1971–)
*Allen, R., *Literary Life in German Expressionism and the Berlin Circle* (Göppingen, 1974)
Apollonio, U., *Futurist Manifestos* (London, 1973)
Arendt, H., *The Origins of Totalitarianism* (New York, 1951; reprinted 1966)
Becher, J. R., *Abschied* (Berlin and Weimar, 1970)
—— *Gesammelte Werke*, 18 vols (Berlin and Weimar, 1966–81)
Benjamin, W., *Gesammelte Schriften*, 6 vols (Frankfurt a.M., 1974)
Benn, G., *Gesammelte Werke*, ed. D. Wellershoff, 4 vols (Wiesbaden, 1959–61)
—— *Doppelleben*, in: *Gesammelte Werke*, IV, 69–176
Bergonzi, B., *Heroes' Twilight. A Study of the Literature of the Great War* (London, 1965)
Berning, C., 'Die Sprache des Nationalsozialismus', *Zeitschrift für deutsche Wortforschung*, 17 (1961), 171–82; 18 (1962), 108–18, 160–72; 19 (1963), 92–112
Bithell, J., *An Anthology of German Poetry 1880–1940* (London, 1941)
Bollnow, O. F., *Die Macht des Worts* (Essen, 1966)
Bork, S., *Mißbrauch der Sprache* (Berne and Munich, 1970)
Bracher, K. D., *Die Auflösung der Weimarer Republik* (Stuttgart and Düsseldorf, 1957)
—— *Deutschland zwischen Demokratie und Diktatur* (Berne, Munich, and Vienna, 1964)
Bracher, K. D., Sauer, W. and Schulz, G., *Die nationalsozialistische Machtergreifung* (Cologne and Opladen, 1960)
Brecht, Arnold, *Aus nächster Nähe: Lebenserinnerungen 1884–1927* (Stuttgart, 1966)
Brenner, H., *Die Kunstpolitik des Nationalsozialismus* (Munich, 1963)
Brod, Max, *Streitbares Leben* (Munich, 1960)
—— *Der Prager Kreis* (Stuttgart, Berlin, Cologne, and Mainz, 1966)
Bronnen, A., *O.S.* (Berlin, 1929)
—— *Roßbach* (Berlin, 1930)
—— *Vatermord* (Emsdetten, 1954)
—— *Gibt zu Protokoll* (Hamburg, 1954)

Broszat, M., *Der Nationalsozialismus. Weltanschauung, Programm und Wirklichkeit* (Stuttgart, 1960)

Butler, R. d'O., *The Roots of National Socialism* (London, 1941)

Carossa, H., *Ungleiche Welten*, in: *Sämtliche Werke* (Frankfurt a.M., 1962), II

Coleridge, S. T., *Biographia Literaria*, 2 vols (Oxford, 1973)

Cowper, W., *Cowper's Poems*, ed. H. I'A. Fausset (London, 1966)

Craig, G. A., 'Engagement and Neutrality in Weimar Germany', *Journal of Contemporary History*, 2, no. 2 (April, 1967)

Daiber, H., *Vor Deutschland wird gewarnt* (Gütersloh, 1967)

Dehmel, R., *Ausgewählte Briefe aus den Jahren 1883–1902* (Berlin, 1923)

—— *Ausgewählte Briefe aus den Jahren 1902–1920* (Berlin, 1923)

De Jonge, Alex, *The Weimar Chronicle — Prelude to Hitler* (New York and London, 1978)

Denkler, H., and Prümm, K., *Die deutsche Literatur im Dritten Reich* (Stuttgart, 1976)

Döblin, A., *Briefe* (Olten and Freiburg im Breisgau, 1970)

Eliot, T. S., *On Poetry and Poets* (London, 1956)

—— *The Complete Poems and Plays of T. S. Eliot* (London, 1975)

Empson, W., *Seven Types of Ambiguity* (Harmondsworth, 1961)

Enright, D. J., *The Apothecary's Shop* (London, 1957)

Esslin, M., *Pinter: A Study of his Plays* (London, 1973)

Eyck, E., *A History of the Weimar Republic*, translated by H. P. Hanson and R. L. G. Waite (Cambridge, Mass., 1962–63)

Fest, J. C., *Das Gesicht des Dritten Reichs* (Munich, 1963)

—— *Hitler* (London, 1974)

Friedmann, H., and Mann, O., *Deutsche Literatur im zwanzigsten Jahrhundert* (Heidelberg, 1959)

Friedrich, H., *Die Struktur der modernen Lyrik* (Hamburg, 1956)

Frind, S., 'Die Sprache als Propagandainstrument in der Publizistik des Dritten Reichs' (dissertation, University of Berlin, 1964)

Frye, N., *Anatomy of Criticism* (Princeton, 1971)

Fussell, P., *The Great War and Modern Memory* (New York and London, 1975)

Gardner, B. (ed.), *The Terrible Rain: The War Poets 1939–1945* (London, 1966)

Gay, P., *Weimar Culture* (Harmondsworth, 1974)

George, S., *Werke*, 2 vols (Munich and Düsseldorf, 1958)

Gilman, S. L., *Nationalsozialismus — Literaturtheorie* (Frankfurt a.M., 1971)

Glum, F., *Der Nationalsozialismus. Werden und Vergehen* (Munich, 1962)

Goebbels, J., *Michael. Ein deutsches Schicksal in Tagebuchblättern* (Munich, 1934)

Goldstücker, E., *Weltfreunde. Konferenz über die Prager deutsche Literatur* (Prague, 1967)

Gray, R., *The German Tradition in Literature 1871–1945* (Cambridge, 1965)

Grieswelle, D., *Propaganda der Friedlosigkeit. Eine Studie zu Hitlers Rhetorik* (Stuttgart, 1972)

Großmann, S., *Ich war begeistert* (Berlin, 1931)

Grosz, G., *A Little Yes and a Big No* (New York, 1946)

Gunn, T., 'On the Move', in: *The New Poetry* (Harmondsworth, 1962)

Hamburger, M., *Reason and Energy* (London, 1957)

—— *From Prophecy to Exorcism* (London, 1965)

—— *The Truth of Poetry* (Harmondsworth, 1972)

Hamburger, M. and Middleton, C., *Modern German Poetry 1910–1960* (London, 1966)

Heller, E., *The Disinherited Mind* (1952; reprinted Harmondsworth, 1961)

Heselhaus, C., *Deutsche Lyrik der Moderne* (Düsseldorf, 1961)

Hesse, H., 'Recent German Poetry', *The Criterion*, I, October 1922–July 1923 (London, 1967)

Heuss, Th., *Hitlers Weg* (Stuttgart, 1932)

Hiller, K., *Köpfe und Tröpfe* (Hamburg and Stuttgart, 1950)

Hitler, Adolf, *Mein Kampf,* translated by R. Manheim (London, 1969)

Hohoff, C., *Dichtung und Dichter der Zeit II* (Gernsbach, 1952–57; Düsseldorf, 1963)

Hufnagel, G., *Kritik als Beruf. Der kritische Gehalt im Werk Max Webers* (Frankfurt a.M., 1971)

Johnson, Samuel, *Lives of the English Poets I* (Letchworth, 1968)

Johnston, J. H., *English Poetry of the First World War* (Berne and Munich, 1973)

Kafka, F., *Tagebücher 1910–1923* (New York, 1948–49)

—— *Briefe 1910–1924* (New York, 1958)

—— *Briefe an Felice* (New York, 1967)

Kästner, E., *Fabian* (1931), in: *Gesammelte Schriften,* 7 vols (Cologne 1959), II

Keller, E., *Nationalismus und Literatur* (Berne and Munich, 1970)

Kessler, H. G., *Tagebücher 1918–37* (Frankfurt a.M., 1961)

Ketelsen, U-K., *Völkisch-nationale und national-sozialistische Literatur in Deutschland 1890–1945* (Stuttgart, 1976)

Keyserling, Graf H., *Das Spektrum Europas* (Heidelberg, 1928)

Klemperer, V., *'LTI'. Die unbewältigte Sprache* (Munich, 1969)

Kokoschka, O., *My Life* (London, 1974)

Kraus, K., *Die Dritte Walpurgisnacht* (Munich, 1967)

Kunisch, H., *Handbuch der deutschen Gegenwartsliteratur* (Munich, 1969)

Laqueur, W., *Weimar — A Cultural History 1918–1933* (London, 1974)

Larsen, E., *Weimar Eyewitness* (London, 1976)

Leavis, F. R., *Revaluation* (London, 1969)

—— *New Bearings in English Poetry* (Harmondsworth, 1972)

Loerke, O., *Tagebücher 1903–39* (Heidelberg and Darmstadt, 1955)

—— *Literarische Aufsätze aus der Neuen Rundschau* (Heidelberg and Darmstadt, 1967)

Loewy, E., *Literatur unterm Hakenkreuz* (Frankfurt a.M., 1966)

Lukács, G., *Werke,* 17 vols (Neuwied and Berlin, 1962–75)

Mahler-Werfel, A., *Mein Leben* (Frankfurt a.M. and Hamburg, 1960)

Mandelstam, N., *Hope against Hope* (London, 1971)

Mann, Thomas, *Briefe 1889–1936* (Kempten-Allgäu, 1961)

—— *Briefe 1937–1947* (Kempten-Allgäu, 1963)

—— *Gesammelte Werke,* 13 vols (Frankfurt a.M., 1974)

Marcuse, L., *Mein zwanzigstes Jahrhundert* (Munich, 1960)

Markov, V., *Russian Futurism* (London, 1968)

Maser, W., *Hitlers 'Mein Kampf' — Entstehung . . . Stil . . . Quellen* (Munich and Eßlingen, 1966)

Mehring, W., *Die verlorene Bibliothek* (Icking and Munich, 1964)

Meinecke, F., *Die deutsche Katastrophe* (Wiesbaden, 1947)

Mosse, G. L., *The Crisis of German Ideology* (London, 1966)

Mühsam, E., *Unpolitische Erinnerungen* (Berlin, 1961)

Muschg, W., *Die Zerstörung der deutschen Literatur* (Berne, 1956)

—— *Von Trakl zu Brecht* (Munich, 1963)

Musil, R., *Der Mann ohne Eigenschaften* (Hamburg, 1952)

—— *Prosa, Dramen, späte Briefe,* ed. A. Frisé (Hamburg, 1957)

—— *Tagebücher, Aphorismen, Essays und Reden,* ed. A. Frisé (Hamburg, 1955)

—— *Tagebücher,* ed. A. Frisé (Reinbek bei Hamburg, 1976)

—— *Tagebücher. Anmerkungen. Anhang. Register,* ed. A. Frisé (Reinbek bei Hamburg, 1976)

Nietzsche, F., *Gesammelte Werke*, Musarion edition, 23 vols (Munich, 1922–29)
—— *Kritische Gesamtausgabe*, ed. G. Colli and M. Montinari, 30 vols (Berlin, 1967–)
Owen, W., *War Poems and Others*, ed. D. Hibberd (London, 1973)
Parsons, I. M., *Men who March Away — Poems of the First World War* (London, 1965)
Pick, O., 'Erinnerungen an den Winter 1911–12', *Die Aktion* (28 October 1916), col. 605
Pinthus, K., 'Rede für die Zukunft', *Die Erhebung. Jahrbuch für neue Dichtung und Wertung*, ed. A. Wolfenstein, 1 (Berlin, 1920)
Plath, Sylvia, *Ariel* (London, 1979)
Pleßner, H., *Die verspätete Nation* (Stuttgart, 1959)
Proß, H., *Die Zerstörung der deutschen Politik* (Frankfurt a.M., 1959)
Rathenau, W., *An Deutschlands Jugend* (Berlin, 1918)
—— *Briefe*, 4 vols (Dresden, 1926–28)
Rauschning, H., *Die Revolution des Nihilismus* (New York, 1938)
—— *Gespräche mit Hitler* (Zurich, Vienna and New York, 1940)
—— *Men of Chaos* (New York, 1942)
Ridley, H., 'National Socialism and Literature — a Study of Five Authors in Search of an Ideology' (dissertation, University of Cambridge, 1966)
Rilke, R. M., *Sämtliche Werke*, 6 vols (Frankfurt a.M., and Wiesbaden, 1955–66)
—— *Gesammelte Briefe*, 6 vols, ed. R. Sieber-Rilke and C. Sieber (Leipzig, 1936–39)
—— *Rainer Maria Rilke. Marie von Thurn und Taxis. Briefwechsel* (Zurich, 1951)
—— *Rainer Maria Rilke. Katharina Kippenberg. Briefwechsel* (Wiesbaden, 1954)
—— *Briefe an Sidonie Nádherný von Borutin* (Frankfurt a.M., 1973)
—— *Rainer Maria Rilke. Lou Andreas-Salomé. Briefwechsel* (Frankfurt a.M., 1975)
Ritchie, J. M., *Periods in German Literature I* (London, 1966)
Rosenberg, A., *Der Mythus des zwanzigsten Jahrhunderts* (Munich, 1930)
Rubiner, L. (ed.), *Kameraden der Menschheit* (Potsdam, 1919)
Schirach, B. v., *Ich glaubte an Hitler* (Hamburg, 1967)
Schoenberner, F., *Bekenntnisse eines europäischen Intellektuellen* (Icking and Munich, 1964)
Schonauer, F., *Deutsche Literatur im Dritten Reich* (Olten and Freiburg im Breisgau, 1961)
Schöne, A., *Über politische Lyrik im zwanzigsten Jahrhundert* (Göttingen, 1969)
Schreyer, L. and Walden, N., *'Der Sturm': ein Erinnerungsbuch an Herwarth Walden und die Künstler aus dem Sturmkreis* (Baden-Baden, 1954)
Sengle, F., 'Wunschbild Land und Schreckbild Stadt. Zu einem zentralen Thema der neueren deutschen Literatur', *Studium Generale*, Heft 10 (1963)
Singh, G., *Eugenio Montale: A Critical Study* (Yale, 1973)
Soergel, A., *Dichtung und Dichter der Zeit* (Leipzig, 1927)
Sontheimer, K., *Antidemokratisches Denken in der Weimarer Republik* (Munich, 1962)
Sorge, R., *Sämtliche Werke*, 3 vols (Nuremberg, 1962–67)
Sorley, C., *The Letters of Charles Sorley* (Cambridge, 1919)
Speer, A., *Spandau. The Secret Diaries* (London, 1976)
Spengler, O., *Briefe 1913–36* (Munich, 1963)
Stern, F., *The Politics of Cultural Despair* (Berkeley and Los Angeles, 1961)
Stern, G., *War, Weimar and Literature* (Pennsylvania, 1971)
Stern, J. P., *Hitler: The Führer and the People* (London, 1975)
Sternberger, D., Storz, G., and Süskind, W. E. *Aus dem Wörterbuch des Unmenschen* (Hamburg, 1957)
Strothmann, D., *Nationalsozialistische Literaturpolitik* (Bonn, 1960)
Symons, J., *The Thirties* (London, 1975)
Taylor, R., *Literature and Society in Germany 1918–1945* (Sussex, 1980)

Toller, E., *Eine Jugend in Deutschland* (1933), in: *Prosa, Briefe, Dramen, Gedichte* (Reinbek, 1961)

Tolley, A. T., *The Poetry of the Thirties* (London, 1975)

UNESCO, *The Third Reich* (London, 1955; published under the auspices of the International Council for Philosophy and Humanistic Studies and with the assistance of UNESCO)

Valéry, P., *Variété V* (Paris, 1945)

Vermeil, E., *The German Scene* (London, 1956)

Viereck, P., *Metapolitics — The Roots of the Nazi Mind* (New York, 1961)

Volkmann, E., *Deutsche Dichtung im Weltkrieg 1914–1918* (Leipzig, 1934)

Waite, R. G. L., *The Psychopathic God Adolf Hitler* (New York, 1977)

Walden, N., and Schreyer, L., *'Der Sturm': ein Erinnerungsbuch an Herwarth Walden und die Künstler aus dem Sturmkreis* (Baden-Baden, 1954)

Weber, M., *Gesammelte Politische Schriften* (Munich, 1921)

Wellek, R., and Warren, A., *Theory of Literature* (London, 1966)

Whitman, W., *Leaves of Grass*, ed. M. Cowley (London, 1960)

—— *A Collection of Critical Essays*, ed. R. H. Pearce (Englewood Cliffs, 1962)

Wilson, E., *Axel's Castle* (London, 1964)

Wolff, K., *Autoren, Bücher, Abenteuer* (Berlin, 1965)

—— *Briefwechsel eines Verlegers 1911–1963* (Frankfurt a.M., 1966)

Wulf, J., *Literatur und Dichtung im Dritten Reich* (Gütersloh, 1963)

—— *Theater und Film im Dritten Reich* (Gütersloh, 1964)

Zuckmayer, C., *Als wärs ein Stück von mir* (Vienna, 1966)

Zweig, S., *Die Welt von gestern* (Stockholm, 1941)

3. GENERAL ACCOUNTS OF EXPRESSIONISM

In recent years especially there has been a plethora of articles and books about Expressionism. The following list includes those items which have been particularly valuable and illuminating.

*Allen, R., *German Expressionist Poetry* (Boston, 1979)

*Anz, T. and Stark, M. (eds.) *Expressionismus. Manifeste und Dokumente zur deutschen Literatur 1910–1920* (Stuttgart, 1982)

Arnold, A., *Die Literatur des Expressionismus* (Stuttgart, Berlin, Cologne, and Mainz, 1966)

Benn, G., Introduction to *Lyrik des expressionistischen Jahrzehnts* (Wiesbaden, 1955)

*Best, O., *Theorie des Expressionismus* (Stuttgart, 1976)

Brinkmann, R., *Expressionismus: Forschungsprobleme 1952–1960* (Stuttgart, 1961)

—— *Expressionismus: Internationale Forschung zu einem internationalen Phänomen* (Stuttgart, 1980)

——Expressionismus — europäische Moderne auf deutsch oder deutsche Seelenkrankheit? Festschrift für E. W. Herd (Dunedin, 1980)

*Bronner, S. E. and Kellner, D. (eds.), *Passion and Rebellion. The Expressionist Heritage* (London, 1983)

Bruggen, Max van, *Im Schatten des Nihilismus: die expressionistische Lyrik im Rahmen und als Ausdruck der geistigen Situation Deutschlands* (Amsterdam, 1946)

Denkler, H., *Gedichte der 'Menschheitsdämmerung'* (Munich, 1971)

Dürsteler, H. P., *Sprachliche Neuschöpfungen im Expressionismus* (Thun, 1954)

Durzak, M., *Zwischen Symbolismus und Expressionismus: Stefan George* (Stuttgart, Berlin, Cologne, and Mainz, 1974)

Edschmid, K., 'Über den Expressionismus in der Literatur und die neue Dichtung', *Tribüne der Kunst und Zeit*, 1 (Berlin, 1920)

—— *Frühe Manifeste* (Hamburg, 1957)

—— *Lebendiger Expressionismus* (Vienna, Munich, and Basle, 1961)

—— *Briefe der Expressionisten* (Frankfurt a.M. and Berlin, 1964)

Elliott, D (ed.), *Germany in Ferment* (Durham, 1970)

Friedmann, H. and Mann, O. (eds), *Expressionismus. Gestalten einer literarischen Bewegung* (Heidelberg, 1956)

Furness, R. S., *Expressionism* (London, 1973)

Gruber, H., 'The Political-Ethical Mission of German Expressionism', *GQ*, (1967), 186–203

Hesse, H., *Blick ins Chaos* (Berlin, 1920)

Hiller, K., 'Begegnungen mit Expressionisten', *Der Monat,* XIII/148 (January 1961), 54–59

*Hucke, K-H., *Utopie und Ideologie in der expressionistischen Lyrik* (Tübingen, 1980)

*Hüppauf, B. (ed.), *Expressionismus und Kulturkrise* (Heidelberg, 1983)

*Kemper, H-G., and Vietta, S., *Expressionismus* (Munich, 1976)

Klarmann, A. D., 'Expressionism in German Literature: a Retrospect of Half a Century', *MLQ*, 26 (1965)

*Knapp, G. P., *Die Literatur des deutschen Expressionismus. Eine kritische Einführung* (Munich, 1979)

Kolinsky, E., *Engagierter Expressionismus* (Stuttgart, 1970)

*Korte, H., *Der Krieg in der Lyrik des Expressionismus: Studien zur Evolution eines literarischen Themas* (Bonn, 1981)

Krispyn, E., *Style and Society in German Literary Expressionism* (Gainesville, Florida, 1964)

*Lange, V. (ed.), 'German Expressionism', *Review of National Literatures*, 9 (1978)

*Levison, K. M., 'War Imagery in German Expressionist Lyric' (dissertation, University of Harvard, 1975)

Lukács, G., '"Größe und Verfall" des Expressionismus', in: *Werke*, 17 vols (Neuwied and Berlin, 1962–75), IV (1971), 109–49

Mann, K., 'Der literarische Expressionismus' (1934), in: *Prüfungen* (Munich, 1968), pp. 193–95

Mann, O. and Rothe, W. (eds), *Deutsche Literatur im zwanzigsten Jahrhundert* (Berne and Munich, 1967)

Martens, G., *Vitalismus und Expressionismus* (Stuttgart, Berlin, Cologne, and Mainz, 1971)

Martini, F., *Was war Expressionismus?* (Urach, 1948)

—— 'Deutsche Literatur zwischen 1880 und 1950. Ein Forschungsbericht', *DVLG*, 26 (1952)

Mautz, K., 'Die Farbensprache der expressionistischen Lyrik', *DVLG*, 31 (1957), 198–240

*Meixner, H. and Vietta, S. (eds), *Expressionismus — sozialer Wandel und künstlerische Erfahrung* (Munich, 1982)

Mittner, L., 'Die Geburt des Tyrannen aus dem Ungeist des Expressionismus', in: *Festschrift zum 80. Geburtstag von Georg Lukács* (Berlin, 1965)

Myers, B. S., *The German Expressionists* (New York, 1957)

Newton, R. P., *Form in the 'Menschheitsdämmerung'* (The Hague and Paris, 1971)

Pascal, R., *From Naturalism to Expressionism* (London, 1973)

Paulsen, W., *Expressionismus und Aktivismus* (Berne, 1935)

—— 'Die deutsche expressionistische Dichtung des 20. Jahrhunderts und ihre Erforschung', *Universitas*, 17, Heft 4 (April 1962)

—— *Aspekte des Expressionismus* (University of Massachusetts, 1967)

Perkins, G., *Contemporary Theory of Expressionism* (Berne and Frankfurt, 1974)

★Pickar, G. B. and Webb, K. E. (eds), *Expressionism Reconsidered* (Munich, 1979)

Pinthus, K., 'Zur jüngsten Dichtung', *Die Weißen Blätter*, 2, Heft 12 (July–September 1915)

—— *Menschheitsdämmerung* (1920; reprinted Hamburg, 1959)

Pörtner, P., *Literatur-Revolution 1910–1925*, 2 vols (Darmstadt, 1960 and 1961)

Raabe, P. (ed.), *Expressionismus. Aufzeichnungen und Erinnerungen der Zeitgenossen* (Olten and Freiburg im Breisgau, 1965)

—— (ed.), *Expressionismus. Der Kampf um eine literarische Bewegung* (Munich, 1965)

—— 'Franz Kafka und der Expressionismus', *Zeitschrift für Deutsche Philologie*, 86 (1967), 161–75

Raabe, P. and Greve, H. L., *Expressionismus: Literatur und Kunst 1910–23* (Stuttgart, 1960)

Reso, M., *Expressionismus. Lyrik* (Berlin, 1969)

Ritchie, J. M., 'The Expressionist Revival', *Seminar*, 2, No. 1 (Spring 1966)

★Ritter, M. A., 'The Development of Urban Poetry in Germany through Early Expressionism' (dissertation, University of Texas, 1978)

Rothe, W. (ed.), *Expressionismus als Literatur* (Berne, 1969)

★Rötzer, H. G. (ed.), *Begriffsbestimmung des literarischen Expressionismus* (Darmstadt, 1976)

Samuel, R. and Hinton Thomas, R., *Expressionism in German Life, Literature and the Theatre 1910–1924* (Cambridge, 1939)

Schirokauer, A., 'Expressionismus der Lyrik', *Germanistische Studien* (Hamburg, 1957)

Schneider, F. J., *Der expressive Mensch und die deutsche Lyrik der Gegenwart* (Stuttgart, 1927)

Schneider, K. L., *Der bildhafte Ausdruck in den Dichtungen Georg Heyms, Georg Trakls und Ernst Stadlers* (Heidelberg, 1954)

—— *Zerbrochene Formen* (Hamburg, 1967)

Schonauer, F., 'Expressionismus und Faschismus. Eine Diskussion aus dem Jahre 1938', *Literatur und Kritik*, Heft 7 (October 1966)

Sokel, W. H., *The Writer in Extremis* (Stanford, 1959). The German edition of this book is called *Der literarische Expressionismus* (Munich, 1959)

★—— 'Expressionism from a Contemporary Perspective', in: *Erkennen und Denken* (1983), pp. 228–42

★Stark, M., *Für und wider den Expressionismus* (Stuttgart, 1982)

Steffen, H., *Der deutsche Expressionismus. Formen und Gestalten* (Göttingen, 1965)

Steffes, E., 'Wirksame Kräfte in Gehalt und Gestalt der Lyrik im Zeitalter des Expressionismus' (dissertation, University of Munich, 1956)

Stieber, H., 'Frühverstorbene nach 1910' (dissertation, University of Munich, 1955)

Stuyver, W., *Deutsche expressionistische Dichtung im Lichte der Philosophie der Gegenwart* (Amsterdam, 1939)

Thomke, H., *Hymnische Dichtung im Expressionismus* (Berne and Munich, 1972)

Usinger, F., 'Die expressionistische Lyrik', *Imprimatur*, 3 (1961–62), 115–25

Vietta, S. (ed.), *Lyrik des Expressionismus* (Tübingen, 1976)

Weisbach, R., *Wir und der Expressionismus* (Berlin, 1973)
Weisstein, U., *Expressionism as an International Literary Phenomenon* (Paris and Budapest, 1973)
★—— 'German Literary Expressionism — an Anatomy', *GQ*, 54 (1981), 262–83
Willett, J., *Expressionism* (London, 1970)
★Wright-Drygulski, B., 'Expressionist Utopia: The Pursuit of Objectless Politics' (dissertation, University of California, 1977)
Ziegler, K., 'Dichtung und Gesellschaft im deutschen Expressionismus', *Imprimatur*, 3 (1961–62), 98–114

4. AUGUST STRAMM

a. Primary Literature

Radrizzani, R. (ed.), *August Stramm: Das Werk* (Wiesbaden, 1963)

b. Secondary Literature

Adler, J. D., 'August Stramm', *Kroklok*, 3 (1972)
—— 'On the Centenary of August Stramm', *PEGS*, 44 (1974)
★—— 'The Arrangement of the Poems in Stramm's *Du/Liebesgedichte*' *GLL*, 33 (1979/80), 124–34
—— and White, J. J. (eds), *August Stramm. Kritische Essays und unveröffentliches Quellenmaterial aus dem Nachlaß des Dichters* (Berlin, 1979)
Benzmann, H., 'Die Dichter des Sturm', *Westermanns Monatshefte*, 127/1 (October 1919), no. 758
Blümner, R., 'August Stramm', *Der Sturm*, 16, Heft 9 (1925)
Bozzetti, E., 'Untersuchungen zu Lyrik und Drama August Stramms' (dissertation, University of Cologne, 1961)
Bridgwater, P., *August Stramm. 22 Poems* (Wymondham, 1969)
★—— 'The War Poetry of August Stramm', *New German Studies*, 8 (1980), 29–53
Brinkmann, R., 'Zur Wortkunst des Sturm-Kreises', in: *Unterscheidung und Bewahrung, Festschrift für H. Kunisch* (Berlin, 1961), pp. 62–78
Emrich, W., *Rudimentär* (programme of the Forum Theatre Production) with a note by Wilhelm Emrich, 'Zur Konzeption des Forum Theaters', ed. C. Rateuke (Berlin, 1973)
Gebhardt, W., 'Das Sturm-Archiv Herwarth Waldens', *Jahrbuch der deutschen Schillergesellschaft*, 2 (Stuttgart, 1958), 348–65
Haller, R., 'August Stramm', in: *Expressionismus als Literatur*, ed. W. Rothe, pp. 232–50
Hering, C., 'Gestaltungsprinzipien im lyrisch-dramatischen Werk August Stramms' (dissertation, University of Bonn, 1950)
—— 'Die Überwindung des gegenständlichen Symbolismus in den Gedichten August Stramms', *Monatshefte*, 51, no. 1 (January 1959), 62–74
—— 'The Genesis of an Abstract Poem. A Note on August Stramm', *MLN*, 76 (1961), 43–48
—— Interpretation of Stramm's poem 'Untreu', in: H. Denkler, *Gedichte der 'Menschheitsdämmerung'*, pp. 97–105
Heynicke, K., 'Zum 100. Geburtstag von August Stramm', *Die Horen*, 94 (1974), 31–34

Jansen, H., 'Der Westfale August Stramm als Hauptvertreter des dichterischen Früh-expressionismus', in: *Westfälische Studien, Festschrift für Alois Böhmer* (Leipzig, 1928)

Jones, M. S., 'An Investigation of the Periodical *Der Sturm*, its Contributors and their Place in the Theory and Practice of Expressionism' (dissertation, University of Hull, 1974)

★—— 'The Cult of August Stramm in *Der Sturm*', *Seminar*, 13 (1977), 257–69

Krolow, K., 'August Stramm', *Die Zeit*, 11, no. 26 (July 1956), 30 f.

Last, R., *Stramm Concordance* (Hull, 1972)

Michelsen, P., 'Zur Sprachform des Frühexpressionismus bei August Stramm', *Euphorion*, 58, Heft 3 (1964), 276–302

Perkins, C. R. B., 'August Stramm's Poetry and Drama: a Reassessment' (dissertation, University of Hull, 1972)

—— 'August Stramm: His Attempts to Revitalize the Language of Poetry', *New German Studies*, 4, no. 3 (Autumn 1976), 141–55

Pokowietz, T., 'August Stramm', in: *Expressionismus. Gestalten einer literarischen Bewegung*, ed. H. Friedmann and O. Mann, pp. 116–29

Rittich, W., 'Kunsttheorie, Wortkunsttheorie und lyrische Wortkunst im "Sturm"' (dissertation, University of Greifswald, 1933)

Schreyer, L., 'Der Dichter August Stramm', *Deutsches Volkstum* (Hamburg, 1925)

—— *Erinnerungen an Sturm und Bauhaus* (Munich, 1956)

Schreyer, L. and Walden, N., *'Der Sturm': ein Erinnerungsbuch an Herwarth Walden und die Künstler aus dem Sturmkreis* (Baden-Baden, 1954)

Soergel, A., *Dichtung und Dichter der Zeit*, pp. 585–623

Stramm, I., 'Tropfblut, Gedanken an den Vater August Stramm', *Deutsche Rundschau*, 70, no. 9 (1947), 218–19

—— 'Mein Vater, der Expressionist', *Neue literarische Welt*, 7 (10 April 1952)

—— *August Stramm. Dein Lächeln weint* (Wiesbaden, 1956)

Der Sturm. Herwarth Walden und die Europäische Avantgarde. Berlin 1912–32 (Veranstaltet von der Nationalgalerie in der Orangerie des Schlosses Charlottenburg, Berlin, 24 September 1961 bis 19 November 1961)

5. GEORG HEYM

a. Primary Literature

A complete edition of Heym's work is being published in six volumes by K. L. Schneider. So far, the following editions have appeared:

Dichtungen und Schriften,   I: *Lyrik*, ed. K. L. Schneider and others (Hamburg and Munich, 1964)

      II: *Prosa und Dramen*, ed. K. L. Schneider and C. Schmigelski (Hamburg and Munich, 1962)

     III: *Tagebücher, Träume, Briefe*, ed. K. L. Schneider and others (Hamburg and Munich, 1960)

     VI: *Dokumente zu seinem Leben und Werk*, ed. K. L. Schneider and G. Burckhardt (Munich, 1968)

Volume VI contains much useful biographical information and a host of contemporary reviews of Heym's work. Details of these reviews have *not* been reproduced in this bibliography.

b. Secondary Literature

Bick, J., 'Cross or Judas-Tree: a Footnote to the Problem of Good and Evil in Georg Heym', *GQ*, 46, no. 1 (January 1973), 22–29

Brand, G. K., 'Die Ahnung des Krieges, Georg Heym', in: *Die Frühvollendeten* (Berlin and Leipzig, 1929)

Dammann, G., 'Untersuchungen zur Arbeitsweise Georg Heyms an seinen Handschriften', *Orbis Litterarum*, 26 (1971), 42–67

Eykman, C., 'Die Funktion des Häßlichen in der Lyrik Georg Heyms, Georg Trakls und Gottfried Benns', *Bonner Arbeiten zur Deutschen Literatur* (1965)

Grote, C., 'Wortarten, Wortstellung und Satz im lyrischen Werk Georg Heyms' (dissertation, University of Munich, 1962)

Kohlschmidt, W., 'Der deutsche Frühexpressionismus im Werke Georg Heyms und Georg Trakls', *Orbis Litterarum*, 9 (1954), 3–17 and 100–19

*Korte, H., *Georg Heym* (Stuttgart, 1982)

Krispyn, E., 'Georg Heym and the Early Expressionist Era' (dissertation, University of Pennsylvania, 1963)

—— 'Georg Heym und der Neue Club', *Revista de Letras*, IV (1963), 262–71

—— *Georg Heym — A Reluctant Rebel* (Gainesville, 1968)

Lange, H., 'Bildnis des Dichters Georg Heym', *Das innere Reich* (April–September 1935), 209–29

Leschnitzer, F., 'Georg Heym als Novellist', *Das Wort*, 2, no. 10 (October 1937), 27–29

—— 'Über drei Expressionisten', *Das Wort*, 2, no. 12 (1937), 44–53

Loewenson, E., *Georg Heym oder Vom Geist des Schicksals* (Hamburg and Munich, 1962)

Mahlendorf, U. R., 'Georg Heym. Stil und Weltbild' (dissertation, Brown University, 1958)

—— 'The Myth of Evil: the Re-evaluation of the Judaic-Christian Tradition in the Work of Georg Heym', *GR*, 36, no. 3 (October 1961), 180–94

Martens, G., '"Umbra Vitae" and "Der Himmel Trauerspiel". Die ersten Sammlungen der nachgelassenen Gedichte Georg Heyms', *Euphorion*, 59 (1965), 118–31

Martini, F., 'Georg Heym: "Der Krieg"', in: *Die deutsche Lyrik. Form und Geschichte. Interpretationen*, ed. B von Wiese (Düsseldorf, 1956), II, 425–49

Mautz, K., *Mythologie und Gesellschaft im Expressionismus. Die Dichtung Georg Heyms* (Frankfurt a.M. and Bonn, 1961)

Müller, J., 'Jahreszeiten im lyrischen Reflex. Zur Sprachgestalt einiger Gedichte Georg Heyms und Georg Trakls', *Sprachkunst, Beiträge zur Literaturwissenschaft*, 3 (1972), 56–74

Regenberg, A., 'Die Dichtung Georg Heyms und ihr Verhältnis zur Lyrik Charles Baudelaires und Arthur Rimbauds' (dissertation, University of Munich, 1961)

Rölleke, H., 'Georg Heym', in: *Expressionismus als Literatur*, ed. W. Rothe, pp. 354–74

—— 'Die Stadt bei Stadler, Heym und Trakl', *Philologische Studien und Quellen*, Heft 34 (1966)

Salter, R., *Georg Heyms Lyrik. Ein Vergleich von Wortkunst und Bildkunst* (Munich, 1972)

Schneider, K. L., *Der bildhafte Ausdruck in den Dichtungen Georg Heyms, Georg Trakls und Ernst Stadlers*, (Heidelberg, 1954)

—— (ed.), *Georg Heym. Marathon* (Hamburg, 1956)

Schulz, E. A. W., 'Das Problem des Menschen bei Georg Heym' (dissertation, University of Kiel, 1953)

Schweitzer, R., 'Die Kunstmittel Georg Heyms' (dissertation, University of Graz, 1962)

Seelig, C. (ed.), *Georg Heym. Gesammelte Gedichte* (Zurich, 1947)

Seiler, B., *Die historischen Dichtungen Georg Heyms* (Munich, 1972)

*Sgroi, C. A., 'Georg Heym's Metaphysical Landscape' (dissertation, Ohio State University, 1975)

Sheppard, R., 'From Grotesque Realism to Expressionism: a Linguistic Analysis of the Second Turning-point in Georg Heym's Poetic Development', *New German Studies*, 3, no. 2 (1975), 99–109

Stadler, E., 'Georg Heym: Umbra vitae. Nachgelassene Gedichte', *Cahiers Alsaciens*, 1 (1912), 319–20

Stieber, H., 'Frühverstorbene nach 1910' (dissertation, University of Munich, 1955), pp. 79–86

Uhlig, H., 'Visionär des Chaos. Ein Versuch über Georg Heym', *Der Monat* 6, Heft 64 (January 1954), 417–27

Williams, R., *The Country and the City* (London, 1973)

6. FRANZ WERFEL

Lore B. Foltin's *Franz Werfel* (Stuttgart, 1972), volume 115 of the Sammlung Metzler, contains the following information on Werfel:

a) pp. 1–6: Detailed information about Werfel's 'literarischer Nachlaß' and holdings in archives at various universities in the United States.

b) pp. 6–10: Editions of Werfel's works, details about his correspondence, his interviews, bibliographies of his work.

c) pp. 10–16: Lists of full-length studies of the writer, dissertations, essays about him in literary histories and magazines.

d) pp. 17–112: Werfel's life and work with details of dates of publication of everything he wrote and (apparently) of everything written about him.

e) pp. 113–15: Suggested topics for research on Werfel; pp. 115–16: Lists of other specific studies of the writer and of aspects of his work.

f) pp. 117–20: A register of the people mentioned in the preceding pages.

g) pp. 120–24: A full register of Werfel's works.

In view of the copious detail and easy availability of this study I have included in my bibliography only those works which have been especially useful to me. When I have referred to novels and plays in the text, full details of the edition used are supplied in the footnotes.

a. Primary Literature

Werfel, Franz, *Das lyrische Werk*, ed. A D. Klarmann (Frankfurt a.M., 1967)

b. Secondary Literature

Arnold, M., 'Lyrisches Dasein und Erfahrung der Zeit im Frühwerk Franz Werfels' (dissertation, University of Freiburg in der Schweiz, 1961)

Bauer, R., 'Kraus contra Werfel: eine nicht nur literarische Fehde', in: *Sprache und Bekenntnis. Sonderband des Literaturwissenschaftlichen Jahrbuchs* (Berlin, 1971), pp. 315–34

Buber, M., 'Vorbemerkung über Franz Werfel', *Der Jude*, 1/2 (1917), 109–12

Fischer, H., 'Sprachwirrwarr bei Franz Werfel', *Neue Literarische Welt. Zeitung der Deutschen Akademie für Sprache und Dichtung*, 3, no. 1 (10 January 1952). See also the editions for 25 January, 25 February and 25 March 1952.

Foltin, L. B., *Franz Werfel 1890–1945* (Pittsburgh, 1961)

Foltin, L. B. and Spalek, J. M., 'Franz Werfel's Essays: a Survey', *GQ*, 42 (1969), 172–203

Fox, W. H., 'Franz Werfel', in: *German Men of Letters* (London, 1964), III, 107–25

Goldstücker, E., 'Rainer Maria Rilke und Franz Werfel. Zur Geschichte ihrer Beziehungen', *Acta Universitatis Carolinae, Germanistica Pragensia I* (Prague, 1960)

Golffing, F., 'Franz Werfel. "Das lyrische Werk"', *Germanistik*, 9 (1968), 218

Grenzmann, W., 'Franz Werfel. Im Vorraum der christlichen Welt', in *Dichtung und Glaube* (Frankfurt a.M. and Bonn, 1967)

Heinzel, A., 'Franz Werfel als Lyriker', *Pädagogische Zeitschrift*, 4, Heft 8 (1949)

Hesse, H., 'Franz Werfels "Gerichtstag"', *Vivos Voco* (Leipzig), 1, no. 2/3 (November-December 1919), 204–05

Ihering, H., 'Der Fall Werfel', *Das Tagebuch*, 10 (1929), 2177–80

Junge, C., 'Die Lyrik des jungen Werfel: ihre religiöse und strukturelle Problematik' (dissertation, University of Hamburg, 1956)

Kahler, E., Review of Franz Werfel's *Gedichte aus den Jahren 1908–1945*, *Commentary* (January 1948), 186–89

Keller, E., 'Franz Werfel — sein Bild des Menschen' (dissertation, University of Zurich, 1958)

Kenter, H., 'Franz Werfels "Gerichtstag": die geistige Wende einer dichterischen Sendung', *Das literarische Echo* (1920–21), 1292–97

Klarmann, A. D., 'Musikalität bei Werfel' (dissertation, University of Pennsylvania, 1931)

—— 'Gottesidee und Erlösungsproblem beim jungen Werfel', *GR*, 14 (1939), 192–207

—— 'Franz Werfel's Eschatology and Cosmogony', *MLQ*, 7 (1946), 385–410

—— 'Franz Werfel, the Man', *GQ*, 19 no. 2 (March 1946), 113–20

—— 'Das Weltbild Franz Werfels', *Wissenschaft und Weltbild*, 7 (1954)

Krügel, F., 'Franz Werfel and Romanticism', *Seminar*, 3, no 2 (1967), 82–102

Kurella, A., 'Briefe an Franz Werfel', in: *Tätiger Geist. Zweites der Ziel-Jahrbücher*, ed. K. Hiller (Munich and Berlin, 1918), pp. 222–28

Kutzbach, K. A., 'Franz Werfel als geistiger Führer', *Die Neue Literatur*, Heft 1 (January 1932), 13–17

Lea, H., 'The Unworldly Character in the Works of Franz Werfel' (dissertation, University of Pennsylvania, 1962)

Leide, H., 'Mensch und Welt in der Lyrik Franz Werfels. Ein Beitrag zur Geschichte des Expressionismus' (dissertation, University of Berlin, 1954)

Politzer, H., 'Dieses Mütterchen hat Krallen' (Prag und die Ursprünge RMRs, Franz Kafkas und Franz Werfels), *Literatur und Kritik* (February 1974), 15–33

Rehfeld, W., 'Die Erlösung zur Geistigkeit. Ein Beitrag zur Untersuchung der Geistesmetaphysik Franz Werfels unter besonderer Berücksichtigung der Zeitkritik in der Geschichtsdeutung des Dichters' (dissertation, University of Berlin, 1956)

Rheinländer-Möhl, A., 'Umbruch des Geistes in seiner Auswirkung auf die literarische Situation der Gegenwart. Nachgewiesen an der zeitbedingten und artfremden Romankunst Franz Werfels (dissertation, University of Münster, 1936)

Schumann, D. W., 'The Development of Werfel's "Lebensgefühl" as Reflected in his Poetry', *GR*, 6 (1931), 27–53

Siemsen, A., 'Zwei Dichter der jüdischen Emigration: Franz Werfel und Alfred Döblin', *Judaica*, 1, Heft 2 (1 July 1945), 157–62

Specht, R., *Franz Werfel. Versuch einer Zeitspiegelung* (Berlin, Vienna and Leipzig, 1926)

Spencer, G. K., 'Franz Werfel's Expressionist Vision: a Textual Study of his Lyric and Dramatic Work between 1910 and 1920' (dissertation, University of Hull, 1972)

Stadler, E., Review of Franz Werfel's *Wir sind*, in: Stadler, E., *Dichtungen* (Hamburg, 1955), II, 23–24

Torberg, F., 'Gedenkrede auf Franz Werfel', *Wort in der Zeit*, 8–9 (1965), 19–27

Trost, P., 'Die dichterische Sprache des frühen Werfel', in: Goldstücker, E., *Weltfreunde. Konferenz über die Prager deutsche Literatur*, pp. 313–18

Voss, C., 'Das Problem der Wirklichkeit und seine Lösung im Werk Franz Werfels' (dissertation, University of Munich, 1957)

7. KURT HEYNICKE

a. Primary Literature

Heynicke, K., 'Seele zur Kunst', *Das Kunstblatt*, 1 (1917), 348

—— 'Der Willen zur Seele', *Masken*, 13, no. 16 (1917–18), 263

—— *Neurode. Ein Spiel von deutscher Arbeit* (Berlin, 1935)

—— *Der Weg ins Reich* (Berlin, 1935)

—— Various poems in: *Jahresring* (1965/66 and 1971/72)

—— *Das lyrische Werk*, 3 vols (Worms, 1969–74)

b. Secondary Literature

No. 36 in the series *Dichter und Denker unserer Zeit* (Dortmund, 1966) contains an exhaustive bibliography of all Heynicke's works, articles and essays, compiled by Hedwig Bieber. Therefore the following list is restricted to those works which have proved most relevant to my study.

Auden, W. H., *Collected Shorter Poems 1930–1944* (London, 1950)

Benzmann, H., 'Die Dichter des "Sturm"', *Die Flöte*, 1 (1918), 195–96

—— 'Kurt Heynicke', *Hellweg*, 3, Heft 13 (1923), 217–18

Berger, B., Heynicke, K. and Bieber, H., *Kurt Heynicke. Dichter und Denker unserer Zeit* (Dortmund, 1966)

Bock, K., 'Kurt Heynicke', *Das Neue Rheinland*, 1 (1919–20), 303–05

Daiber, H., *Vor Deutschland wird gewarnt* (Gütersloh, 1967)

Dietrich, R. A., 'Kurt Heynicke wird 70 Jahre alt. Dichtung als Bekenntnis. "Außenseiter mangels Nihilismus". Lyriker aus der Zeit der "Menschheitsdämmerung"', *Westdeutsches Tageblatt*, 21 September 1961

Elster, H. M., 'Von der "Sturm"-Lyrik zum Unterhaltungsroman. Kurt Heynicke wird heute 70 Jahre alt', *Der Tagesspiegel*, 21 September 1961

Hochhuth, R., 'Unsere "abgeschriebenen" Schriftsteller in der Bundesrepublik', in: *Die Hebamme* (Hamburg, 1971), pp. 335–46

Hoffbauer, J., 'Kurt Heynicke und sein Lebenswerk', *Der Schlesier. Breslauer Nachrichten*, 13, no. 38 (1961), 6

Jones, M. S., 'An Investigation of the Periodical "Der Sturm"...' (see under Stramm), pp. 645–75

Klein, J., 'Die Mumi singt. Zur Lyrik Kurt Heynickes', *Welt und Wort*, 25, Heft 7 (1970), 208–13

Loerke, O., *Der Bücherkarren. Besprechungen im Berliner Börsen-Courier 1920–28* (Heidelberg and Darmstadt, 1965), pp. 111–13

Mahr, G., '"Ich unterscheide mich von der Gegenwartslyrik und ihrer Artistik"; Gespräch mit Kurt Heynicke', *Die Horen*, 94 (1974), 31–34

—— 'Vom Expressionisten zum Dichter unserer Tage — Kurt Heynicke', *Die Horen*, 94 (1974), 60–64

—— Review of K. Heynicke's *Das lyrische Werk*, in: *Frankfurte Hefte*, 31, Heft 3 (March 1976), 62–64

Menz, E., 'Sprechchor und Aufmarsch. Zur Entstehung des Thingspiels', in: *Die deutsche Literatur im Dritten Reich*, ed. H. Denkler and K. Prümm, pp. 330–46

Meridies, W., 'Alle Finsternisse sind schlafendes Licht. Zum Lebenswerk des Dichters Kurt Heynickes', *Schlesien*, 17, Heft 4 (1972), 218–24

Saeckel, H., 'Kurt Heynicke', *Ostdeutsche Monatshefte*, 6, Heft 2 (1925), 232–38

—— 'Rückkehr zum Volk. Gedanken zum Werke Kurt Heynickes', *Der Bücherwurm*, 12 (1926–27), 33–35

Weiglin, P., 'Kurt Heynicke', *Neue Literarische Welt*, 3, no. 6 (1952), 14

8.   WILHELM KLEMM

a.   Primary Literature

Klemm, W., *Gloria! Kriegsgedichte aus dem Feld* (Munich, 1915)

—— *Verse und Bilder* (Berlin, 1916)

—— *Traumschutt* (Hannover, 1920)

—— *Aufforderung* (Wiesbaden, 1961)

—— *Geflammte Ränder* (Darmstadt, 1964)

—— *Ergriffenheit* (Nendeln, Liechtenstein, 1973)

—— *Entfaltung* (Nendeln, Liechtenstein, 1973)

—— *Verzauberte Ziele* (Nendeln, Liechtenstein, 1973)

—— *Die Satanspuppe* (Nendeln, Liechtenstein, 1973)

See also *Simplizissimus* (1907–21), *Jugend* (1911–14), *Licht und Schatten* (1912–15), *Die Aktion* (1914–25), *Die Neue Rundschau* (1916–17), *Akzente* (1965 and 1968) and *Jahresring* (1968–69) for more examples of Klemm's poetry.

b.   Secondary Literature

Benzmann, H., 'Wilhelm Klemm: Aufforderung', *Zeitschrift für Bücherfreunde*, 10 (1918–19), col. 266

Brockmann, J., 'Untersuchungen zur Lyrik Wilhelm Klemms' (dissertation, University of Kiel, 1961)

—— Analysis of W. Klemm's 'Betrachtungen', in: H. Denkler, *Gedichte der Menschheitsdämmerung*, pp. 154–67

F (Paul Fechter ? Otto Flake ?), 'Wilhelm Klemm: Gloria', *Zeitecho* (1915), 366

Heuss, Th., 'Die Kriegsgedichte von Wilhelm Klemm', *März* (24 July 1915), 62

Hoffmann, C., 'Ausblick in die Literatur', *Das Kunstblatt*, 1 (1917), col. 378

Hoffmann, D., 'Gedanken filtern langsam ins Graue', *Frankfurter Neue Presse*, 17 August 1961

—— 'Rose, Symbol des Schweigens. Wilhelm Klemm: *Aufforderung'*, *Christ und Welt*, 8 December 1961

Krolow, K., 'Erregbar, zart und rigoros' (review of W. Klemm, *Aufforderung*), *Deutsche Zeitung*, 5/6 August 1961

—— 'Wilhelm Klemm: Aufforderung' (review of W. Klemm, *Gesammelte Verse*), *Neue Deutsche Hefte*, 8 (November-December 1961), 108–110

Pinthus, K., 'Verse und Bilder', *Leipziger Tageblatt*, 14 December 1916

—— 'Der Lyriker Wilhelm Klemm', *Die Aktion* (25 August 1917), cols 461–62

—— 'Gloria und Verse und Bilder', *Zeitschrift für Bücherfreunde* 8 (1917), col. 556; see also 9 (1917), col. 557

—— Introduction to W. Klemm, *Aufforderung* (Wiesbaden, 1961), pp. 137–42

—— 'Wilhelm Klemm. 15. Mai 1881 in Leipzig — 24. Januar 1968 in Wiesbaden', *Jahresring* (1968), 313–22

Wendel, H., 'Wilhelm Klemm. Gloria', *Die Neue Zeit* (12 November 1915), col. 222

INDEX OF NAMES

References are only given to the footnotes if the author's name does not appear with a quotation in the main text. This applies especially to the mottoes used throughout the book.

SOME RECENT AND FORTHCOMING
VOLUMES IN THE SERIES
PUBLICATIONS OF THE INSTITUTE OF GERMANIC STUDIES

30 *Goethe Revisited; essays for the 150th anniversary of his death,* ed. by E. M. Wilkinson (in collaboration with John Calder (Publishers) Ltd, London)
ISBN 0 85457 110 8   192 pp.   1984   £5.95

31 *Minnesang in Österreich,* hrsg. von Adrian Stevens und Fred Wagner (in collaboration with Verlag Karl M. Halosar, Vienna)
ISBN 0 85457 111 6   iv, 244 pp.   1984   £12.95

32 *London German Studies II,* ed. by J. P. Stern
ISBN 0 85457 112 4   viii, 198 pp.   1983   £7.90

33 *Adalbert Stifter heute: Londoner Symposium 1983,* hrsg. von J. Lachinger, A. Stillmark und M. W. Swales (in collaboration with the Adalbert-Stifter-Institut, Linz)
ISBN 0 85457 119 1   viii, 167 pp.   1985   £5.95

34 *Geschichtsbewußtsein in der deutschen Literatur des Mittelalters,* hrsg. von Christoph Gerhardt, Nigel Palmer und Burghart Wachinger; (in collaboration with Max Niemeyer Verlag, Tübingen)
ISBN 0 85457 123 X   viii, 190 pp.   1985   £19.95

35 *Paths and Labyrinths. Nine papers from a Kafka Symposium,* ed. by J. P. Stern and J. J. White
ISBN 0 85457 124 8   xii, 159 pp.   1985   £6.95

36 *Modern Swiss Literature. Unity and diversity,* ed. by John L. Flood (in collaboration with Oswald Wolff (Publishers) Ltd)
ISBN 0 85457 125 6   x, 146 pp.   1985   £10.95

37 *Geistliche und weltlich Epik des Mittelalters in Österreich* hrsg. von David McLintock, Adrian Stevens und Fred Wagner. (in collaboration with Alfred Kümmerle Verlag, Göppingen)
ISBN 0 85457 130 2   1986   *at press*

38 *London German Studies III,* ed by J. P. Stern
ISBN 0 85457 131 0   x, 211 pp.   1986   *at press*

Prices, which are for UK only, include postage. They are liable to adjustment without notice. For overseas orders, add 20% to the price quoted.

All publications are obtainable direct from the Institute of Germanic Studies, 29 Russell Square, London WC1B 5DP. A complete list is available on application.

Customers in North America may place their orders through Humanities Press Inc, Atlantic Highlands, NJ 07716.